# SEXUAL LIBERATION AND RELIGION IN NINETEENTH CENTURY EUROPE

# SEXUAL LIBERATION AND RELIGION IN NINETEENTH CENTURY EUROPE

J. MICHAEL PHAYER

**CROOM HELM LONDON**
**ROWMAN AND LITTLEFIELD**

© 1977 J. Michael Phayer

Croom Helm Ltd, 2-10 St John's Road, London SW11

ISBN 0-85664-230-4


First Published in the United States 1977
by Rowman and Littlefield, Totowa, N.J.

Library of Congress Cataloging in Publication Date

Phayer, J. Michael.
    Sexual liberation and religion in nineteenth century Europe.

    Bibliography: p. 165
    Includes index.
    1. Sex and religion – History.   2. Germany – Christianity.
    3. France – Christianity.
    I. Title
HQ63. P47    261. 8'34'1    76-30351
ISBN O-87471-947-X

Printed in Great Britain by Biddles Ltd, Guildford, Surrey

# CONTENTS

FOR PAT

# INTRODUCTION

Popular belief and behaviour changed with the advent of modernisation. How and why they changed is what concerns us in this book. The process treats the historian to a fascinating chapter in social history; how did people manage to steer straight ahead in matters of religion while veering off sharply in sexual conduct? Because we commonly associate sexual liberation with modern secularity and religious piety with tradition and the past, they seem to run off in opposite directions. But the experiences of European people in the first half of the nineteenth century do not bear this out. Most Germans and Frenchmen, especially people in the lower class, became more sexually permissive while remaining religious.

Perhaps it has been the sensitivity of secular humanists that has kept us from plunging into an analysis of this relationship. Doing so sometimes casts an unflattering light on religion and, at other times, displays it in full retreat. On the other hand, perhaps it is simply the lack of an informed acquaintance with Baroque religious tradition that has protected the nakedness of the relationship from the historian's eye. For whatever reason, the result has been unfortunate in several ways.

In the first place, the discrepancy between religious tradition together with its moral code of behaviour and modern sexual freedom poses a dilemma for Western society. Modernisation has introduced principles of behaviour that often contradict those which religion has sought to maintain. While relishing personal sexual freedom modern people hesitate to jettison their religious tradition. Meanwhile, many churches have fought a rear-guard action to adjust the Christian code to recent circumstances, such as abortion and divorce, and contemporary situations (pre-marital and extra-marital sexuality and homo-sexuality). Others, alternately, steadfastly hold tight to traditional moral guidlines and jeopardise the credal belief of their members.

It is by no means clear what the resolution of this dilemma will be. Much hangs in the balance. If the Western tradition of moral monotheism disappears, what values or value systems will society adopt? Besides fragmenting and pluralising us, how will they change us? At the very least we may be assured of a deep character transformation in Western society. Alternately, should the traditional code which has been put in question reaffirm itself, hard and difficult decisions loom on the horizon, given the new pattern of sexual behaviour.

Second, entirely practical considerations compel us to deal with the origin of the dilemma. Ever since historians have interested themselves in the history of sexual behaviour, gnawing doubts about the subject have beset them. Statistics have convinced some of the fact of significant sexual change. But while we have groped to find the causes of this new conduct, doubters have asked if it is at all likely that any massive change in an area of such fundamental human behaviour as sexuality could occur. And to such Cartesian minds the glimpses into the causes of sexual change on the part of those who affirm a sexual revolution seem all too fleeting.

This study demonstrates that a change in mentality cut common people adrift from traditional sexual controls and allowed them greater sexual freedom and indulgence. The process occurred in such a way that, incredible as it may sound, the proletariat never considered whether their newly found sexual liberation might be in conflict with the moral teachings of their Church.

The circumstances that furnish the historical evidences of this proposition vary. Determining just which Germans were affected by sexual change and which were not poses no problem. Early nineteenth-century sources allow us to follow this development with amazing precision. By comparing tax records from state archives with parish records from church archives it may be asserted that differences in sexual behaviour constitute one of the earliest earmarks of class society. At the same time, the continuance of traditional religious practices and customs permits us to bring into focus a more complete and composite picture of the early nineteenth-century Central European proletariat than we have hitherto known.

Because most of the documents in question derive from Catholic Germany, it is difficult to say to what extent the experience of Protestant Germans ran parallel. There are suggestions and evidence indicating both a similarity with Catholic Germany and a different relationship between belief and behaviour.

It is not as simple to pry open the mentality of French common people. In the last analysis, it is not so much their sexual as their religious behaviour that permits us to demonstrate the interplay of secular and religious influences among the proletariat. We are forced along this circuitous path in the case of France because we cannot be precise about French illegitimacy ratios due to the fact that French women commonly placed their new-born children in orphanages where they were registered simply as foundlings, regardless of legitimate or illegitimate birth. Thanks to popular religion and new methods of analysing it, we will be able to find a way around this obstacle.

Two developments surrounding French popular religion will command our attention, but before identifying them we must take time to explain the term 'popular religion'. It denotes the religious experience of the laity (but not exclusively), their pious predilections, their passing religious fancies. The view from the pew need not be opposed to official religion. The two are not wholly self-contained. The survival of organised religion depends on a substantial concordance between what is officially taught and decreed and what is popularly believed and performed.

France radiated wave after wave of religious impulses in the nineteenth century. Three powerful expressions of popular piety—the mission cross, Philomena and the Marian movement—testify both to the controversial and dynamic nature of religion in France. But how do they provide us entree into the proletarian mentality? Two developments help us here. An analysis of the French mission cross troubles after the July Revolution shows that common people did not make the distinctions between religion and politics and religion and secular pastimes that characterised their social betters. As it turns out, those devoted to the cross were also devoted to more sexual indulgence than others.

Secondly, the sensational cult of a newly discovered saint, Philomena, provides clues to the mentality of common people. Philomena became the first beneficiary of a new trend in popular devotion toward a virginal ideal. The process of dechristianisation, articulated by a number of distinguished historians since Gabriel Le Bras, hardly conditions us for an eruption of fresh piety. But the success of Philomena in the latter 1830s is beyond question. Since she is as new today in the study of history as she was to French people in 1834, it will be necessary to do some spadework and lay the foundations of historical research into her cult, which holds great promise for the study of religion and society in nineteenth-century France. Thus, ironically, a person whose historical existence cannot even be established becomes a tool in the researcher's hands to establish historical fact. Philomena holds particular promise because by using nomenclature to chart her progress by class, we can determine the religious attitude of common people and, at the same time, show that piety and promiscuity were proletarian bedfellows.

There are many whose generous assistance has enabled me to write this book and I can only hope that it at least partially measures up to their efforts on my behalf. Karl Bosl of Munich University first stirred my interest in many of the questions dealt with herein. I am thankful to him for this and for his generous doses of encouragement. I am grateful to Peter N. Stearns for his many insights that enabled me to express my own ideas with greater precision and conviction, and for his invaluable editorial help. A fellowship from Marquette University enabled me to do some of the research and I am also indebted to the Marquette University library staff, and especially to Harry J. Onufrock who patiently tracked down and obtained innumerable obscure titles, and to John Berens who helped prepare the manuscript. One owes thanks to colleagues who read parts of the manuscript and made valuable suggestions and necessary corrections; and special thanks to those who generously put manuscripts which they are preparing for publication at my disposal: Edward Shorter, Timothy N. Tackett, Michael R. Marrus and William H. Sewell, Jr. The help of my wife, Patricia, in researching French birth registers, typing and correcting innumerable drafts, making graphs, proof-reading and indexing has been indispensable and I am above all grateful to her.

# 1 THE SECULARISATION OF SEX

Abrupt changes in sexual attitudes and behaviour surged through Central Europe around 1800. Since this vastly altered the pattern of daily life and powerfully contributed to the formation of the modern character, we will want to study the consequences of the new outlook. But, initially, a more intriguing and compelling question faces us: why did the change occur? While it is a mistake to imagine that a set formula can be found to explain sexual change for all people everywhere, in Central Europe certain external conditions brought about a sudden secularisation of sex among the proletariat.

The notion of a sexual revolution taking place in modern Western society is a fascinating one. It rests, partly, on startling bastardy statistics that show sharp increases in illegitimacy after 1750.[1] But statistics do not tell all. Those who have doubted that any such thing as a sexual revolution ever took place demand to know how it came to happen. If there was a sexual revolution, would not a new attitude towards sex have had to trigger it? Frankly, it must be admitted that explaining attitudinal changes has proven much more elusive than gathering data for statistical support of the idea of dramatic sexual transformation. If celibates, who cannot write, abruptly decide to have sex, *how* are we going to find out what changed their minds?

This question embraces several problems. For one thing, historical evidence must be largely circumstantial because, again, of our subjects' illiteracy. Secondly, one is handicapped by the lack of historical studies on pre-modern Central European society that tackle this question.[2] But, more than anything else, we are hampered by an inability to break out of our own mind-sets so as to gain the freedom to think about sexuality in a context far different from that surrounding our own experiences. We customarily think of sex as the domain of the individual. Within certain limits, which are constantly being tested, we regard sex as an inviolably personal matter. As a result, when asked to explain attitudes towards sex different from our own, we throw up our hands, or rack our brains in search of likely and compelling causes of a change in sexual behaviour, and produce a list tailored to suit the individual sexuality of the contemporary world: capitalism, education, social class, 'the wish to be free', and so on.[3] Is this good history? What allows us to assume that factors controlling our sexuality are historical constants? In

13

fact, the modern attitude towards sex would have boggled the minds of our Baroque ancestors, for whom sexual response answered to more than personal whim. It fell under the purview of the family, the community, and what might be called the cosmic view. If we look at the world through their glasses, rather than our own, we will better understand how people finally came to entertain thoughts of explicit sexuality.

First of all, the family. In traditional German society parental discipline, which was normally stern and at times brutal, probably acted as a restraint to sexual indulgence.[4] The inheritor's inclination to marry and satisfy the sexual drive was a threat to the patriarch that had to be contained. One method of doing this was to frighten children with the spectre of ghosts and evil spirits. We may never find out how commonly this happened, but we must not confuse the open, carefree sexuality of the aristocracy, whose domestic servants fondled the genitals of blue-blooded little children, with the situation of the peasants.[5] It is certain that the sexual mentality of the aristocracy—Tridentine in standard but hedonist in practice—could not and did not find place among their common subjects.[6] And it is a safe assumption that they did not encourage the sexual appetites of their children and heirs.[7]

As a person matured, his or her sexual drives mired down in the family's economic designs. Through the marriage contract the family often sacrificed their nubile members in profitable deals. Not the heart but the purse determined who had intercourse with whom in pre-modern Central Europe. To say that people 'made love' is to speak euphemistically: married couples who could hardly tolerate each other produced a numerous progeny.[8]

But it is not true to say that personal sensitivities were completely bypassed. The Bavarian custom known as the *Heimgarten* provided for this. It worked somewhat as follows. A courter, accompanied perhaps by a 'marriage maker', paid a visit to the home of the prospective bride. She had become a 'prospect' because of her dowry, which either the marriage maker, a mutual friend, or the young man's father himself fancied to be worthwhile. Since the purpose of the visit was still a kind of 'open secret', the family voiced all manner of objections when asked to give the young couple some privacy by clearing out of the room. Once alone, the suitor began to speak of domestic concerns and matters of the heart. He might even go so far as to propose, or at least broach the topic of marriage in some way. This little tête-à-tête was called a Heimgarten. Soon—'after about thirty minutes—the 'marriage maker'. and the parents returned to see if they had taken to one another or not'.[9] If the couple announced their engagement, or, more likely, somehow signalled positively, a day *zum Sehen* was set aside to have a look around, for business matters now had to be worked out. The family of whichever party was to move away from home visited the homestead of the other, making an exhaustive inspection of fields, livestock, farm buildings and the home itself. If a great deal was amiss or too much in poor repair, or if there was too large a debt outstanding, 'negotiations' simply broke off. Thus, although personal dispositions were assigned a role, traditional society did not allow them to determine the marital contract. Real estate considerations weighed in more heavily. The marriage bond would be held together by more than sacramental grace.

Elsewhere in Central Europe the affective element in arranged marriages counted for even less, if this can be imagined. In Westphalia something similar to the Heimgarten took place. On a specified day the prospective bridegroom called on the homestead of his would-be fiancée. Although the purpose of his visit was perfectly obvious, no one at first mentioned it or even alluded to it. Communication took place by custom. As an excuse for his visit, the caller was always to ask for a light for his pipe—a rather limp excuse, one would think. At any rate the woman of the house—not the one whose hand was being sought, who was evidently also present in the room—offered him a chair, and poked about in the stove for an ember for his tobacco while making small talk about the weather and this and that. In the meantime, she took a pan and placed it on the stove, the signal for him that the moment of truth had come. If she then proceeded to prepare some kind of dough for *Pfannenkuchen*, he was to immediately pull out his watch and assert that he would not be able to stay any longer. If, on the other hand, she began to prepare bacon and eggs, he was to proceed with the proposal, assured in advance of its acceptance. The young man and woman then made the promises of faithfulness to one another, which constituted an official engagement. It is obvious that in these rather awkward negotiations the prospective bride is being given the opportunity to 'speak' for herself and to determine whether she wants to become engaged, although it is not clear just how she does this. Has she already made up her mind, having at least met the person in question at some church social function, or must she reach a decision during the few minutes that pass while the fumbling with the pipe and coals transpires, and then somehow signal her inclination to her mother? We are left hoping it was not the latter, but not knowing for certain. What the entire affair—the family-arranged marriages and engagement ordeals—do point out to us is that sex was impersonal. Even the choice of a sex partner was taken out of the individual's hands.[10]

Thus, familial economic considerations overruled affective relationships, or would have had there been any, for it is not clear that romance figured in the lives of farmers' children. We would like to think that Heimgarten cases were exceptions, confined only to parts of Germany, but unfortunately, this was not the case; nor was the custom infrequent in France.[11] In fact, more extreme examples pointing to the same disregard of personal inclination can be cited. During the Napoleonic era, prospective brides in the Rhineland, upon being asked by French bureaucrats to give the names of the bridegrooms with whom they would soon (a week) be married, were unable to supply them![12] It was not at all unusual for the prospective bride and bridegroom to have seen each other on only a few occasions before engagement.

At other times they knew only too well for whom they were intended. The ambitious Saipalt family of the Burgenland in Austria married one of its daughters to a farmer who was 21 years older than her, and a second daughter to a childless farmer, who at age 67 and 37 years older than her, was not likely to produce any heirs.[13] Call it what one will, human exploitation or family solidarity, the marital aspirations of these girls ran aground on the family's rocky determination to be distinguished members of the tiny Schläning settlement in Upper Austria. In nearby Antau 12 per cent of the married women had husbands who were at least 15 years older than them, and 6 per cent of them were 20 or more years junior to their mates. In this respect little Antau was typical of Europe.[14]

If a girl survived being bespoke through a family arrangement, she still had to be careful not to transgress the restraints imposed by her community. In general, this meant postponing marriage a number of years, no sleeping around in the meantime, and in most parts of Catholic Germany and, possibly, some parts of France, it meant not conceiving a child before wedlock (pre-nuptial pregnancy). The community's concern about bastardy was rooted in its anxiety over the food supply for the existing population. About once every decade during Baroque times Europe was hit by a famine.[15] Bad weather terminating in poor crop yields caused scarcity. Sickness and disease followed in the footsteps of undernourishment and put an end to the misery of many. While it is true that a few reaped great profits by exporting grains during times of want[16] nature herself was perceived by common people everywhere as the primary culprit. The last of these killer famines occurred in the early 1770s. Central Germany was one of the hardest hit areas. The yearly average of bread prices in Munich more than trebled during the crisis years. A glance at Table 1 shows the effect of the famine on the rural population of Gars, a large area situated between Munich and Salzburg. Most of those who died in 1771-2 probably succumbed to some illness resulting from malnutrition. But, as Peter Laslett wrote, this is splitting hairs; in common parlance we would say they starved. Many of them were infants, but most, 2,120 out of 3,359, were adults. Thus, during the worst year of the famine in Gars, twice as many adults died as in an average year. Few German communities escaped the early 1770s without a surge of mortality like that of Gars, and none of them escaped the bitter misery of these years. Hunger drove people to eat their entire harvest, leaving no seeds for the following year's crop. The second year of famine would then be worse than the first. To stay alive, people commonly ate

Table 1: Archdiaconate Gars, Bavaria, July 1769 to June 1774

| Year | Births | Deaths | Population |
|------|--------|--------|------------|
| 1769 | 1539 | 1643 | 49,522 |
| 1770 | 1466 | 1698 | 49,307 |
| 1771 | 1580 | 3359 | 48,860 |
| 1772 | 1202 | 1862 | 47,555 |
| 1773 | 1598 | 1433 | 46,771 |

Source: OAM *Relatio Synodalis,* Gars.

wild berries and grass.[17] Contemporaries have left us a number of accounts of their excruciating experiences during these years.[18] Under such conditions bastardy constituted a luxury which no community would tolerate and for which few people had energy anyway. In the crisis of the 1770s society even became peevish towards the poor, who, they believed, brought on the catastrophe themselves through their improvident marriages and consequent proliferation of their number.[19] With famine a recurring nightmare and death no stranger to any family, it is not surprising that the community would not tolerate illegitimacy. If it had only been a matter of what happened to the poor, others might have been relatively unconcerned. But it has been shown that famines brought farmers to their knees as well.[20] Hard times were community concerns, not only the worry of the poor. The low bastardy ratios of the Old Regime in Europe are customarily ascribed to this fact.[21] Hence, it can be no accident that the illegitimacy ratio for 1772-3 in Gars, the year of the highest mortality, was the lowest of that area during the last 35 years of the eighteenth century.[22]

To keep their numbers in balance and to avoid tempting God's wrath, German communities penalised those responsible for sexual excess. This could happen in several ways and may sometimes have included bodily punishment. In Bavaria a *Hausvater* (head of household) was fined if his farm hands violated curfew, and the offender himself seems to have been whipped.[23] We may question just how commonly corporal punishment was administered, but fines for bastardy were enforced. German communities even regularly imposed fines on newly-wed couples whose children were born too soon.[24] In the Paderborn principality the fine for this was higher than most others such as drunkenness, missing church, or disorderly conduct, so we know that Baroque communities took this matter seriously.[25] In Piesport on the Mosel in western Germany, the parish synod, all laymen, kept close account of their parish newly-weds, fining those who violated the rule and exacting a public penance from those who could not afford it.[26] Thus did German Catholic communities apply the brakes to sexual activity.[27]

At one time the French mentality surely must have resembled that of the Germans, but by the latter part of the eighteenth century a transition had come over Western Europe. The catastrophe of 1770-4 did not strike France as harshly as Germany. Deaths rose sharply in 1770 and 1772 but they did not come close to exceeding births, whereas in Gars, Germany, there were twice as many burials as baptisms.[28] Vienna, Berlin and Augsburg felt the famine far more urgently than did Paris, whose increase in mortality hardly compares to those of Central European cities.[29] To find a French famine which surpasses that of 1770-4 in Germany it is necessary to go back more than a hundred years to 1661-2.[30] In the intervening years conditions ameliorated in France to the extent that historians see the famine of 1770-4 as a new type of crisis, the effects of which were primarily social, not demographic. Thus, food riots commonly occurred and the government's poverty programme broke down under the burden of increased indigency, but population decimation receded into the background.[31] French people gradually put away their paranoia about plagues and famines. Magical devices associated with pilgrimages for warding off misfortune declined proportionately.[32] In time some Frenchmen became indifferent towards the pilgrimage itself.[33] Accordingly, communities gradually eased their vigilance against bastardy, which rose during the eighteenth century from about 3 to 10 per cent. It resulted more often from affective relationships and less from exploitative ones (master—subject).[34] A certain lassitude towards bastardy may be discerned here, although other indicators—concern over population, age at which women married, abstinence from marital intercourse during Lent and Advent—show that society was not letting its guard down altogether.[35] In France, too, there is evidence showing some correlation between food prices and

bastardy rates. But in comparison to Germany, parental discipline over
the sexual behaviour of children grew lax, as did the community's over
pre-nuptial conceptions.[36] In the Sologne area of central France,
parents found 'no difficulty in intermingling their illegitimate with their
legitimate children', and were 'little bothered when their daughters
became pregnant before being married'.[37]

In the cruel world of the Baroque era Central European people found
famines something of a mixed bag. For the unlucky they meant death,
or the death of a loved one (or, to put it more accurately, one on whom
you depended). But for the lucky survivors the famine could usher in an
unexpected change of life—marriage. In the five-year period running
from 1766 to 1771, 383 marriages annually took place on the average in
Gars, Bavaria. In the ensuing five years an average of 427 matrimonies
were solemnised.[38] So the same famine that visited death on one member of the family brought good fortune—marriage—to another. (In
Gars more people married in the peak years of the famine than at any
other time over a ten-year span.) No wonder the emotions of pre-modern
people appear stunted and strange to us.

The upshot of all this is, of course, that the people who married after
the famine had been sitting around cooling their heels up until then.
This is a second way in which the community repressed sexuality. Many
had to live through part of their fertile years as celibates, and for some
it amounted to a lifetime proposition. 'Castration by voluntary continence', P. Chaunu has called it. In the Burgenland in Austria more than
35 per cent of the fertile population was not married in 1762.[39] Had
the domestics been dispersed evenly among the households, every other
one would have counted an unmarried hand under its roof. In Kranzburg,
Bavaria, 31.7 per cent of the adult population was unmarried in 1771. In
Upper Bavaria in 1794 about 41 per cent of the males between the age of
22 and 50 were single, as were 37 per cent of the women.[40] Although
the number of penalised people varies quite considerably from region to
region, this kind of sexual abstinence was typical of pre-modern Europe.
Those not doomed to lifelong celibacy married for the first time rather
late, usually between 25 and 30.[41]

It is not altogether clear in what manner the community pressured
people into delaying marriage. The priest warned farm hands from the
pulpit not to marry improvidently, thereby abandoning the station in
life God had chosen for them.[42] But—not to belittle the influence of
the local clergy—we must suppose that unmarried youths were con-
fronted by more than moral restraints. The community seems to have
had at least partial control over the assignment of non-inherited

properties (and, therefore, who could marry and start a new family in the community). More importantly, farmers could control access to the commons (pasturage rights), and exact a tax from smallholders, day labourers and non-farmers, which, if not paid, relieved them of any obligation to see the families in question through difficult years of food shortage.[43] Thus, anyone contemplating marriage would have been wise to consider how the community at large viewed the venture. Finally, a young man had to apply to his jurisdictional lord, or to the reeve who represented him, for a marriage licence. The politics involved in getting over this hurdle varied, but the possibilities for chicanery are easily envisioned.

By now it is obvious that marriage was a communal as well as familial concern. Did village patriarchs as well as relatives and respected neighbours take a hand in deciding the marital fate of young women? Distasteful as this may seem to us, it is possible that distinguished members of the community did take part in these decisions. Late eighteenth- and early nineteenth-century light drama was pervaded by plots played out on variations of the 'true love versus money' (arranged) marriage.[44] It appears to have been an unwritten law amongst playrights that, although it was legitimate to amuse people by toying with this tension, in the end familial or patriarchal authority had to prevail. Felix Christian Weisse's *Jubelhochzeit* plays on the predicament of a young German woman, Dorchen, who loves a man who has enlisted in the army and is presumed by everyone but Dorchen to be missing in action. Out of economic necessity Dorchen's family urges her to marry Berthold, the wealthy but much older and quite beery village miller. Repulsed by him, she puts off consent, bringing down the ire of the entire clan on herself: 'Heh, Mädchen, Du musst Berthold heiraten. Berthold ist reich. . .' Eventually, even non-family members pressure her. Despicable as the miller may be, they point out that he is important to the little settlement and has to be kept happy. When Dorchen still dallied, a decision was imposed on her: if her true love had not returned by the time (a few weeks away) of the golden wedding of Robert—the elder of her family and one of the village patriarchs—she must marry the miller. The lord of the area sanctioned this arrangement. Communal pressure was so intense that Dorchen could not refuse these terms. Only the unexpected return of her lover provides this soap opera with a Hollywood ending. We cannot conclude from literary evidence that women were chattels in the hands of the community as well as the family. But the possibility suggests itself since we know that marriage was a very important community event.

Along with the two societal inhibitors of sexuality there was a third, internal one—the cosmic view. For Baroque man, who saw his world as an extension of the spirit world, reality was a blur. As in other pre-modern societies, the cosmic view was the key to the enigma of a life stalked closely by death.[45] Religious service and its corollary, super-stition, were life's proper end because these functions, Baroque man believed, gave him some control over his sacral environment.[46] Sexuality, like everything else, was embedded in the cosmic view, and was therefore subject to the manipulation of religion and superstition. This could lead to bizarre sexual aberrations, which come to light now and then as historians unearth them, but usually it simply meant that impersonal forces exercised control over sexuality.[47]

Baroque religion had been unimaginably mechanical. God was a fac-totum. If man sinned, He punished: it stormed, a plague struck, or war broke out. So long as nature eluded man's control, the common people, imbued with the cosmic view, saw disasters as automatic divine retribu-tions for man's transgressions.[48] God used three ways, the preacher's manual read, to drive sin from His land: 'first, the preacher; second, the authorities; and, third, war, plagues, and famine.'[49] The motivation of the congregation to obey their priest, who warned them not to have sex before marriage and even not to marry at all so as not to over-burden the community's food supply, was strong.[50] Given the nature of the times, we may be certain that the faithful took him at his word.

Baroque preachers from Abraham a Sancta Clara to the obscure Christoph Selhamer put great emphasis on chastity in their sermons, which denounced sexual excess in plain language. These and other preachers provided details of sexual temptations and sins of which the overwhelming majority of their parishioners were certainly innocent. Johann Christoph Beer spoke in lurid phrases about the sexual escapades of his flock in south-western Germany. His sermons uncovered one dalliance after another: mothers let their daughters entertain midnight visitors who got them pregnant; farm hands put straw dummies on their beds so that the *Hausmutter* would think all were chastely asleep, while in reality they romped about lasciviously. On and on he went: we would have to conclude there were no more highly sexed people in all of Germany than his parishioners—were it not for the fact that during his 32 years of service the bastardy ratio never exceeded 4 per cent a year![51]

Besides being explicit, Baroque preachers were also extraordinarily crude. Ignatius Ertle of the Upper Palatinate included in his repertoire of stories an incident involving an older farmer and his wife, who, like the Saipalt women in Austria, was much younger than her husband. 'Durl', the farmer's wife, began consorting sexually with young hired farm hands. Suspecting his wife's marital infidelity, the farmer asked her to prepare him a special meal. She complied, believing it would make him, blind, and leave her free to enjoy the company of the hired help. After eating the specially concocted dish, the old farmer feigned blindness and observed all of the sexual escapades of his wife. Finally out of patience, he told her that he wanted to die, and she should lead him to the well, and then come running up behind and push him in with all her might. She readily agreed, but at the last moment he stepped aside, letting her fly headlong down the dark shaft into the water where he left her to drown![52] Through such earthy stories, the threat of immediate punishment, and the prospect of terrible suffering in a fiery hell, religion helped suppress sexual permissiveness. There was nothing very Pauline about this morality at all. As usually preached, and always conceived by the rustic, it was a simple *quid pro quo* arrangement: when man sinned, God intervened, letting him feel His wrathful hand by wreaking havoc with crops or health. What would happen when that hand ceased to punish?

Baroque man also believed that magic gave him entrée into the world of cosmic forces. Indeed, it is questionable to what extent he could distinguish between religion and magic. European Baroque culture was shot through with superstition. Everything about life and death was impounded by it. It is difficult to determine how superstition affected sexuality. It repressed it, certainly, but it seems that it also gave sexuality an avenue of expression, albeit in an impersonal manner. We know that hundreds of natural phenomena—certain trees, plants, flowers, bugs, animals and animal appendages—held sexual fascination for common people.[53] Baroque popular culture fostered a vivid sexual imagination, out of which grew countless colourful colloquialisms.[54] Folklorists know of the myriad lore of treasured sexual trinkets, amulets, images and potions that they made and used.[55] Young Munich women put a drop of their blood in a man's beer as a love charm. If he proved to be unfaithful, they said the 'Our Father' backwards to put a curse on him.[56] A number of exotic superstitions surrounded the eating of certain kinds of bread or certain portions of the loaf. One of these, which was current in both northern and southern Germany, held that a girl's breasts would develop fully if she ate this bread.[57] It was also a fertility food. There were even superstitious practices for controlling premature ejaculation, nocturnal emissions, abortion, and for removing hexes causing impotency.[58] Superstitions surrounding weddings abounded. In Austria, where the Saipalt family lived, people sought out a *Hochzeitslader* (the person who extended invitations to the wedding guests) who was something of a village joker, because his antics would attract the evil spirits to himself and away from the newly-weds![59] Some newly-weds refrained from intercourse their first three nights together: the bride must not be exposed to evil spirits and cause the marriage to be unhappy![60] Prokop von Templin, a Baroque preacher, claimed to know of betrothed couples who feared to be married in church lest the devil bewitch them, and of other married couples who were unable to have intercourse because of bewitchment.[61]

The predicaments of Dorchen and the Saipalt women plagued females everywhere in Central Europe during Baroque times. Reconciling the family's well-being with their own marital happiness was a principal cause of anxiety and even terror for them. We know this because of the frequency with which they had recourse to the cosmic view—to religious and superstitious practices—to relieve it. While others made pilgrimages to cure an illness or to insure against bad weather, young women made them in the hope of securing a personally acceptable spouse.[62] In the Rhineland, St Andrew was a favourite saint for arranging a happy marriage. Elsewhere maidens appealed to St Anne: 'Mutter Ann, verschaff mir'n Mann!' (Mother Anne, get me a man!) But so great was concern over this problem that many nubile women could not leave matters in St Andrew's or St Anne's hands. By one or other of a dozen tricks of magic they sought to divine the identity of their future mates.[63] One of these involved taking off one's clothes and walking backwards out of the room in the hope of divining one's future mate (presumably by seeing him first or last).[64] Similarly, the devil could be induced to reveal the identity of one's future mate, if a woman made a pact with him while standing naked among the (outdoor) stations of the cross at night around Christmas time.[65] The use of an egg to divine magically the identity of one's mate was common (and more convenient than the other methods, one might add!).[66]

These few examples do not begin to expose the world of sexual superstitions and religious taboos in the pre-modern mentality, but they reveal to us the human context of sexual restraint and anguish.

The combined influence of the various social, legal and psychological factors we have discussed overwhelmed Baroque people, making sexual abstinence or restraint not so much a matter of personal choice as a simple fact of life. To grasp the situation as the ordinary person experienced it, we would do well to think of the awesome forces aligned against sexual permissiveness—parents, stem family members, community and religion, not to mention the enormous weight of custom—

and avoid two simplistic conclusions. First, the notion that Baroque communities sustained discipline through threat of physical force alone is naïve. The force or fines that existed served to remind the individual of the community's concern about public behaviour and discipline. The internal familial and psychological inhibitors were immensely more compelling, and sufficed to restrain or sublimate the sexual impulses of most people. Secondly, the concept of a man or woman confronting his or her sexual impulses with the imperative 'Thou Shalt Not Commit Adultery' (and all the sins implied therewith), and then making a moral choice on that basis alone, does violence to everything we know about their depersonalised world. Morality was but one of many factors contributing to celibacy or sexual restraint, and the rustic never paused, as we have done, to analyse the various inhibitors working together to smother sexual indulgence.

The liberal reforms of the Napoleonic era penetrated the thick walls of local custom, drastically altering the very conditions of everyday life in Central Europe. When this happened attitudes towards sex changed. Knowing how the new outlook differed from the old is the point of critical interest, but let us first briefly enumerate the factors upsetting traditional society. First and foremost among these reforms was the declaration of personal freedom. With the suppression of serfdom, ordinary Germans were at last free to come and go as they pleased, without fear of legal reprisal. On the positive side, guarantees against deprivation of liberty without due process and freedom from malicious prosecution were written into law.

Legal reforms insured the independence of the judiciary, giving teeth to these newly declared laws. The guarantee of personal freedom cut deeply; it not only severed subject from lord, but also, to a certain extent, father from son and mother from daughter. Thus, parents could no longer dictate religious choice after a certain age (while their children were still minors). More importantly for us, they could no longer impose marriage partners on their children.[68]

Secondly, penal reforms were achieved. Although corporal punishment (whipping, stocks, etc.) was not eliminated, specific conditions and cases were established which governed its use. *These did not include fornication.*[69] In fact the protection of the law was extended to bastard children and their mothers. This reflected the reformers' interest in population growth. Bastards became *'enfants naturels de la patrie'.*

Thirdly, since we have noted the importance of the community in the suppression of sexuality, it is important to stress the demise of village society. It fell victim to agricultural reforms (enclosure) and administrative schemes that regrouped rural settlements into large self-governing units and districts. This process destroyed the former ready control of the community over the individual, who found himself now dealing with bureaucrats rather than patriarchs. This is important because it allows us to understand that the anonymity and freedom of the big city are not necessarily components of a sexual revolution. Rural people, as we will see, suffered few inhibitions when they switched to a more indulgent sexual behaviour.

All of these innovations were taking place at a time of rapid economic change and unprecedented land speculation. The secularisation and subsequent auctioning of Church property allowed thousands of ordinary Germans to purchase small plots of land at a time when war was keeping grain prices where farmers liked to see them. Meanwhile the nightmare of famine began to fade from consciousness.[70]

It was at this point and under these circumstances that attitudes towards sex in Central Europe underwent a sudden transition. When secular authority, having abolished sexual restraints in law, established foundling programmes, sexuality and morality had taken on a new relationship without the rustics becoming any the wiser.[71] As Christians and believers, they were now faced with a personal choice as to how the moral code of their religion would determine their sexual life. But, alas, the rustics never made the connection. When they saw penalties for fornication being dropped, and foundling homes built where unwed mothers could place their babies while preserving anonymity, illiterate people concluded that sexual indulgence had become legal, and they equated civil with moral legality.[72] This was quite natural since they had never sorted out the several constraints to sexual impulse, nor viewed sexuality as an exclusively personal matter. In Catholic Germany, where the rustic could not account for the sudden unexpected turn of events, it all seemed like an extraordinary stroke of good luck! It was just as the young woman delightfully put it when asked why she kept having illegitimate children: 'Kindermachen sei erlaubt. . .Der König hat's erlaubt!' (It's OK to make babies. . .The king has OK'd it!)[73]

Sexual behaviour now existed in a vacuum, and the lower class seemed content to let it free-fall. The bourgeoisie rushed in to fill the vacuum with new and often preposterous notions about sex. In other words, bourgeois families quickly supplied their own controls over sexual behaviour (indeed, were already doing so during the Enlightenment). Farmers just stuck to traditional ways. But how did the rural proletariat react to the vacuum? When the community's sanctions against premarital sex disappeared, the Baroque relationship between sinful transgression and divine retribution ceased to be axiomatic. *With that, an aspect of life that had been associated with the cosmic view evaporated and the moral basis of sexuality was abruptly and completely undercut.* The rustic never gave the morality of sexual behaviour a second thought. Once he took it to mind that God was unconcerned about sexuality because He did not punish bastardy, his attitude towards sex became secular. Now he could be as sexually permissive as he wished and go right on believing in his religion and his God. In fact, not to do so never occurred to him. As a result, right after 1800, during the period of liberal reform in Germany, the clergy began to complain bitterly that morality was no longer associated with God and religion.[74] 'Chastity and the fear of God', as one cleric put it, 'have been blasted apart'.[75]

In France and, possibly, parts of Protestant Germany, the switch to a relaxed sexuality began earlier and progressed more gradually, although this surely varied from province to province since the French Restoration clergy commonly blamed immorality on the Revolutionary period. But, as we will discover, it makes little difference whether the secularisation of sex was spontaneous and gradual as in France, or induced and abrupt as in Germany. Both paths allowed the lower-class family to incorporate permissive sexuality into their life-style without so much as dropping a single popular belief or missing a cherished religious devotion. Sex had become a wholly secular activity.

Substantiating the argument about the secularisation of sex may only be accomplished indirectly, because the people with whom we are dealing were illiterate. How the lower class behaved in matters of sex and religion is really the best clue, and we discuss these points in the ensuing chapters. But there is nothing very surprising about the argument, since middle-class attitudes towards sexuality had become secular as well. True, many of the manuals dealing with sexuality counselled moderation. S. Tissot, an eminent Swiss physician, maintained that the emission of semen corresponded to the loss of 40 ounces of blood. Anyone who masturbated or slept around or practised contraception lost his vigour, and, consequently, produced sickly children when he did engage in fruitful intercourse.[76] After the notions of Tissot, which he set forth in a book that went through ten editions during the Restoration, had outlasted themselves around 1860, subsequent generations of doctors emphasised the nervous, rather than physical, debilitations deriving from sexual stimulation.

Meanwhile, the advantages of sexual abstemiousness were being heralded in Germany as well. One popular writer, J. E. Aronson, asserted that an overactive sex life between husband and wife led to such common complaints as nervousness, fatigue, loss of hair and headaches. He counselled married couples to refrain from intercourse after great mental, physical, or emotional exertion (great joy, sorrow, anger, etc.), after an evening of entertainment such as a ball, after heavy eating, and never before at least four hours had expired since dining (better yet, not at all in the evening but only in the morning). Aronson gave explicit instructions regarding the proper place for intercourse (never outdoors as this debases women to the animal level) and the proper position (always horizontal with the man on top, as other positions are either unhealthy or impede conception).[77] Like Tissot, Aronson believed that sexual intercourse and masturbation weakened the body. Other writers advocated greater sexual indulgence, but the middle classes generally held to a code which counselled continence before marriage and moderation thereafter.[78]

Now it is not necessary for us to think that bourgeois couples practised sexual restraint to the extent advocated by the new secular moralists. In fact, the attack of the latter on birth control indicates that the bourgeoisie were already easing their sexual inhibitions and dallying with sex for pleasure. We know that contraception became a more common practice as the nineteenth century wore on.[79] The point is not whether the middle classes were having more sex than formerly, but the nature of their thinking about sex. And on this point the manuals agree. Writers used *secular* considerations to win compliance: 'your hair will fall out', 'you will lose your strength'. Thus, around 1800 the literate bourgeoisie required guidelines for sexual conduct and emerged with a secular code governing sexuality which in practice often taught about the same thing as the old Tridentine code.

All of this simply tells us that the secularisation of sex was not a uniquely proletarian experience. Nor was the rural proletariat boldly plotting new paths in human sexuality. Rather, they were passive agents in the change in attitude towards sex that preceded the sexual revolution. Having never perceived sex as an exclusively or even principally moral issue, there was no cause for them to do so after 1800. The threats of the preacher's manual, referred to earlier, made sense because they correspond to the experience of the Baroque world, not because of specifically religious force. Once we have eliminated the notion that Pauline or Tridentine standards were the only pillars sustaining chastity in pre-modern society, we can see how extraordinary it would have been had rustics treated sex in the context of morality in early modern times. Moral constraints collapsed when the other inhibitors to sexuality were removed. Sexual licence could ensue because the rural proletariat did not set up other blocks to check sex as other classes did. But that is getting ahead of ourselves. The secularisation of sex, we may conclude, was an abrupt and colossal change in sexual attitudes brought on by the liberal reforms of the Napoleonic era in Central Europe, which left the rural proletariat without any effective restraints to sexual permissiveness.

## Notes

1. Edward Shorter, *The Making of the Modern Family* (New York, 1975), Ch. 3; for figures on illegitimacy, see the charts by the same author in 'Illegitimacy, Sexual Revolution and Social Change in Modern Europe', *Journal of Interdisciplinary History*, pp. 237-72.
2. There are many exceptions among whom are P. Chaunu, 'Malthusianisme démographique et malthusianisme economique', *Annales, E.S.C.*, XXVII, 1 (Jan-Feb. 1972); Peter Laslett, *The World We Have Lost* (New York, 1965);Helmut Möller, *Die kleinbürgerliche Familie im 18. Jahrhundert* (Berlin, 1969). Others speak expansively about the 'old values' of pre-modern times without ever analysing them: L. A. Tilly, J. W. Scott, M. Cohen, 'Women's Work and European Fertility Patterns', *Journal of Interdisciplinary History*, VI, 3 (Winter 1976), pp. 418-47.
3. Edward Shorter puzzles over these factors in 'Illegitimacy, Sexual Revolution and Social Change', pp. 237-72.
4. Helmut Möller, *Die kleinbürgerliche Familie*, pp. 75ff. and 196ff.
5. Philip Aries, *Centuries of Childhood: A Social History of Family Life*, trans. Robert Balkick (London, 1962).
6. Eberhard Straub, *Repraesentatio Maiestatis oder Churbayerische Freudenfeste, Miscellanea Bavarica Monacensia*, XIV (1969), Ch. 5, *'Der Hof—Ideal und Wirklichkeit'*.
7. We cannot say whether young men and women commonly committed the 'sin of Onan'. Masturbation among children was noticed by the supervisors of early industrial sweat shops (R. P. Neuman, 'Masturbation, Madness, and the Modern Concepts of Childhood and Adolescence', *Journal of Social History* [Spring 1975], pp. 1-27), but traditional society was often silent about it. This reticence may mean that no one masturbated, or that everyone did and no one fussed about it, or that youth did it privately out in the fields or in the barns. See Shorter, *The Making of the Modern Family*, Ch. 3.
8. Möller, Ch. 7. p. 287. During his seminars Karl Bosl used to say that family patriarchs frequented country taverns where, in their cups, they amused themselves with a game of 'marriage monopoly' by plotting the matches of their still small children.
9. *Historisch-Politische Blätter*, VI (1840), pp. 419-28. The word 'Heimgarten' had broader meanings as well: see Grimm's *Deutsches Worterbuch*. The custom was also known as *'punkeln'*. K. Rob. V. Wikman discusses the Heimgarten custom in *Die Einleitung der Ehe: Eine vergleichend ethno-soziologische Untersuchung über die Vorstufe der Ehe in den Sitten des Schwedischen Volkstums* (Turkü [Finland], 1937),p. 232 and *passim*.
10. *Historisch-Politische Blätter*, XVI (1845), pp. 463-72, 505-20, 587-600.
11. Shorter, *The Making of the Modern Family*, Ch. 4.
12. *Historisch-Politische Blätter*, XVI (1845), p. 592.
13. Ordinariatsarchiv Eisenstadt (OAE), *Pfarrbeschreibung*, Grosspetersdorf, 1728.
14. Shorter, *The Making of the Modern Family*, Appendix III.
15. Wilhelm Abel, *Massenarmut und Hungerkrisen im Vorindustriellen Europa*

(Hamburg, 1974), pp. 156 and 173-4.

16. Ibid., pp. 213ff.

17. Pfarrarchiv Niederkirchen *Gedenkbuch;* Abel, *Massenarmut,* p. 268.

18. Both of Wilhelm Abel's recent works contain accounts. See *Massenarmut und Hungerkrisen im vorindustriellen Deutschland* (Göttingen, 1972), pp. 46-51; and the larger work with the same title, pp. 211-12 and 254-7; Phayer, *Religion und das Gewöhnliche Volk in Bayern in de Zeit von 1750 bis 1850, Miscellanea Bavarica Monacensia,* XXI (1970), Ch. 2.

19. Abel, *Massenarmut* (all subsequent references are to his larger work published in 1974), pp. 201-2.

20. Ibid., p. 277.

21. Peter Laslett, *The World We Have Lost* (New York, 1965), Ch. 6.

22. Ordinariatsarchiv München (OAM), *Relatio Synodalis,* Gars.

23. Ordinariatsarchiv Passau (OAP), 07090 Hofkirchen, 1828. This account was written by an older country curate who looked back on his pre-1800 experience.

24. Ordinariatsarchiv Trier, *Visitation,* Piesport, 1715; Ordinariatsarchiv Paderborn, *Visitationsbuch,* XIV 1ba, *Bewerungen,* 1769.

25. Bistumsarchiv Paderborn, *Visitationsbuch,* XIV 1ba.

26. Bistumsarchiv Trier, *Visitation,* Piesport, 1715-50.

27. The evidence for Protestant communities is not conclusive; many communities imposed fines for pre-nuptial pregnancies, but in Mulsum, Saxony, they increased rapidly between 1750 and 1800, occurring in more than a fourth of all marriages. See Möller, pp. 73-74; Willy Klenk, *Das Dorfbuch von Mulsum* (Frankfurt a.M., 1959), p. 271; Shorter, 'Illegitimacy', see charts; John Knodel, 'Two and a half Centuries of Demographic History in a Bavarian Village', *Population Studies,* XXIV, 3 (Nov. 1967), pp. 353-6.

28. Jacques Dupaquier, 'Sur la population francaise au XVIIe et XVIIIe siècle', *Revue Historique,* CCXXXIX (Jan.–March 1968), p. 60.

29. Abel, p. 252.

30. Francois LeBrun, *Les hommes et la Mort en Anjou au 17 et 18 siecle,* (Paris 1971), pp. 329-38.

31. Thomas M. Adams, *An Approach to the Problem of Beggary in 18th Century France: The Depots de Medicité* (Diss., Wisc., 1972), I, pp. 270-3 and II, p. 528; see also F. Braudel and E. Labrousse (eds.), *Histoire Economique et Sociale de la France* (Paris, 1970), II, pp. 675ff.

32 LeBrun, pp. 400-1.

33. Michel Vovelle, *Piété Baroque,* pp. 398 and 444.

34. J. Depauw, 'Amour illégitime et société a Nantes au XVIIIe siècle', *Annales E. S. C.„* XXVII, pp. 4-5 (July-Oct. 1972), p. 1181; Shorter, 'Illegitimacy', see charts.

35. Dupaquier, p. 71; Adams, pp. 95-6 and 117-19.

36. Shorter, 'Illegitimacy', see charts.

37. Gerard Bouchard, *Le Village immobile: Sennely-en-Sologne au XVIIIe siècle* (Paris, 1972), p. 234.

38. OAM, *Relatio Synodalis,* Gars.

39. OAE, *Pfarrbeschreibung,* 1762.

40. Robert Lee, 'Zur Bevölkerungsgeschichte Bayerns 1750-1850: Britische Forschungsergebnisse', *Vierteljahrschrift f. sozial-und Wirtschaftsgeschichte,* 62, 3 (1975), 331.

41. Möller, pp. 26ff; Laslett, pp. 82-6.

42. Franz Karl Rienle, *Lexikon der christlichen Glaubens-und Sittenlehre* (Augsburg, 1796), I, pp. 162-3.

43. M. Hofmann, 'Die Dorfverfassung im Obermaingebiet', *Jahrbuch f. fränkische Landesforschung,* VI-VII (1941), pp. 151; Sebastian Hiereth, 'Die Bildung der Gemeinden im Isar-Kreis nach den Gemeindeedikten von 1808-1818',

*Oberbayerisches Archiv f. vaterländische Geschichte,* LXXVII (1952), pp. 1-34.

44. See, for example, Felix Christian Weisse's *Die Liebe Auf dem Land;* Heinrich Joseph von Collin's *Kindespflicht und Liebe;* Carl Rudolf's *Ein Vater auf Kundigung.*
45. Laslett, *The World We Have Lost,* pp. 71ff.
46. J. Michael (Fintan) Phayer, *Religion und das gewöhnliche Volk in Bayern in der Zeit von 1750 bis 1850, Miscellanea Bavarica Monacensia,* XXI (1970) Chs. 3 and 4.
47. Emmanuel LeRoy Ladurie, *Les Paysans de Languedoc* (Paris, 1969), pp. 336-7, 342; E. P. Thompson, *The Making of the English Working Class* (New York, 1964), pp. 370-2; Jeffry Kaplow, *The Names of Kings* (New York, 1972), pp. 124-5.
48. Phayer, Ch. 3; Möller, Ch. 6; Bernhard Groethuysen, *The Bourgeois: Catholicism vs. Capitalism in Eighteenth Century France* (New York, 1968), *passim.*
49. Karl Franz Rienle, *Lexikon der christlichen Glaubens und Sittenlehre* (Augsburg, 1796), I, p. 832.
50. Ibid., I, pp. 162ff; Karl Böck, *Johann Christoph Beer, 1690-1760. Ein Seelsorger des gemeinen Volk, Münchener Historische Studien, Abt. Bayerische Geschichte,* II, pp. 49ff; Georg Lohmeier (ed.), *Bayerische Barockprediger* (Munich, 1961), pp. 210-88.
51. I will discuss the credibility of German parochial records in the next chapter.
52. Lohmeier, pp. 970117.
53. Dr Aigremont, *Volkserotik und Pflanzewelt* (Halle a.S., n.d.), *passim.*
54. Ibid., *passim.* For example, in the seventeenth and eighteenth centuries the rose stood for the nubile virgin or the young woman: *Die schönste Rose wird endlich zur Hagebutte* (the most beautiful girl will someday be ugly and fat); it was also a symbol for the vulva: *nach Rosen gehen, Rosen suchen,* or *Rosen pflucken* meant to make love, or sleep around, or have intercourse with a virgin; *Rosengasse,* or *Rosengarten,* or *Rosenwinkel* referred to the part of a city where prostitutes lived; more crudely, *Rosendurchbohren* was an expression for taking a girl's virginity.
55. Many are listed and pictured in Liselotte Hansmann and Lenz Kriss-Rettenbeck, *Amulett und Talisman* (Munich, 1966), esp. pp. 208ff.
56. I. Grassl, 'Münchener Brauchtum und Leben im 18. Jahrhundert' (Diss., München, 1940), p. 19.
57. W. Gaerte, *Volksglaube und Brauchtum Ostpreussens* (Würzburg, 1956), pp. 45-6.
58. Möller, pp. 237-8.
59. Niko Kuret, 'Der Slowenische Anteil am Pannonischen Hochzeitsbrauchtum', *Burgenländische Forschungen,* Heft 61, p. 114.
60. Johann August Ephraim, *Nützliches Allerley aus der natur und dem Leben* (Leipzig, 1788), II, pp. 146ff.
61. L. A. Veit and L. Lenhart, *Kirche und Volksfrömmigkeit des Barock* (Freiburg, 1956), p. 238.
62. Robert Böck, 'Die Marienwallfahrt Kösslarn und ihre Mirakelbücher', *Bayerisches Jahrbuch für Volkskunde,* 1963, p. 51.
63. E. Moser-Rath, 'Brauchdokumentation in baroker Homiletik', *Festgabe für Joseph Dünninger* (Berlin, 1970), p. 364.
64. Moser-Rath, p. 364.
65. Böck, p. 43.
66. I have come across numerous variations of this custom. See, for example, W. Gaerte, p. 32.
67. Migration was sometimes restricted to German-speaking territories.
68. Reinhart Koselleck, *Preussen zwischen Reform und Revolution* (Stuttgart,

1967), pp. 52-78; Ernst Rudolf Huber, *Deutsche Verfassungsgeschichte seit 1789* (Stuttgart, 1967), I, pp. 95-384.

69. For Prussia, see Koselleck, Appendix III; for Bavaria, see *Regierungsblatt*, 1808, p. 2254.

70. I see these causes as external and preliminary to the transformation in sexual mentality and behaviour. Other direct and internal causes are discussed in subsequent chapters.

71. OAM, *Pfarrbeschreibung*, 1811.

72. Fritz Valjavec,*Geschichte der abendländischen Aufklärung* (Munich, 1961), p. 218 and *passim*.

73. Hauptstaatsarchiv, Munich, MI 46556/9271 Seinsheim to Minister of Interior. Quote derives from the research notes of Edward Shorter, who generously put them at my disposal.

74. Rupert Kornmann, *Gutachten über den Priestermangel* (Landshut, 1817), p.7; anon., *Freimütige Darstellung der Ursachen des Mangels von Katholischen Geistlichen* (Ulm, 1817), p.9; anon. [Constantin Höfler], *Concordat und Constitutionseid der Katholiken in Bayern* (Augsburg, 1847). p.11.

75. OAP 07090 Haller, 1828.

76. Angus McLaren, 'Some Secular Attitudes toward Sexual Behaviour', *French Historical Studies*, VIII 8 (Fall 1975), pp. 604-25. See also Theodore Zeldin, 'The Conflict of Moralities', *Conflicts in French Society: Anti-clericalism, Education and Morals in the Nineteenth Century*, T. Zeldin (ed.) (New York, 1970), pp. 13-50.

77. J.E. Aronson, *Die Kunst das Leben des schönen Geschlects zu verlängern, seine Schönheit zu erhalten und es in seinen eigentumlichen Krankheiten vor Missgriffen zu bewahren* (Berlin, 1817), pp. 154ff. This book went through four editions between 1790 and 1810.

78. See the article by Neuman cited above and Carl N. Degler, 'What Ought To Be and What Was: Women's Sexuality in the 19th Century', *American Historical Review*, 79, 5 (Dec. 1974), pp. 1467-90.

79. Edward Shorter, 'Female Emancipation, Birth Control, and Fertility in European History', *AHR*,LXXVIII, 3 (June 1973), pp. 605-40.

# 2 PROLETARIAN SEXUALITY

At the beginning of the nineteenth century Munich, the royal residential city of Bavaria, found itself deluged with illegitimate children. In 1811 the bastardy ratio soared to 43 per cent in St Peter's, one of the big parishes.[1] *Unser Liebe Frau,* Munich's other big parish, regularly counted one illegitimate birth for every two and a half legitimate.[2]

Meanwhile, the rural clergy of Catholic 'Old Bavaria' began noticing the same trend.[3] From the remotest corners of the kingdom—a markedly rural province even in comparison to other German territories, none of which boasted an urban centre to compare with some in England and France—clerical reports echoed those of Munich.[4] 'It's unusual,' wrote the curate of Birnbach, 'to find a not yet deflowered country girl.'[5] One of his colleagues from tiny Grafenau maintained that there were only a few women 'who don't already have one or even more illegitimate children. . . a virgin—*rara avis!'* [6]Many had the impression that 'amongst the youth virginity has become practically legendary'.[7] Bucolic Bavaria, it seems, vibrated to a new free and unrestrained tempo. And time after time curates noted the result of the fashionable life-style when they wrote 'illegitimate' after a name as they registered it in their baptismal logs. These descriptions of town and country life point to abrupt changes in moral attitudes and sexual behaviour. In fact, they suggest that Germans were caught up in a sexual revolution.

To demonstrate sexual licence is one thing; to assert that it constitutes a revolutionary change, another. These two questions concern us in this chapter. Documenting sexual licence is a simple matter of tracing the simultaneous diversification of social class and sexual behaviour in rural Germany as close as possible to the moment of their inception. But this does not establish a sexual revolution. The second question is more complex than the first. We have reasoned that the reforms of the Napoleonic era triggered the secularisation of sex which set the stage for greater sexual involvement. The argument is based on the assumptions that the parochial baptismal records for the period 1750 to 1850 are accurate, and that women were not aborting themselves to avoid illegitimate birth before 1800. These assumptions must be tested.

## Bavaria

On the basis of the enormity of the illegitimacy ratio, it is tempting to picture Bavaria in a state of total change in matters of sexuality around 1800. By the 1820s most parishes were reporting an unprecedented 1 : 3 or 1 : 4 illegitimacy ratio. Even before 1834, the year of the Home Laws which encumbered marriage by giving local communities control over marriage licences, any number of parishes—including very remote, rural ones—supported an incidence of bastardy that matched and sometimes even surpassed Paris's 35 per cent.[8] While it is true that these statistics support the notion of a sexual revolution occurring in Germany and Europe around this time, they can also mislead us.

Surprisingly enough, not everyone, it seems, was party to the sexual permissiveness. The reports of immorality cited above came from clerical alarmists—dyed-in-the-wool pessimists who were sceptical of social change and nostalgic over the past. Most of the clergy observed more accurately. These, without exception, singled out 'poor people', fingering them as the culprits in the new sexual behaviour. To cite a typical example: twelve bastards were born in 1829 in Than, Lower Bavaria. Poor people, the pastor reported, fathered eleven of them.[9] Disregarding for the moment the vague term 'poor people', let us pause to put our crude impressions in balance. The high bastardy ratio suggests that a sexual revolution swept the countryside, but the observations of the clergy, who maintained that sexual permissiveness did not infect the non-poor, counteract this notion. They tell us that at the local level, the new permissiveness attracted only a segment of the population. Others, amazingly, though co-religionists and parish neighbours, held aloof. Thus, if we follow the clergy's account, we cannot indiscriminately speak of a sexual revolution sweeping the countryside.

Oberkreutzberg, a parish in the Bavarian Forest (Upper Palatinate), provides a neat model of the 'spottiness' of the new sexual behaviour, and shows how a relatively small, well-defined group experienced it. Oberkreutzberg consisted of some 1,700 people, scattered about in numerous settlements, who broke down into three groups. Roughly 850 were independent farming families (*halb* and *ganz Bauern*). Some 300 were employees of a glass factory along with their dependants. The rest, somewhat less than one-third of the parishioners, were small property-owners. After 1800 the breezes of sexual permissiveness wafted through the Bavarian Forest; in 1828, 31 per cent of Oberkreutzberg's births were illegitimate.[10]

The farmers, however, held aloof from the sexual indulgence in full swing elsewhere in the parish. They fathered no bastards in 1828. Set apart by themselves in tiny settlements, hamlets and small villages, these families constituted the traditional element of society. Not all, to be sure, were big farmers, but there were enough of them to accommodate the work needs of any non-self-employed cotters' or smallholders' children in their midst, and to allow the Oberkreutzberg parishioners to continue to cherish the notion that they still basically resembled the society of the Old Regime.

The glass workers, disliked by their curate because of their 'uppity-ness' and independence (stemming from their work) constituted a second distinct segment of the parish. Not only did they earn their livelihood apart from the soil, but physically they lived apart from the others in woodland areas. Probably enjoying some form of symbiotic home economy like domestic workers, they were disliked by their curate for their loose morals as well, which led, by his reckoning, to a few illegitimate births amongst them each year.

Mainly responsible for Oberkreutzberg's numerous bastards was the large contingent of 'poor people'. Their marginal economies forced the familial unit to break up, or to alter, earlier than those of other Ober-kreutzbergers. 'Because of their poverty, they let their daughters wander off to find work. There, by and by, they get pregnant.'[11] This group—probably not much more than one-fourth of the parishioners—accounted for almost all the bastards.

Can we accept the Oberkreutzberg case as typical? The pattern and frequency of bastardy give us cause to think so. It follows the tedious script of contemporary observers who specifically blamed 'poor people' for the new sexual behaviour.[12] Fortunately, the records of another parish, Dietramszell, an area of nine square kilometres in the midst of the high plateau stretching from Munich to the Alps, provide statistical evidence with which we can test contemporary reports. At the same time, Dietramszell will enable us to come to grips with the exasperating phrase 'poor people'.

Dietramszell counted 202 property-owners in 1812. Only those owning full units or half-units may be considered independent farmers. The size and frequency of property ownership show that many property units were little more than places of residence whose owners earned their living wholly or mostly apart from them. Strictly speaking, pro-perty units should only be thought of as farms when they possess a thoroughly isolated, rural quality, or when several were grouped to-gether in a small settlement, where each owner nevertheless won his livelihood entirely from his farm (in Figure 2 these settlements are shown and designated as having less than 30 inhabitants).[13]

We can see from a glance at Table 2 that the value of the 202 property units differed immensely, and that Dietramszell counted many small property-owners.[14] This was by no means unusual for Bavaria or Germany. In fact, the ratio of small property-owners to larger ones was somewhat lower in Dietramszell than elsewhere.[15] Hence, it cannot be regarded as exceptional.

Table 2: Number and Size of Properties According to the *Hoffuss* System in Dietramszell, Bavaria

| Size | 1/1 | 3/4 | 1/2 | 1/3 | 1/4 | 1/6 | 1/8 | 1/12 | 1/16 | 1/24 | 1/32 |
|------|-----|-----|-----|-----|-----|-----|-----|------|------|------|------|
| Number | 5 | 0 | 43 | 0 | 48 | 0 | 15 | 0 | 74 | 0 | 17 |

The six varieties of property-owners in Dietramszell break down further into three groups according to distinct roles each played in the community's economic life: farmers (1/1 and 1/2 unit of property), smallholders (1/4 and 1/8), and cotters (1/16 and 1/32). Rural Bavaria consisted of these three fairly well-defined groups of roughly equal size.[16] Who, then, we may now ask, were the sexually permissive 'poor people'? We would naturally assume that the phrase excludes farmers and includes cotters and day labourers. And so it did:

Parents with means keep their children at home and give them the necessary supervision. . .For the poor this control is either impossible or so difficult that [illegitimate] pregnancies often occur in this class.[17]

'Experience shows,' runs another typical report, 'that it is precisely the cotters' and day labourers' daughters who are the most frivolous and who bear the most illegitimate children.'[18] No matter, then, whether they were actually poor, we know to whom the label 'poor people' was applied.

But what of smallholders? Surely they cannot be lumped together with the day labourers? After all, they owned considerably more property. Yet a linkage was exactly what the clerical observers intended. They maintained that 'deflowering' befell smallholders' daughters, because these in particular found it necessary to send their children, still of tender age, away from home so as not to overtax the family economy.[19] In short, they could not afford to keep children over the age of about twelve at home. We know, of course, that in fact it was

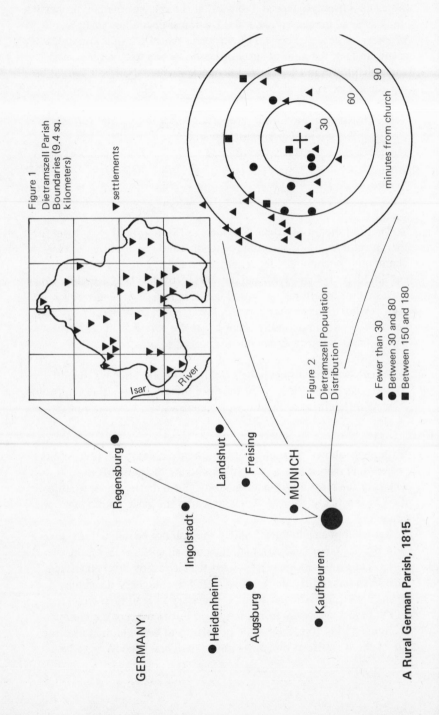

Figure 1
Dietramszell Parish
Boundaries (9.4 sq.
kilometers)

▲ settlements

Isar
River

Figure 2
Dietramszell Population
Distribution

▲ Fewer than 30
● Between 30 and 80
■ Between 150 and 180

30   60   90

minutes from church

GERMANY

● Regensburg

● Ingolstadt

● Landshut

● Freising

● Heidenheim

● Augsburg

MUNICH
●

● Kaufbeuren

**A Rural German Parish, 1815**

the smallholders who furnished the rural economy with domestic help.
Once beyond the pale of parental control, the curates reckoned, the
sexual energies of these youths knew no reins.[20] Hence, when it was
asserted that 'poor people' supported all the bastardy, this definitely
meant smallholders—though certainly not all of them—as well as
cotters and day labourers.

Since we have both the tax and parochial records of Dietramszell at
hand, it is a simple matter to check contemporary observations against
the record. In 1817 20 per cent of the parish new-born were bastards.
Who was party to the illegitimacy? The lines break cleanly: farmers
fathered no bastards, but amongst smallholders and cotters (including
day labourers) illegitimacy had become commonplace. Twenty per cent
of the births among the former (smallholders) and nearly 29 per cent
among the latter were illegitimate. These two groups—together about
two-thirds of the Dietramszell parish families—accounted for all the
bastardy.

We see how true this is if we look closer at the Dietramszell families
into which illegitimate children were born in 1817. In about half of the
cases the presence of young legitimate children and their parents and of
an illegitimate child and its unmarried parent make it clear that the sib-
ling who did not inherit the family property fathered the bastard. In the
remaining instances, the father or mother of the illegitimate child had
not yet inherited the family property, but would in time, there being
no rival siblings in the household. They had refused to bide their time
until their elders died and passed the family plot on. To these grown
children of smallholder, cotter or day labourer origin a new era had
dawned; they believed, in a way their parents or grandparents had not
dared to believe, that society could and would support them and their
children. Meanwhile, as far as middle-class farmers were concerned,
society was being turned on its ear—the poor, 'propertyless people
with no prospect of marriage'—were populating the countryside with
bastards.[21]

The situation is compounded if we bear in mind that families of
farmers were usually twice as large as those of cotters and half again
larger than those of smallholders. This means that there were considerably more unmarried adults living in these families than in those of
smallholders and cotters, yet they held aloof from the prevailing sexual
permissiveness. Unlike their neighbours and co-religionists, these celibates were content to live life out in the traditional manner and in
accord with a traditional sexual code. As those who were not content
to do so began to settle into a new life-style, social tension grew up

within Dietramszell. In 1822 the farmers of Linden, one of the settlements of the Dietramszell parish, wrote a letter to King Ludwig of Bavaria bemoaning the disappearance of the traditional farm hand. In

Table 3:    Size of Property and Average Size of Family (Including Farm Hands) in Dietramszell, Germany

| Property Size | 1/1 | 1/2 | 1/4 | 1/8 | 1/16 | 1/32 |
|---|---|---|---|---|---|---|
| Family Size | 8 | 6.5 | 5.9 | 5.5 | 4.3 | 3.5 |

recent times, they said, farm hands had become either lazy, or—even worse, to their way of thinking—money-grabbing and immoral.[22]

Accustomed to the swollen and, for many, threatening world population figures of recent years, we cannot help but be amazed at Dietramszell's diminutive population of roughly 1,200. It becomes all the more astonishing to be informed that so much diversity in sexual behaviour could exist among so few people. Yet, circumstances obtained within the ten square kilometre boundaries of the parish which made their small world appear immensely greater to them than it does to us, and which allowed localisation of sexual behaviour to an extent that we would not have imagined possible in so small and sparsely populated an area. To begin with, although Dietramszell had begun to feel the effects of modernisation, its population still lived and worked under physical conditions that more resembled the previous millennium than the coming hundred years. This is hardly surprising, since it was the very lack of farm mechanisation that necessitated a large, if dispersed, rural population. Communication and transportation lagged exasperatingly, a factor which would not have been of overriding importance had the entire population lived in one, or even two or three, villages. But Dietramszell, fully rural like most of the rest of Germany and Europe, counted some 34 settlements, which, in view of the fact that most people were still afoot, cannot be described as close to one another (see Figure 2; the distances from the various settlements to the parish centre at Dietramszell are walking-time measurements). All of the people may have congregated in the Dietramszell church on Sunday; many may have seen each other on market days, and many of the youth may have frequented the same few entertainment places, but it would most certainly be an exaggeration to think of all of the people as close neighbours or to imagine that they were normally in ready and easy contact with one another. On the contrary, a study of their settlements reminds us of the lingering insular quality of life.

Since isolation imposed itself in varying degrees on all the Dietramszell parishioners, it is important to know who was neighbour to whom. While no rigid geographical boundaries may be established to hermetically seal off the various kinds of Dietramszell property-owners one from another, nevertheless a certain pattern emerges pointing in the direction of socially monolithic settlements. Day labourers tended to live amongst day labourers and cotters in a large village, and farmers amongst farmers in a hamlet, and so on. In terms of the sexual permissiveness that had mushroomed up amongst the Dietramszell people, this means, of course, that those who were party to it tended to be neighbours and isolated from those who were not. On the other hand, the maturing and mature sons and daughters of farmers, for whom economic considerations still largely determined marital choice, tended to be neighbours. As a result of these socio-spatial considerations the tiny Dietramszell parish becomes somewhat magnified, lending greater credence to the astonishing sexual diversity that sorted its parishioners out.

Table 4: Socio-Spatial Structure of a Rural Parish—Dietramszell, Germany

| Number of Properties Per Settlement | Size of Property | | | | | |
|---|---|---|---|---|---|---|
| | Farmers 1/1 − 1/2 | | Small Farmers 1/4 − 1/8 | | Cotters/Day Labourers 1/16 − 1/32 | |
| 1      = Farm | 1 | 2 | 1 | 1 | 2 | 1 |
| 2 - 5  = Hamlet | 1 | 20 | 3 | 1 | 6 | 4 |
| 2 - 9  = Small Village | 0 | 8 | 9 | 2 | 10 | 1 |
| 10-20 = Medium Village | 2 | 9 | 23 | 5 | 24 | 8 |
| 20 +   = Large Village | 1 | 4 | 12 | 6 | 32 | 0 |

But the area's social geography is by no means a *deus ex machina* through which the diversity may be explained. Class residence was not, after all, nearly as distinct as class bastardy statistics, and, even more importantly, these lines of geographical social distinction were largely erased from seed time to harvest time by occupational contacts among most types of property-owners. At the end of a long day's work the cotters' children returned from the fields to their homes in the village where they socialised amongst themselves, but the *boarding* farm hand returned to the farmer's homestead. Are we, consequently, required to believe that a persistent awareness amongst the virile and nubile farm hands and farmers' children that the former would some day inherit and return to small farms such as they had known during childhood, or that they might choose city life and migrate to, let us say, Munich, kept them socially and sexually apart at such a carefree age? By no means. Not future prospects but recent past developments cooled their attraction for one another. We noted above that the Dietramszell farmers had become discontented with their farm hands, who seemed insubordinate, money-minded and oversexed. This was a common complaint in Bavaria and throughout Germany in the nineteenth century, but it is a tale only half told. The farmers themselves had become oriented more to profit and less to subsistence. To whatever degree this process had advanced by 1825, the old patriarchal relationship between farmer and farm hands had eroded. The employer no longer treated the farm hand as an intimate member of the family whom one loved and scolded, and with whom one prayed and ate, but as an employee whose worth was set by his work. Whatever psychological difficulties this might have caused farm hands, they adjusted as best they might, which is why by the early part of the nineteenth century farmers had begun wondering what had happened to the loyal, obedient and mindless farm hand of days gone by.[23] In this manner the emotions that characterise a parent—child relationship were giving way to those of the employer—employee, creating a gulf too wide for potential affective relationships between the farmer's mature children and his farm hands to span. Nascent class consciousness inhibited sexual permissiveness among the possessing group.

The German Heimgarten custom provides us with additional reason —based on etymological evidence—to claim that sexual permissiveness was a class phenomenon. Heimgarten, it will be recalled, referred to the traditional manner by which a young man and woman decided whether or not to exchange marital vows. Marriage may have been more romantic among smallholders and cotters, but during the Old Regime the double exchange of vows and property held for them as well. And, like others, they had to postpone marriage until miserable family plots fell into their hands. After 1800, awash in the currents of sexual permissiveness, business and inheritance considerations soon dissolved. Social contact between the sexes became frequent, and traditional peasant frocks gave way to more suggestive, revealing and fashionable clothing.[24] In the abeyance of property concerns only the Heimgarten custom continued to occupy smallholders. But unmoored from practical considerations, this drifted swiftly along in the prevailing currents. By the 1820s, Heimgarten was no longer a little tête-à-tête , but, rather, just about

any clandestine meeting between two 'poor people' in love. Before long
outraged complaints were to be heard of Heimgarten taking place in the
hayloft, or, in the summertime, out in the green meadow. Obviously, it
was becoming more spontaneous, arising, perhaps, just from youthful
nocturnal carousing, or in connection with some dance—now held ever
more frequently—somewhere in the vicinity.[25] Cotter parents did not
object to the new twist that sexual permissiveness had given to the traditional Heimgarten. In fact, they sometimes actually made it a point to
vacate the cottage of an evening to ensure the necessary privacy for a
successful Heimgarten.[26] Not surprisingly, the meaning of the word
itself began to change. Farmers began to suspect with good reason that
the revised Heimgarten helped sustain the high bastardy ratio. It no
longer bore any resemblance to their traditional custom, and, of course,
it was of no use to them in its new form. For whatever reason—because
of disgust with sexual looseness or from shame or embarrassment arising
from the new connotation the word had taken on—they dropped the
Heimgarten altogether. The word itself, no longer part of the German
language, seems to have fallen victim to the social upheaval of the new
morality. What happened to the Heimgarten is further evidence that,
although a sexual revolution may have swept through the countryside,
it found only pockets of enthusiasts—not blanket reception.

To sum up, the remarkable records of Dietramszell provide two bits
of information: they offer factual evidence that sexual permissiveness
did indeed infect smallholders and cotters but not farmers, and they tell
us that both smallholders and cotters were included under the rubric
'poor people'. Oberkreutzberg and Dietramszell may not be microcosms
of central Europe in the 1830s, but, on the other hand, their surprising
social and economic variety is not a poor likeness of Bavaria and even of
Germany. Shortly after 1800 clear lines began to separate those conta-
minated with the new permissiveness from those who were not. The
sexual revolution was not a tidal wave that engulfed the country, but a
swift current that swept along finding its channel wherever 'poor people'
chanced to live.

The concept of a sexual revolution is at least implicit in the source
material we have been using. Consider, for a moment, the credibility of
the Dietramszell records. The priest wrote down the following information for each family in his parish: house name and number, family name,
number and age of each family member; marital status, confirmed and
not yet confirmed, communicants and non-communicants, number legiti-
mately born in previous years, and the number illegitimately born. How
likely is it that a person would take such pains only to falsify his record

by assigning bastard children exclusively to smallholding and cotter families? The same may be said of all the baptismal registers of the Bavarian clergy. Those who doubt that a sexual revolution occurred must somehow explain why the records were systematically falsified by imputing bastardy to one class but not another.

Still, class discrepancies in sexual behaviour do not in themselves establish the fact of a differential sexual revolution. There are several reasons for this but the point we must take up here concerns credibility again. Record books of Bavarian parishes indicate that illegitimacy had fluctuated from between 5 and 10 per cent of all births during the 1770s, 1780s and 1790s.[27] Naturally, the careers of many priests who kept these records extended into the nineteenth century.[28] Now anyone who doubts that a sexual revolution took place must be prepared to deal with the alternatives. Why did the clergy, working in the same parishes after 1800 as before, suddenly decide to record bastards giving rise to a 20 per cent jump in the illegitimacy ratio?[29] Why did they describe in detail the familiarity between the sexes at the beginning of the nineteenth century and completely ignore it twenty years earlier? Why were they unconcerned if sexual licence led to an abortion in 1790 but upset if it led to an illegitimate birth in 1810? Finally, those who doubt a sexual revolution do so in the face of a specific historical assertion: the 1820 to 1830 records of the parish clergy trace the origin of the new sexual permissiveness back to the Napoleonic period.[30] It makes more sense to take the record at face value. After 1800 bastardy surged. Although we have yet to discuss other criteria, the evidence allows us to speak theoretically in terms of a sexual revolution, and, further, positively to assert the existence of this revolution in the lives of many lower-class rural people.

### Westphalia

What was happening in Bavaria happened elsewhere as well in rural Germany. A Westphalian writing in the *Historisch-Politische Blätter* about his homeland during the first half of the nineteenth century distinguished three cultural areas: the Sauerland in the Ruhr, Münster to the north, and Paderborn to the east.[31] Before Napoleon redrew the political map of Germany, the latter two areas had been ecclesiastical principalities, whereas the first belonged partly to the Earl of Berg and partly to the Duke of Westphalia. These several traditions, along with the peculiarities of the land in each territory, had left their mark on the Westphalians, allowing the correspondent of the *Blätter* to identify each in some detail. Before discussing them in turn, let us pause to note the

the author's overall impression of the sexual behaviour of his native people. The Sauerländer, immersed in business, seemed hardly to have had time for it. Their sexual behaviour, he thought, was faultless. The Münsterländer, on the other hand, could no longer sustain the sexual discipline of former times (Old Regime), and the Paderborn population, in his opinion, had allowed themselves to become downright debauched. These differences in sexuality were so pronounced that the writer found it easier to distinguish Westphalian cultural areas on this score than on any other.

Statistics confirm that the author knew his Westphalians. During the 1820s and 1830s the Sauerländer managed an illegitimacy ratio which hardly exceeded 1 per cent of all births—certainly one of Germany's lowest, while bastardy amongst their neighbours to the north mounted to the vicinity of 6 to 12 per cent. Meanwhile, the lascivious Paderborn people, with 15 to 30 per cent of all births illegitimate, rivalled the Bavarians of southern Germany (see Figure 3).[32] The baptismal logs on which these estimates of bastardy are based—confirming the correspondent's impressions—are doubly useful because they sometimes list the occupation of the illegitimate child's father. This information is vital because no such close superimposition of tax and parish data is possible in Westphalia as it was in Dietramszell, Bavaria. Out of the 61 cases where the Westphalian occupations are known, only two fathers of bastards had middle-class standing—a Tirolean merchant and an army officer, neither of whom in all likelihood claimed Westphalia as his home. In addition to these two, three men holding positions as clerks, probably natives, fathered illegitimate children. All of the rest—not one farmer among them—may be counted among the rural proletariat: artisans, farm hands, day labourers, shepherds and the like (with the exception of the very few Sauerland cases, for obvious reasons, as we shall see). Thus, we may note at the outset that Westphalians, like Bavarians, parted company when it came to questions of sexual permissiveness.

The fact that the Sauerland had industrialised while the other two Westphalian regions had not constitutes the greatest single difference amongst them. The Sauerländer, as a consequence, appeared to be developing both mentally and physically in a different manner from their neighbours. Big and muscular, they were as strong and healthy as anyone in Germany, a fact that might best be attributed to their exogamous marriages. Because of their economic activity, the Sauerländer often came into contact with 'foreigners', and, in the opinion of the correspondent, had intermarried with them frequently enough to have

Figure 3.    Bastardy in Westphalia.  1820 - 1840

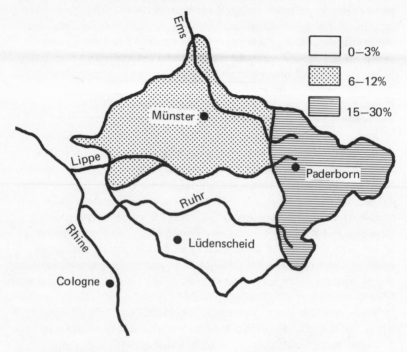

0–3%

6–12%

15–30%

Source: see footnote 37

completely dissolved pure native blood. It is unclear just how often
these marriages with outsiders, as well as those amongst the Sauerländer
themselves, came about because of economic considerations as opposed
to affective relationships. The working people, it seems, like the entre-
preneur, tried to marry prosperously. This need not mean that they
always strove to marry into families of better economic standing than
their own, but that in deciding upon marriage partners, the element of
economic aptitude, if not money itself, figured importantly. Marriage
meant an economic as well as a romantic partnership.

It is difficult to imagine that affective relationships, like those of the
Zurich Highlanders, were not involved in leading these working-class
people to marry.[33] Yet the astonishingly low bastardy ratio attests to
the fact that romantic love was not indiscriminate. The Sauderländer,
thrifty, practical, business-minded people, took care not to become en-
tangled in relationships that could become financially draining, such as
caring for an illegitimate child. It would be fascinating to know if and

to what extent they became divorced or deserted, but our correspondent makes no mention of this aspect of life. The health and physical vitality of the Sauerländer manifested itself in their physical surroundings and their mental attitudes. The industrial villages—especially these—were neat, clean and sturdy. The village streets and country roads were well kept, giving the whole area a prosperous, positive look. The people themselves, three-fourths of whom worked in industry, shared this appearance. They loved nature for different reasons than most Germans: the mountains for their iron, the valleys for their timber, the rivers for their water power which made the factories hum. Of the three Westphalian areas it is clear that on the whole the Sauerland was wealthiest, and that, on the average, its people enjoyed a higher standard of living than their neighbours.

Life was as wretched around Paderborn as it was good in the Sauerland. Both the people and their dwellings reflected misery. Small and skinny, they married early and endogamously. Starting marriage penniless and soon burdened with children, many of the Paderborn people lived in and out of poverty from childhood to old age. Evidently, only a relatively few hard-working ones managed to eject themselves completely from a relentless orbit of poverty. Their misery produced poor mental attitudes; they were lazy, superstitious and spendthrifts. Only dire necessity propelled them to work, and, should they ever have found themselves with extra *Groschen*, they drank them away in the first tavern they came across. Not surprisingly, their living quarters ranked among the worst in all Germany. Constructed of a few planks of literally begged, borrowed, or stolen wood, they consisted of two rooms; one was large enough for a bed and whatever animals the couple owned, the other—unduly graced with the name 'living room'—was not much more than an outsized crate complete with holes for windows. The whole ensemble resembled a shack much more than a house. The correspondent's rhetoric warns us that he nurtured the same prejudices towards the 'poor' as did Bavarian farmers. But this need not distract us, since we are here concerned with the question of class involvement in the sexual revolution. Furthermore, research on the population and economy of the Paderborn principality around 1800 bears him out. The area was overrun with 3,900 cotters and 1,700 day labourers who could not begin to be absorbed as farm hands on the 2,300 farms. Nor could they find work in industry, which lagged so far behind that of the Sauerland that it could only just sustain its estimated 2,700 workers.[34] No textile industry obtained at all except in the westernmost part of the Paderborn area.

In the mind of the correspondent, one principal cause accounted for the destitution in Paderborn—their impetuous marriages. In sharp contrast to the Sauerländer, unbridled passion alone determined marriage partners amongst day labourers in Paderborn. During the early adult, pre-marriage years, young men and women slept around. There was hardly a day labourer's daughter left who had not had sexual relations with a *braunen Heinrich* (lusty rustic).

> But they consider this to be customary and moral, and live with the conviction that a good marriage, like a piece of cloth, must first be broken in before it can become useful house linen.[35]

Unrestrained as they must have been, the day labourers did not sustain the high bastardy quota all by themselves. Sexual taboos amongst farm hands had fallen as well. Any farmer who wished to keep his volatile female domestics in service had to maintain constant surveillance over them. As in Dietramszell, then, both groups of rural people, constituting the smallest property-holders, were involved in the new sexuality. It appears that in the Paderborn region, perhaps more so than in Bavaria, the day labourers accounted for the high illegitimacy. The area was ridden with large villages, where, as we saw, day labourers tended to concentrate. The Westphalian writer, who had never seen more wretched villages than these anywhere in Germany, attributed most of the poverty and bastardy of the area to the loose women *(Barackenbewohnerin)* of these places rather than to the populations of the smaller settlements.

Because of its economy, Münster resembled Paderborn more than it did the Sauerland, but beyond that the two former ecclesiastical territories were easily distinguishable. Whereas the Paderborn day labourers left a strong imprint on the life-style of that region, the farmers set the tone of life around Münster. The countryside was dotted with full-sized farms rather than with sprawling proletarian villages. Naturally, there were small farms as well, which provided the farm-hand class of workers, and a certain quota of day labourers. But both of these seemed to have been absorbed in a rural economy dominated by the large farms to a degree no longer possible in the adjacent Paderborn economy, and in a manner that still allowed the tempo of life to be coloured by the customs of the farmers. Their great stone homesteads, whose kitchens alone were large enough to accommodate the entire household—family and farm hands—all at once, contrast with the draughty wooden shacks that sheltered many of the nearby Paderborn people.

Since the Münster economy was local and rural, few opportunities for outside contact presented themselves. Consequently, tradition and custom carried on uninterrupted, and, in contrast to their Westphalian neighbours to the south, the Münsterländer generally preferred to marry amongst themselves. The farmers, it turns out, married much like their counterparts in Bavaria. Relatives and respected neighbours recommended their children to each other, leaving the final decision in the hands of each family's most distinguished member. This signals to us that the Westphalian farmers were as far removed from sexual permissiveness as their Bavarian counterparts. Statistics bear this out; not one farmer contributed to the illegitimacy that his fellow Münsterlander were sustaining.

Bastardy, again, was the work of the farm-hand class. When compared to other areas of Germany the bastardy ratio of the Münsterländer seems only moderate, but the farmers were little inclined to view any illegitimacy amongst farm hands with equanimity. Although thirty years earlier (around 1800) almost no illegitimacy at all existed, it had in the meantime become common. Baptismal logs suggest that those occupied as farm hands sustained more bastardy than any other group. In Herzefeld eight out of the eleven identified fathers of illegitimate children born between 1820 and 1826 were farm hands (along with two cotters and one small farmer).[36] This could simply be explained by the fact that in an area of many large farms the farm-hand class was large, quite possibly larger than the day labourer group.

Difficult as it may be to pin down exactly who was responsible for illegitimacy in Westphalia, a few definite conclusions may now be drawn. The sexual permissiveness penetrated the industrial Sauerland hardly at all, if bastardy alone is to be the measure of revolutionary change in sexual conduct. We may suppose that the vibrant economy of the Saüerlander allowed them to marry earlier than the very mature children of the Münsterländer farmers. But how are we to explain the loose pre-marital sex of their other neighbour, the Paderborn day labourer? Clearly, sexual licence came to different areas in different ways. Secondly, in both rural areas of Westphalia farmers lived and married according to custom while others around them adopted new sexual attitudes and conduct, suggesting, as in Bavaria, pockets of diversity in the two former ecclesiastical territories, in addition to general differences among the three Westphalian regions.

Bavaria and Westphalia prove that sexual behaviour became varied in Central Europe around 1800. We will see that other areas had similar experiences. Secondly, quantitative evidence based on Dietramszell tax and parish records force us to insist upon class differences in sexual behaviour. In fact, distinctive sexual conduct among rustics constitutes the first hard historical evidence pointing to the existence of a rural proletarian class. By 1800 rural popular morality was turning askew— where there had been one there were now two popular moralities amongst rural common people. Farmers clung to traditional ways, but the rural lower class adopted a non-Tridentine morality. On the threshold of urbanisation and industrialisation in Germany, rural sexuality had become a matter of class instead of community.

Since we have posited the rural proletariat as the source of sexual dynamism in early modern society, and since we will be discussing this class throughout much of what follows, it is worth while to pause here long enough to allow an image of these people to crystallise into an historical statement. In terms of numbers the rural proletariat constituted about 30 to 50 per cent of the rural population; in terms of occupation they mostly depended on piece-work and agrarian wage work, since they were themselves increasingly propertyless; and, finally, in terms of sex, they displayed licence while those around them maintained restraint.[37] There are many other ways through which we will come to identify the rural proletariat, and still other as yet undiscovered characteristics. For the moment, these bits of information may serve as a foundation on which to build as we attempt to understand what propelled them towards a sexual revolution.

## Notes

1. Ordinariatsarchiv Munich (OAM), *Pfarrei Beschreibung (Pf. Besch.)*, 1811.
2. OAM *Status Animarum, circa* 1810.
3. 'Old Bavaria' means Upper and Lower Bavaria and the Upper Palatinate. Archival records provide evidence of rural illegitimacy about ten years later than for Munich. It should not be assumed that this is chronologically correct or even that illegitimacy was more widespread in the cities than throughout the countryside.
4. Ordinariatsarchiv Passau (OAP), file no. 07090; and OAM, catalogue title, *Visitation Beantwortung (Vis. Beant.)*. During the 1820s the Archbishop of Munich and the Bishop of Passau required all of their parish clergy to submit written reports to the chancery regarding the state of morality and practice of religion. These reports—hundreds of them—have been preserved in the diocesan archives.
5. OAP, 07090 Birnbach, 1829.

6. OAM, *Vis. Beant.*, Ruprectsberg, 1823.
7. *Generalien Sammlung (Gen. Samm.)*, Regensburg (ed. Joseph Lipf), p. 272 (1832). OAM, *Vis. Beant.*, Herbertshausen, 1824; Lenggriess, 1826. OAP, 07090 Dekanat Vilshofen, 1828.
8. OAP, 07090 Deanery reports, 1828; OAM, *Seelenstandbeschreibung*; for Paris I am following Louis Chevalier, *Classes laborieuses et classes dangereuses* (Paris, 1958), p. 383.
9. OAP, 07090 Than, 1828.
10. OAP, 07090 Oberkreutzberg, 1828.
11. Ibid.
12. Since virtually everyone agreed on this point, specific citations would be too numerous to list. Three random references are OAP, 07090 Than, 1828; Dekanat Aigen am Inn, 1829; and Dekanat Schatz an Ordinariat, 1828.
13. Pankraz Fried, *Herrschaftsgeschichte der Altbayerischen Landgerichte Dachau und Kranzberg im Hoch- und Spät-mittelalter sowie in der frühen Neuzeit* (Munich, 1962), p. 16.
14. In cases where other than farm work obtained, the tax assessment considered the lucrativeness of the trade or work being pursued independently of property. It did not happen that a small property-holder could establish himself in one of the more respectable trades or more profitable businesses.
15. Pankraz Fried, 'Historisch-statistische Beiträge zur Geschichte des Kleinbauerntums (Söldnertums) im westlichen Oberbayern', *Mitteilungen der Geogr. Ges. in München,* LVII (1966), p. 19 (table).
16. Although there were many fewer farmer families, they were as numerous as cotters and smallholders by a head count. I discuss rural social structure in more detail in 'Lower Class Morality: the Case of Bavaria', *JSH* (Fall 1974) pp. 79-95.
17. OAP, 07090 Schöllnach, 1828.
18. OAP, 07090 Than, 1829.
19. OAM, *Vis Beant.*, Kohlgrub, 1826.
20. OAM, *Vis. Beant* Schliersee, 1826; Tegernsee, 1826; Oberammergau, 1826; Lenggriess, 1826; OAP, 07090 Obing, 1827; Schöllnach, 1828.
21. OAP, 07090 Grafenau, 1829.
22. OAM, *Vis. Beant.*, Dietramszell, 1822.
23. Rolf Engelsing, *Zur Sozialgeschichte deutscher Mittel-und Unterschichten* (Göttingen, 1973), pp. 190ff.
24. *Gen. Samm*, Munich, I, 73 (1823); OAP, 07090 Alholming, 1829.
25. OÁM, *Vis.Beant.*, Tettenhausen, 1828.
26. OAM, *Vis. Beant.*, Garmisch, 1826.
27. OAM, *Pfarrmatrikelnbücher.*
28. I have read their reports and know this to be fact.
29. It is nonsense to claim that this rise in Bavarian bastardy may be explained by a traditional 'bed now, marry later' practice or that pre-marital 'sexual relationships were common' in pre-modern society; see page 414 of L. A. Tilly, J. W. Scott, M. Cohen, 'Women's Work and European Fertility Patterns', *Journal of Interdisciplinary History,* VI, 3 (Winter 1976). Again, the need to qualify our historical judgements is evident. In *some* parts of France and *some* parts of Protestant Germany, pre-marital sex did become more common during the eighteenth century, and certain families did have records of bastardy generation after generation; see Laslett, Ch. 4, Möller, pp. 90ff. and Klenk, pp. 171. It would be convenient if we possessed a map

which showed which areas of Europe were strict in these matters and which were lenient, but until we do, it only confuses the issue to generalise.

30. I have searched the archives for eighteenth-century reports of parish clergy bearing on sexuality. There are none, although other reports, which would have taken this matter up had there been anything to take up, are not lacking. The 1820-30 data are in OAM, *Visitation Beantwortung,* and OAP 07090, *Sittenverfall* collections.

31. *Historisch-Politische Blätter,* XVI (1845), pp. 463-72, 505-20, 587-600.

32. These figures, it should be noted, are estimates which are based on statistics drawn from the following archives: Landesarchiv der Evangelischen Kirche von Westfalen (Bielefeld)—*Kirchengemeinden* Elsey, Iserlohn, and Lüden-scheid; Bistumsarchiv Münster—*Pfarreien* Dülmen, Appelhüsen, Werne, and Herzfeld; and, finally, for the diocese of Paderborn where the baptismal registries have not been deposited in the central archives, the parish archives of Korbach, Rüthen, and Arolsen. Illegitimacy ran highest in the Paderborn area, and I suspect it would have been even higher had I been able to get information from parishes that were actually within the boundaries of the old ecclesiastical principality of Paderborn.

33. Rudolf Braun, *Industrialisierung und Volksleben: Die Veränderungen der Lebensformen in einen landlichen Industriegebiet vor 1800 (Zürcher Oberland)* (Zurich, 1960). On Westphalian industrial growth and industrial families, see Joachim Kormann, *Die Manufakturen im Rheinland* (Bonn, 1972), and 'Prussian Mercantilism and the Rise of the Krefeld Silk Industry', *Transactions of the American Philosophical Society,* LVIII (n.s.), 7 (1968), Pt. IV, 'Tight Little Families'.

34. Hansjörg Gruber, *Die Entwicklung der pfälzische Wirtschaft 1816-1834* (Saarbrucken, 1969), pp. 67ff; F. W. Henning, *Dienste und Abgaben der Bauern im 18. Jahrhundert* (Stuttgart, 1969), pp. 168-9.

35. *Historisch-Politische Blätter,.* XVI (1845), p. 511.

36. Bistumsarchiv Münster, *Taufbuch* Herzfeld. This evidence is far from conclusive since there were 49 illegitimate births during the span of these six years.

37. The size of the class would vary considerably from area to area, but the Dietramszell proportions by no means exaggerate the lower-class element. It would be ludicrous to think that all proletarian women were sexually permissive. What the bastardy statistics imply is discussed in Chapter 3.

# 3 PROLETARIAN FAMILIES

The data we have reviewed reveal widespread sexual activity among lower-class, rural Bavarians and Westphalians during the first part of the nineteenth century. There was nothing unusual about this for Germany. Even Pomerania counted triple the number of illegitimate births around 1830 than a hundred years earlier.[1] Research has established that the new sexual conduct penetrated throughout Central Europe and that it was urban as well as rural.[2] We have suggested that the great change in sexual mentality was occasioned by the Secularisation and the reforms of the Napoleonic era. Yet it seems ridiculous to think that people suppressed sex until the state came along and said, 'OK, go to it'. If common people suddenly abandoned celibacy, they themselves must be part of the explanation for the newly found experience. We must now decide what egged them on to sexual permissiveness.

A problem arises because the people we have been discussing disappear or metamorphose in the course of the nineteenth and twentieth centuries. The farm hand, like his city counterpart, the domestic servant, vanishes almost entirely, while the rural day labourer, steadily absorbed by industry, disappears at the same time. Concomitantly, both groups migrate to the cities as urbanisation goes on apace since about 1830, accelerating after German unification. Our subjects were caught up in this blur as urbanisation and industrialisation ingested them between 1750 and 1870. As a consequence, we are faced with the old familiar question: which came first, the chicken or the egg? Did rural people become sexually permissive because of industrialisation? Or because of urbanisation? It has been asserted that they began to change when, among other things, they began to sense the anonymity of city air.[3] Does this mean that rural people experienced no sexual revolution in their own right? The problem is admittedly complicated because during the nineteenth century people migrated back and forth between town and country, depending on work opportunities and other factors, so hardly knows at any given moment whether they are rural or uban.[4] Nevertheless, it is not likely that the big city was what changed the sexual conduct of the rustic. Westphalia itself is evidence pointing to a self-contained rural sexual revolution. The areas whose economy was most thoroughly agrarian led the way to sexual licence. In Oberkreutz-berg, as in the Sauerland, people doing piece-work or 'factory' work were less promiscuous than agricultural day labourers.

Industrialisation and urbanisation in the Rhine Palatinate also suggest this. In 1790 a shoe manufacturing company was established in the city of Pirmasens. During the Napoleonic era, when people began dressing more according to style and taste than to custom, the company had become Pirmasens' most important business. Many of the city's 4,000 inhabitants worked there—the men in the shops, their wives and children as hawkers far out in the surrounding countryside.[5] As the factory prospered, the city grew. In 1800 it counted only 400 Catholics, but by 1825 there were 1,200. Rural day labourers, who could no longer make ends meet doing pick-up work in the country when their increased numbers surfeited the rural labour market, were drifting into the cities.[6] During these years it is true that Pirmasens sustained greater illegitimacy than the surrounding countryside.[7] In 1809 the Pirmasens' priest wrote to the bishop, 'Perversity is difficult to correct, especially in a city where corruption has become rampant and where the men in charge are without faith, religion, and morals'.[8] Nevertheless, it was clear to him that the city's immorality originated with the influx of day labourers.

> With the powerful development of the shoe industry and the rapid increase in population, most of whom have moved in from the country, . . . many moral lapses also find their way into the city.[9]

Thus, Pirmasens took on its character, at least partially, from the newly arrived day labourers, not they from it.

Bavaria tells the same story. Rural and urban illegitimacy occurred at the same time. The clergy, many of whom attempted analyses of the sexual revolution, did not view it as an effect of urbanisation. Rather, they saw it as a result of the breakdown of authority in traditional rural society.[10] Thus, evidence points to a self-contained rural sexual revolution. It is quite ridiculous to imagine that their bastardy resulted from either prostitution or urbanisation.[11]

Having traced the sexual revolution back to a rural proletarian milieu, we must now grapple with a larger and more cumbersome question: how did the rural proletariat generate it? The Heimgarten custom, once again, provides us with a clue to the riddle, because it points up the significance of the term 'poor people'. Obviously, it was social, more than economic, conditions that gave the expression currency: sexual permissiveness was the common denominator that allowed smallholders, cotters and day labourers to be lumped together. 'The women who sink into easy virtue and who give themselves up to lustful pleasures are mostly those who have no prospect of marriage because of their poverty.'[12] These people were called poor because most of them could not look forward to the day when they would inherit property, and, thereupon, enter into marriage which brought with it full stature in peasant society. This had been the order of things in traditional society, and, as we saw, it remained the custom of farmers—the most substantial element of the rural populace. In the last analysis, then, people were called poor if they could not inherit property. To the farmer, 'poor people' meant the landless.

Actually, the phrase only reflects his prejudices. Land had ceased to be important for lower-class people when marriage was in question. But money, with which one dressed oneself smartly and lived to some degree of success to the dictates of a new life-style, certainly had not. The same 'poor people' who were faulted for sexual misbehaviour were scolded just as frequently for squandering their money on flashy clothes and high living (*Luxus*)! They weaseled money out of their employers by hook or crook, it was said, and contracted bad debts without blinking an eye. In short, they accustomed themselves to a style of living which, in the eyes of farmers, ill suited their lowly station in life.[13] We are dealing with people, then, who undermined the Heimgarten by shifting the emphasis away from property towards personal relationships. They may not have owned much or any land, may not have been able to construct sturdy houses, but they could be dashing in the latest cut of clothes and turn a pretty ankle.

The important point is that it took money for 'poor people'—the rural proletariat—to maintain the new life-style on which their romantic encounters and marriages were based. It is a mistake to confuse property-lessness with poverty.[14] We have already made mention of the fact that certain changes had come over the rural economy of Central Europe. By bringing proletarian youth together and providing them with pocket money, these changes both directly and indirectly caused the sexual revolution among the proletariat.

Consider the occupational contacts of the rural population. During the warmer months of the year, the day labourers, both man and wife, worked for the farmer, where they came into contact with the farm hands. This meant that someone had to baby-sit for their small children and look after what few animals they might have had. To do this, they hired 8-to-12-year-old girls, most of whom would have themselves been day labourer children. During these same months the small farmer required someone to tend his animals while he worked his fields. He hired shepherd boys, about 6 to 12 years old, who were also of cotter or day labourer families. These children, completely left to themselves from six o'clock in the morning until evening, congregated in the fields while tending the herds, where the older ones talked about sex and got into mischief. There, in the meadows and pastures, they also came into contact with older (12-to 25-year-old) farm hands 'who tell them their crude, dirty stories and jokes, and disclose all their immoral ways to them by word or deed'.[15] Their sexual expertise was then carried back to the girls and to the large villages by the shepherds. All of this presumes that these youngsters knew little about sex or had little sexual experience before they left home for the fields, which was not necessarily the case. But the point of extra-familial association and extra-familial sexuality is extremely important.

Table 5:   Socio-Spatial Occupational Contacts from Seed Time to Harvest Time

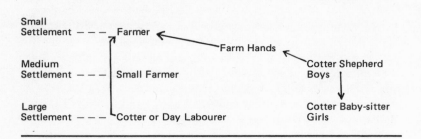

This analysis lends itself to consideration for another reason. Capitalism, profit farming, has been seen as the critical lock which, once turned, changed the patriarchal relationship of the farmer with his farm hands into an exploitive employer—employee relationship, and as a process which displaced people as the average size of farms increased.[16] The enclosure system (*Flurbereinigung*), which constituted a major step along the way towards capitalistic farming, also helped bring about the integration of the rural work-force. Cotters and day labourers depended increasingly on the larger farms for employment, and the shepherds, one or two of whom formerly watched over the flocks for an entire village community on the common meadow, were replaced by the many shepherds (*Hütejungen*) of day labourer origin. Again and again the reports of the German clergy tag these youths with responsibility for the sexual revolution.

Economic opportunity allowed youth to get together in the winter months as well. In Haimhausen, Bavaria, girls congregated on long cold nights to spin or do other profitable light work with their hands. Neighbourhood boys would drop in on them to get acquainted and have fun. Soon, jokes, songs, dances and intimate touches and whispers punctuated turns at spinning or carding. Late at night the boys and girls paired off for the walk home. Now a more provincial and rural parish than Haimhausen could hardly be found in nineteenth-century Central Europe. Yet its bastardy ratio annually fluctuated from between 20 and 25 per cent, and there is no doubt about who supported it.[17]

Before 1800 such spinning bees had not been common. And they certainly did not drag on into the night's latest hours. Curfew was enforced. In some areas the bees were altogether outlawed. In 1783 the bishop of the ecclesiastical principality of Würzburg banned all extrafamilial *Winterabendspinnstuben* (spinning bees).[18] This prelate was not exactly the backward stick-in-the-mud one might envision. The principality operated a school programme that enrolled 28,000 boys and girls in 1795, which was looked upon as a model for surrounding states to emulate.[19] Furthermore, the bishop encouraged his subjects to be industrious and to find extra sources of income. His only reason for curtailing the bees was to preserve public morals.

The Secularisation put an end to the secular authority of prelates. People were free to gather at night to spin, chat and flirt. New laws guaranteeing personal freedom relaxed the grip of the farmer-employer over his farm hands, so that he could not stop them from carousing late into the night. The spinning bees not only brought youths together, but also provided them with the extra money needed to dress smartly and make themselves attractive.

Capitalism, we may conclude, not urbanisation, abetted the sexual revolution in rural areas. The argument that economic change was the spur must be limited to the agrarian scene. It obviously does not apply to Pirmasens or the Sauerland on the upper and lower Rhine. In neither France nor Germany do we always, or even often, know what specifically governs the sexual behaviour of a certain area, a warning signal too often ignored. Why economic change would trigger sexual licence in an economic disaster area like Paderborn and not in neighbouring progressive Sauerland is surely a puzzle. But this is a predominant pattern for rural Central Europe. We cannot overlook the fact that modernisation increased the earning capacity of the rural youth of *both sexes*. We have noted several varieties of work that allowed lower-class children to become wage-earners at very tender ages. And we must realise that these were new experiences.[20]

Nor can we overlook the fact that when contemporaries attempted to explain the new proletarian sexual behaviour, the money factor always played a signal role. Listen to the analysis of the parish priest of tiny, rural Vierkirchen in Bavaria:

> They measure success and happiness in terms of clothes, food and sexual pleasure; to get ahead socially they put others down; to outdo those of whom they are envious, they make bad debts, take unfair advantage of others and swindle them; they try to make money in the slimiest ways.[21]

Others say the same thing in other words: girls leave home to work and then get pregnant; boys spend money on girls (buy them beer) and then get them to go to bed as reimbursement; youths spend all their money on clothes in order to be attractive to the opposite sex. It seems that once profit farming took hold and money began to circulate, there was no keeping them 'down on the farm'.

Although the widespread conformity of the rural proletariat to freer sex puts this aspect of their lives in sharp relief, it was quite evenly interwoven into the fabric of their day-to-day existence. Some historians see the sexual revolution as a question of youth or of lower-class women; others note the new economic factors in early industrial times that lured young proletarian women away from home, but deny that this amounted to anything like a sexual revolution. In fact, sexuality was a routine aspect of a proletarian child-rearing regimen that emphasised individuality, work and play. Let us consider these qualities in some detail, to understand better the context of the capitalistic impulse we have described.

Since romance led to marriage amongst the proletariat, it is in no way surprising that affective bonds would characterise the relationship between them and their children.[22] This is evident by the fact that proletarian parents took pride in their children and expressed their feelings for them by showing them off in public whenever possible. Not caring whether they were legitimate or illegitimate, proletarian parents happily stopped passers-by to display their babies proudly.[23] Instead of restrictively swaddling them in the traditional manner, they dressed them up 'like little dolls' in fancy clothes.[24] Flattering and fussing over them, rural proletarian parents instilled a strong sense of self-awareness into their children. This appreciation of one's physical charms may have been instilled into female children more than male: 'the tiniest girls want to be dressed up, made pretty and flattered,' according to a

Bavarian observer.[25] Farmers did not shower their children with this kind of attention.

In place of the purposefulness, discipline and restraint which prevailed in other homes, proletarian parents were permissive and lenient towards their children. Taking note of this, the clergy of rural Bavaria alluded to the 'childlike indulgence' which governed the attitude of the lower-class parents towards their children.[26] The proletarian parent was accused of being 'lax' towards her child or having 'false principles' of infant and child care.[27] These comments, coming from the closest observers of social change to provide us with records of what they saw, clearly evoke the images of two life-styles. In the sturdy farmer's home the infant is alone, the parents aloof; in the breezy proletarian shack, the baby is fondled and cooed over by attentive parents. In other words, in the countryside it was the proletarian who first picked up attitudes of loving care and sentimental tenderness that had begun to typify the closely knit bourgeois city family.[28] Thus, the situation which today we would call normal, the traditionalists (the farmers and parish clergy) called perverse. This is not so important as it is to recognise that proletarian families were new. Their appearance coincides with the expanded wage opportunities that we have already discussed. It is a mistake to imagine that the relationship of tenderness that characterised the proletarian family relations existed in the pre-modern smallholding family. Consequently, it may not be asserted that the new lower-class family is directly linked to the pre-modern cotter family, carrying on the latter's solidarity with new jobs and cash.[29]

The importance of child rearing cannot be too strongly insisted upon. Proletarian children learned mother's ways with mother's milk. When parents indulged themselves by eating, drinking and dressing in a style that belied their humble homes, could they treat their children any differently? Disdaining traditional children's clothing, the proletarian mother happily boasted to her son, 'I've fixed you up with different [stylish] trousers'.[30] As these proletarian children grew older, they lived and behaved according to an inbred proletarian style which held that money was for self-gratification. 'Johanniskirchen [Bavaria] is full of day labourers and poor people', wrote the town's curate, 'who are none the less possessed by craving for flashy clothes and high living.'[31] 'They wear their wealth on their backs.' Every cleric and administrator in Bavaria could have echoed these words, because as lower-class children grew into young manhood and womanhood, they were armed with an inbred self-assertiveness and clothed with an accustomed garishness which proclaimed their proletarian origins as plainly as a badge.[32]

Better-minded Germans used the words 'Hoffart', 'Luxus', and 'Egoismus' to describe the proletarian character and personality which they found despicable. 'A demonic Egoismus works its mischief in every [lower-class] shack.'[33]

Obviously, two life-styles as well as two sexual codes were coexisting in rural Germany. It is critical to remember that when proletarian youths acted in ways distinctive to their class, they were only doing what they had learned at mother's knee as far back as memory could reach.

If one grew up in a proletarian family, sexual awareness came early. Consciously or unconsciously, lower-class parents awakened the sex drive in their still small children. In the home sexual restraints were minimal or non-existent. Any topic of conversation, including adult stories or jokes, was table talk.[34] Parental sexuality was not hidden, and children, regardless of sex and age, sometimes slept naked in the same bed.[35] Likewise, heterosexual socialising was encouraged. 'Some parents are pleased when their children—just barely weaned—make an impression in the world.'[36] As soon as a young girl began to be admired by neighbourhood boys, her parents took note of it approvingly.[37] Proletarian parents pushed their not yet teenaged children in the direction of carefree living, encouraging them to date, go to dances, enjoy themselves, and stay out at night as long as they wished 'so that they'll have some fun, too, and feel like going back to work'.[38] Even though dances had quasi-religious overtones, as we will see, and regardless of the fact that they inevitably led to sexual liaisons, the rural proletariat saw nothing morally offensive about this favourite recreational pastime. When an illegitimate child resulted from these encounters or from a 'proletarian Heimgarten', it is absurd to think that the couple involved 'were not pursuing sexual pleasure'.[39]

We must not imagine, then, that a sexual revolution occurred when young women, or youth in general, charged out the front door flaunting their parents' authority and exalting their independence by going to bed with the first dance partner.[40] On the contrary, youth only followed a sexual inclination which had been awakened and encouraged by their parents. Again and again, the Bavarian clergy accused proletarian parents of arousing the sexual activities of their children.[41] Nor may we see in the sexual exploits of proletarian youth a rebellion against society at large. As curate Müller of rural Lower Bavaria observed, modern society allowed them this freedom, even if it bellowed about its abuse: no one enforced curfew, no one fussed about abused authority enough to do anything about it, no one penalised adultery. 'Why ever should young people suppress the enjoyment of their sex drives?'[42]

No doubt the new sexual freedom was of enormous importance to

young, proletarian women. They were suddenly free of the anxiety
that was a normal part of maturing in the old patriarchal households
which had subsumed them. Young women immediately responded by
dropping the superstitious practices, with which they had sought to
assuage their anxieties, in favour of their own charms and personalities.
In tiny rural Aholming, diocese of Passau, lower-class girls threw away
traditional garb for sexy and revealing clothes.[43] The outcry against
Luxus indicates that this was common practice everywhere. Thus, young
women found ways to 'catch' their husbands and lovers. Going to dances (unescorted) to find a suitable man, and then letting him buy the
drinks for the evening, was one way to do it.[44] As one Bavarian cleric
put it,

> But since a young man is never so selfless as to spend his money on
> the vanity of a flashy date without something else in mind . . ., the
> young buck takes her virginity for his reimbursement.[45]

In other words, affective relationships replaced erotic superstition and
the delayed impersonal marriage of bygone days. Sex was extricated
from superstition.

In view of their horrendous exploitation in pre-modern Central
Europe, it is hardly surprising that women were often specifically accused of spreading the new sexual looseness by sleeping around. For
many of them this brought the happiness that came with a personally
satisfying marriage, although for others, it must be admitted, it meant
disappointment and social maladjustment. Although lower-class women
were obviously now enjoying sex, this does not necessarily cast them as
the leaders in the proletarian switch to sexual permissiveness.[46] If nubile
women 'instigated' sex by coquetry and cosmetics, it was because of
post-1800 proletarian breeding, which assigned this role to females, and
not because they, in particular, rebelled against authority—parental or
otherwise, or because they were any more involved in the rural economy
than men. They earned enough money to dress and act in the accustomed style of their sub-group's culture—enough to 'be competitive'
in the dating game. This certainly gave them a degree of independence
that they had not known in traditional society.[47] But this element,
while important because it allowed women to be active agents promoting the pre-marital proletarian life-style, must not be over-emphasised.
After marriage these same women readily stayed on in the new occupational roles that early industrial times offered them throughout the
nineteenth century so that they could help support their families.[48]

One final aspect of proletarian home life remains to be considered—work. A baffling problem confronting the historian of *Vormärz* society involves the repeated references in source material to contradictory patterns—idleness and industriousness. Laziness, an inheritance from pre-modern times, is hardly surprising. But whence the sudden impulse to work? We have long known, of course, that it was one of the sterling qualities of the rising bourgeoisie. For some reason we have been slower to realise that work was a lesson imparted as well by proletarian parents to their children.

A *sine qua non* of lower-class existence was that children should not be too great a drag on the family budget. Consequently, proletarian children were put to work much earlier than other youths. During pre-school years this meant begging and scavenging. Poaching was to rural society on the threshold of industrialisation what shoplifting is to our own.[49] 'Not infrequently, parents lead their still very small children to steal garden produce. . . so that more [family] income is realised.'[50] It did not matter if they missed school, or got into mischief, or were without adult supervision all day long. 'Parents of nondescript type homes [day labourers and cotters] no longer care about the innocence of their children,' complained the curate of Martinsried near Munich.[51] What did matter is that they bring home extra money, which played an important role in the family budget.[52] During bad years it allowed the family to subsist, during good ones it allowed them to sustain themselves in the cherished proletarian life-style—with coffee, sweets, colourful clothes, and so on.

By the time a proletarian child became a teenager, he or she might be working away from home for months on end—'in Alpine meadows tending flocks' or 'across the Danube where wages are much higher'.[53] Once away from home a maturing process overtook proletarian youth. They were financially somewhat independent, and, with age, became increasingly aware of this and of their growing earning capacities. Naturally, during these periods they became sexually experienced (if they weren't already). Since close affectionate ties had been the way of their parents, long absences from home brought loneliness. Proletarian youths sought and found new affective bonds to take up the slack. They mixed easily and behaved in a gregarious manner that would be difficult to imagine in the closed, local societies of pre-modern times. Under these circumstances it was inevitable that proletarian girls would, as the Oberkreutzberg curate put it, 'get pregnant by and by'.

We must pause here to insist that the proletarian work ethos extended to women as well as men. We have already mentioned several occupations that drew young women and even small girls into the rural economy. It would be a mistake to think that these were isolated experiences of only a few. Lower-class women were in great demand as domestic workers in the nineteenth century. Not only were they employed in unprecedented numbers, they were even taking over some traditionally male occupations.[54] This provided them with the money both to live the 'high life' of the proletarian single set, and, subsequently, to help finance their own families or their and their husband's families.

In other words, romance led to an illegitimate birth or to marriage, whereupon the proletarian family cycle was again set in motion. This was a new kind of family and the engine that drove it had nothing to do with the cold impulses that kept the pre-modern smallholding family huddled together on a wretched piece of earth. There was no question for them of romantic marriage because their unions, like those of farmers, entailed property transactions. We insist, again, that proletarian families were the product of a new kind of marriage made possible, in the last analysis, by lower-class involvement in a new economy. There is nothing novel about this historical assertion.[55] Rudolph Braun brilliantly demonstrated how piece-work formed an aspect of a symbiotic economy that enabled Zürich Highland cotters to assume modern life-styles and modern mentalities (including romantic marriage).[56] We may conclude that in German territories, as in parts of Switzerland, it was money, derived from hard work within an economy based on profit farming that allowed an endless chain of proletarian 'propertyless marriages' or romances to take place.[57]

By now it is evident that complex historical developments produced the sexual revolution of rural Central Europe. First of all, external and internal constraints—the latter being especially important for the female sex—were terminated. Secondly, economic change ended authoritarian relationships between employer and employee and allowed individual enterprise to determine who could materially profit. For cotters and some smallholders, *a large minority of the European populace around 1800*, this economic engagement resulted in an unaccustomed accumulation of cash )rather than property). Thirdly, very distinct behavioural patterns set the rural proletariat apart from farmers and point to the formation of a new class. Their peculiar life-style did not pivot around new sexual behaviour, but open sexuality was unmistakably an aspect of it and it lends itself to demonstrate the historical fact of a sexual revolution.

Prostitution, urbanisation, and even industrialisation either play a very minor part or none at all in the rural sexual revolution.[58]

Nor may we attribute it to a high incidence of anomie among the lower class. Contemporary reports, it will be recalled, juxtaposed sexual with other kinds of indulgence—extravagance with money, fashionable clothes, and so on. Thus, it was the 'doers' not the 'losers' in the new rural proletarian economy that accounted for most of the bastardy.[59]

Remove the rural proletarian class from the early nineteenth-century Central European scene and the sexual revolution is inexplicable. Affective familial bonds trumpeted the emergence of a new kind of rural family unit. When the children of such a family grew to adulthood, they established anew, or tried to establish, the warm, loving relationships they had known. This had two consequences: a proliferation of propertyless proletarian marriages bore witness to enduring romantic encounters, and a jump in proletarian bastardy bespoke the frequency of more fleeting romantic encounters. Although in some areas as many as 40 per cent of lower-class women probably bore illegitimate children, it would be ludicrous to imagine that the sexual revolution had this consequence for every proletarian woman. But, in either event—that of legitimacy or illegitimacy—affective relationships were pivotal, and of principal concern to them. Thus, established society complained that proletarian parents were proud of (i.e. loved) their children, whether legitimate or not. In sum, illegitimacy and the sexual revolution were a product—actually, a by-product—of the affective relationships which typified rural proletarian families.

Other factors which could contribute to a sexual revolution—marriage rate, pre-nuptial pregnancy, age at marriage—must still be explored, but we now know enough about some of them to suggest that the new pre-marital sexual indulgence seemed socially revolutionary to early modern communities. In Bavaria, for example, the birth rate between 1800 and 1849 was considerably *lower* than during the last half of the eighteenth century. It stagnated alarmingly during the *Vormärz* after the Montgelas era of reform. It has been determined that a startling drop in the marriage rate caused the retardation of the birth rate.[60] In Massenhausen, Bavaria, the marriage rate was 12.7 (per 1,000 adult women) in 1752 and 16.3 in 1801, but only 9.5 in 1830 and 5.3 in 1843.

These astonishing statistics force us to ask which segments of the rural population were abstaining from matrimony. Although we lack data which would disclose the marriage rate by class, there are clear indications that big farmers avoided matrimony. In Dietramszell 71 per cent of the farmers were married in 1817 as opposed to 86 per cent of the smallholders and 87 per cent of the proletarian day labourers. And

of the farmers themselves, the biggest among them were the least likely
to be married (only 60 per cent of the 'ganz Bauern' were married).[61]

The reason for the farmers' celibate ways lies in the fact that they
were going broke. The tax remissions of Massenhausen's biggest farmers
fell by 68.3 per cent between 1750 and 1850, and during this one hundred year span they went bankrupt or sold out at sharply increasing
rates, decade after decade.[62] Since marriages among them had traditionally been promoted by real estate considerations, we may
hypothesise that the farmers' low marriage rate greatly contributed to
the low birth rate in Bavaria. While the farmer's family stood by celi-
bately hoping for the 'right' marriage that would save them from
bankruptcy, the proletariat married for romantic reasons and begot
children out of wedlock. Illegitimate fertility accounted for an increasing proportion of Bavaria's birth rate. When we know more about the
marital ages of farmers and day labourers and about class differentials
in pre-nuptial pregnancy, the extent of the land-owner's bitter anxiety
and the proletariat's happy *élan* will be fully revealed.

We speak, then, with justification of a sexual revolution. The proletarian family was socially revolutionary both as to its nature or ethos
(affective bonds) and as to its effect (increased legitimate and illegitimate fertility). Faced with blanket disapproval on the part of farmers,
they insisted on their life-style even though this led to an unprecedented
jump in bastardy. In time proletarian families would learn to inhibit
sexuality, but for roughly the first half of the nineteenth century, they
revelled in the freedom to love, marry and beget, or just to love and
beget, that modernisation had brought them.

'Poor people' was only the first of many designations that legitimate
and illegitimate non-inheriting sons and daughters came to acquire as
their number grew. Fourth Estate, landless peasant and lower class
would be added in time. But before these names could be given them
and long before they migrated to the cities where they would acquire
new ones—working class, proletariat, etc., these dispossessed people
acquired a life-style that distinguished them from their neighbours.
While this life-style allows us to speak of a sexual revolution, a term we
need not cavil to use, we must cautiously avoid exaggerating its effect
outside the family. For, as we will see, neither with regard to religion
nor in other respects did the proletarian family cut itself off from the
community.

## Notes

1. *Evangelische Kirchen-Zeitung,* XXXIV-XXXV (4 May 1844),, p. 288.
2. Shorter, 'Illegitimacy, Sexual Revolution, and Social Change', see charts; Edouard Ducpetiaux, *De la condition physique et moral des jeunes ouvriers* (Brussels, 1843), I, Pt. 2, Ch. 3.
3. Shorter, 'Female Emancipation', p. 620, enumerates numerous factors which seem to include urbanisation as a necessary ingredient. See his schematisation in 'Sexual Change and Illegitimacy: The European Experience', *Modern European Social History*, Robert J. Bezucha (ed.) (Lexington, Mass., 1972), p. 245.
4. Migration to and from Bavarian cities was intense during the *Vormärz*. Preliminary analysis indicates that the cost of living index may have dictated the proletariat's place of residence. Also, there is evidence that single people were on the move towards the city in bad years and young proletarian families on the move toward the countryside, and vice versa in good years.
5. Hansjorg Gruber *Die Entwicklung der pfälzische Wirtschaft 1816-1834* (Saarbrucken, 1962), pp. 67ff.
6. Ordinariatsarchiv Speyer (OAS), *Smuggler*, Pfarrei Remlinger to ordinariat, Blickweiler, 1828.
7. OAS, *Elenchen.*
8. Pfarrarchiv Pirmasens, *Gedenkbuch.*
9. Ibid.
10. I refer to the correspondence in OAP 07090 and OAM *Vis. Beant.*
11. Tilly, Scott and Cohen, 'Women's Work', generalise to this effect (p. 469). We need regional models of fertility change rather than sweeping statements.
12. OAP 07090 Grafenau, 1829.
13. This complaint runs *ad nauseam* through the reports of the clergy. See OAM, Vis.Beant., Taufkirchen, 1823, Chieming, 1828; Buchbach, 1823; Vierkirchen, 1828; Pfrombach, 1823; Fischbachau, 1827.
14. Tilly, Scott and Cohen make this error on page 464 of their article.
15. *Evangelische Kirchen-Zeitung,* XXXVI-XXXVII (29 March 1845), p. 247.
16. Engelsing, Ch. 6, and Edward Shorter, 'Sexual Change and Illegitimacy', pp. 231-69.
17. OAM, *Vis. Beant.*, Haimhausen, 1824.
18. *Sammlung der hochfürstlich-Würzburgischen Landesverordnungen*, III (13 Nov. 1783).
19. Michael Renner, 'Fuldaer Einfluss auf die Würzburger Schulreform Fürstbischc Franz Ludwig's von Erthal, 1781, *Zeitschrift f. bayerischen Landesgeschichte,* XXXVIII, pp. 368-91.
20. Naturally, women worked in traditional society as well, a point which Tilly, Scott and Cohen are at pains to make: 'Women's Work and European Fertility' pp. 452-3; the point is that with modernisation opportunities for cash paying jobs significantly increased. See Patricia Branca, 'A New Perspective on Women's Work: A Comparative Typology', *Journal of Social History,* IX, 2 (Winter 1975), pp. 129-53.
21. OAM, *Vis Beant.,* 1828.
22. Edward Shorter brilliantly develops this thesis in *The Making of the Modern Family.*
23. OAM, *Vis. Beant.*, 1825.
24. Ibid.
25. OAP 07090 Waldhof, 1828; OAM, *Vis. Beant.*, Taufkirchen, 1823.
26. OAP 07090 Obing, 1827.
27. OAP 07090 Waldhof, 1828; OAM, *Vis. Beant.*, Buchbach, 1823.

28. Again this is Shorter's thesis (Ch. 4 of *Making of the Modern Family*). I think there was a difference, none the less, between rural proletarian and city bourgeois attitudes toward infants and children. While the latter were attentive and loving, they were also firm and disciplinary—two qualities that did not prevail in the rural lower-class home.
29. In their article, 'Women's Work and European Fertility', Tilly, Scott and Cohen refer to an excerpt of Rudolph Braun's fundamental study, *Industrialisierung und Volksleben: Die Veränderungen der Lebensformen in einem ländlichen Industriegebiet vor 1800 (Zürcher Oberland)* (Stuttgart, 1965). If they would consult the original work they would see that the Zurich Highland people were also new both in terms of their *numbers* and in terms of their evolved lifestyle.
30. OAM, *Vis. Beant.*, Taufkirchen, 1823.
31. Ibid.
32. Edward Shorter, "La Vie Intim" Beiträge zu seiner Geschichte am Beispiel des kulturellen Wandels im den bayerischen Unterschichten im 19. Jahrhundert', *Kölner Zeitschrift für Soziologie und Sozialpsychologie*, Sonderheft, 16 (1972), pp. 356ff. This article is indispensable for understanding the proletarian youth.
33. OAM, *Vis. Beant.*, Buchbach, 1823.
34. OAP 07090 Bren, 1828.
35. OAM, *Vis. Beant.*, Garmisch, 1826.
36. OAP 07090 Munchham, 1828.
37. OAP 07090 Waldhof, 1828.
38. OAP 07090 Aidenbach, 1828; see also Kreutzberg, 1828 and OAM, *Vis. Beant.*, Wambach, 1823.
39. Tilly, Scott, and Cohen speculate to this effect in 'Women's Work and European Fertility'.
40. It is true that Church and state hoped to rein in the runaway sexual licence of youth by re-establishing lines of authority within society—those between farmer and farm hand, master craftsman and apprentice, parents and children. But this was so much whistling in the wind because society was not willing to go to extremes to insist upon authority. On the other hand, cotter parents had themselves grown accustomed to challenging their farmer-employers' authority, to which the latters' frequent complaints about proletarian surliness gives testimony.
41. OAM, *Vis. Beant.*, Mittenwald, 1826; Vogtareut, 1827; OAP 07090 Gressl to Chancery, 1828; Peinting, 1828.
42. OAP 07090 Aholming, 1829.
43. Ibid.
44. Shorter, "La Vie Intim", makes this point explicitly.
45. OAP 07090 Waldhof, 1828.
46. Edward Shorter's view in *The Making of the Modern Family* and in other writings seem to revolve around two considerations: women increasingly engage in gainful employment, and appear to have abandoned their accustomed sexual passivity of pre-modern times. Both of these factors can be easily explained with reference to the lower-class family, and, in fact, the source material I have used suggests that it should be construed in this way. Sexual freedom was a product of the proletarian family and it extended to and was equally promoted by youths of either sex.
47. Tilly, Scott and Cohen argue this point effectively, 'Women's Work and European Fertility', pp. 448-62.
48. Branca, 'A New Perspective on Women's Work', argues this point convincingly, pp. 135, 143, 146.
49. Ducpetiaux, I, p. 406, shows that juvenile delinquency was a rural as well as

urban phenomenon.
50. OAM, *Vis. Beant.*, Mettenheim, 1823.
51. OAM, *Vis. Beant.*, 1833.
52. OAP 07090 Obing, 1827.
53. OAM, *Vis. Beant.*, Tegernsee and Oberammergau, 1826; OAP 07090 Schollnach, 1828.
54. Branca, pp. 134 and 143.
55. Shorter's thesis in Chapter 7 of *The Making of the Modern Family.*
56. Braun, *Industrialisierung und Volksleben,* pp. 59-112.
57. Tilly, Scott and Cohen have pointed out that work was demanded of pre-modern woman quite as well as in modern times. This has suggested to them that 'old values' carried over into modern times, allowing the proletarian family to maintain a precarious existence now as then. The only difference being that the old value—family solidarity and work—informed new conditions—a liquid economy. But this is not the only difference by any means. Pre-modern women who provided their sweat and blood for the cause of a married brother's or sister's family did not do so from altruistic motives. The homestead was by custom legally hers in part. Besides, were she to leave it, there were usually no other means at hand to maintain oneself.
But there is an even more important difference between the pre-modern and modern single, female worker. The latter could and did find work far from home and the means of self-support, although not always glamorous, were at hand. The point is then that when she sent money or provisions home it was because she chose to, not because circumstances forced her to. The bond of affection that typified the proletarian family induced her to continue to help her family out with transfusions of cash even when circumstances would have allowed her to discontinue them. The widespread practice among young European women of continuing this kind of support is a tribute to the affective bonds of the modern proletarian family, whose solidarity was founded on family love rather than family real estate.
58. It is gross to assign these indiscriminately as do Tilly, Scott, and Cohen. Even contemporary observers such as Ducpetiaux realised that no exact correlation between urbanisation and illegitimacy could be sustained; I, p. 319.
59. Some women never succeeded in establishing a permanent relationship with a man and bore illegitimate child after illegitimate child. But statistically these recidivists could not have accounted for more than a few per cent of the 20–35 per cent bastardy ratio.
60. Lee, pp. 332ff.
61. OAM, *Pfarr Beschreibung,* Dietramszell.
62. Lee, p. 333.

# 4 POPULAR CULTURE: RELIGION

'Old Time Religion', which accommodates man's spiritual as well as physical cravings, may not be as far from us as we sometimes suppose. There are indications that this kind of religious mentality typified Central Europeans as society began to modernise. Anyone accustomed to think that the pious and the promiscuous have always sorted themselves out with great dispatch will be sceptical of this hypothesis. What it would mean, of course, is that the sexual revolution that we have discussed had little or no effect on popular religious culture. If this is true, then we will want to adjust our judgement about the implications of the sexual revolution for society.

The fact is that the high bastardy ratio among rural Germans tells us nothing at all about their religious feelings and practices. Rather, it tells us just the opposite of what we should expect, because the more sexually indulgent people were during the transition into modernity, the more likely that they were also religious! [1] To understand this behaviour and to penetrate further into the mentality of the rural proletariat in the first half of the nineteenth century, we must look again at the people involved with sexual licence.

The Westphalians, whose varied sexual attitudes we considered in the first chapter, offer a neat paradigm of the unusual relationship between religion and sexual permissiveness. The *Sauerländer*, it will be recalled, were the most modern Westaphalians by virtually every standard. They had got rid of their traditional peasant clothes, become accustomed to factory work, and adjusted to something approaching city life. Belief in ghosts, together with much of the practice of religion, they left behind them when they took the step out of the past into a world more reminiscent of our own.[2] They even jeered at their rural neighbours when they saw them trooping along on a pilgrimage.[3] Would we not naturally expect these people with their enlightened attitudes to be tolerant of varied sexual behaviour or even somewhat experimental in their life-styles? Instead, they turn out to be the most restrained people in the Westphalian area, and, indeed, in all of Germany.

To leave the Sauerland for Münster to the north or Paderborn to the east is to turn back a page of history. The people of both areas preserved and cultivated all the vestiges of a traditional Baroque

culture. A Church regulation of 1686 baldly stated that the people celebrated their superstitious practices with greater devotion than their
observance of the Lord's Day. They changed very little during the next
hundred years. In 1781 when Enlightenment impulses moved their
bishop to proscribe devotions for protection against hailstorms, the
faithful objected, reminding him of the disastrous storm of 1586!
In the parish of Daseburg the people (not the church or curate) levied
a two *Groschen* fine on anyone who absented himself from the devotions on the first Saturday of the months of May, June and July, which
were held for the benefit of the harvest.[4]

Conservative religious inclinations carried over into politics when
the Secularisation threatened the Westphalians with absorption by
Prussia. The people of both Münster and Paderborn vehemently opposed annexation, as Prince Karl August von Hardenberg noted.[5] In
Münster economic considerations played a hand in their attitude, but in
Paderborn the people even resisted the secularisation of monastic property. There is only one way to explain this: still enmeshed in folk
piety, the people vested the cloisters with mysterious religious significance. A Prussian adminstrator confirmed this when he wrote to
Baron *von und zum* Stein that the Paderborn people were too superstitious to be able to withstand the Secularisation.[6]

The events surrounding the Secularisation and Napoleonic era did
nothing to dampen the religious fervour and superstition of the Münster
and Paderborn people. Attendance at Sunday mass remained virtually
universal. There were tumultuous scenes of people reciting their sins
over each others' shoulders, such was their eagerness for the sacrament
of penance. Civil authorities risked a riot if they curtailed traditional
processions or pilgrimages of which the Münster *Almanach* scheduled
no less than 149 between the months of May and August alone![7]
During processions the populace touched handkerchiefs or clothing to
holy pictures intending to use them later to cure illnesses. Belief in
witches was general, and people practised magic and had recourse to
sorcerers to rid their fields of pests as a matter of course.[8] Thus popular religion, unrestrained by the Enlightenment and unimpeded by the
Secularisation, remained overwhelmingly unreflective and possessed of
a mystical if not outright magical nature.[9]

Yet, it is here in the midst of all this continuity with the past
rather than in modernising Sauerland that we find sexual permissiveness. While all else has remained static as far as religious observance is
concerned, the rural proletariat reversed itself in matters of sexuality.
The illegitimacy ratios of the two provinces reflect the switch in sexual

behaviour. Lower-class youth had acquired a new life-style which led them to sleep around. But this did not bother their consciences in the least. On the contrary, even though in Paderborn many people gave themselves unlimited sexual licence, they still thought themselves to be religious and even quite pious.[10] Thus, the new sexual behaviour did not occur at the expense of religion—not, at any rate, in the mind of the rustic. In spite of his newly acquired sexual morality, he never missed a step in the performance of his community's accepted folkways and religious customs.

This association of religious enthusiasm with indiscriminate sexual indulgence seems bizarre to us, but it is not difficult to document. The experience of Bavaria closely resembles that of the Rhineland. In spite of the fact that the rural proletariat had become sexually permissive, the practice of religion did not grow slack, nor did the religious mentality change. Let us review the evidence.

Before 1800 Bavarians had been every bit as superstitious as Westphalians. One of hundreds of superstitious practices occurred in connection with Ascension Thursday, one of the major feast days. After a statue of Christ had been pulled up and and out of sight through an opening in the roof of the church, the people rushed outside where they fell upon a dummy devil which had been cast down from the roof to the ground below. They snatched off bits of it, ripping it to pieces, and then took their fragments home with them, which they further shredded and buried here and there in their fields to ward off evil spirits.[11] Evidently, no sermon could convey the theological meaning of the Lord's ascension as pointedly as the dramatisation. The trouble was that once reduced to such a rudimentary level of conceptualisation, the door was left open to subsequent mechanical and therefore superstitious practices.

Innumerable forms of liturgial play-acting of this sort competed with pilgrimages as the most beloved religious activity of Bavarians. In the 1780s the congregation of Bogenhausen outside Munich conducted no fewer than 26 annual group pilgrimages.[12] (The number of individual or sub-group pilgrimages would have been five to ten times greater.) The clergy were aware that religious non-essentials had become more important for the common people than essentials, but there was little or nothing that they could do about it.[13] When they tried to suppress superstition the people got ugly and surly. 'If a [Catholic] priest doesn't stand with his parishioners [in these matters], they scorn him and treat him like a Lutheran heretic.'[14] Many Protestants behaved in the same way. When some of the popular holy days were discontinued, a community near Nurnberg expressed the following sentiments in a note to their pastor which they attached to a rock and delivered at night through his bedroom window pane:

> Get this straight, you priest: if you don't reinstate the holy days which have been cancelled..., you'll be whipped and stoned. Now your belly has gotten another foot bigger around, because you didn't have to preach for two days. You lazy pig of a priest. The only reason you preached on the church festivals was because of the cookies and cake. He teaches that one shouldn't steal and takes money himself from the poor. You lazy priest.[15]

As the Enlightenment wore on, state and Church strove to suppress religious folklore, but the people continued to resist tenaciously.[16] When Bavaria's early nineteenth-century liberal, Maximillian von Montgelas, continued these policies, attempting to purify religion of superstition in the wake of the Secularisation, he stirred up a hornet's nest of opposition. In Munich the closest thing to a revolution occurred when Montgelas banned one of the people's favourite pilgrimages. Because both town and country people associated the Enlightenment with the suppression of folkways they detested it. 'The very word "Enlightenment" is hated by the lower class,' a contemporary observed.[17] One historian goes so far as to write that superstition actually increased during the first decades of the nineteenth century.[18] In 1809 a country pastor penned the following description of Bavarian people:

> The country folk around here are taken in by unusual, striking events. They love to read and listen to talk about such things, but because of their ignorance of religion they cannot distinguish truth from falsehood... I still well remember how about 8 or 9 years ago ...a rumour suddenly got started around here [Laufen, Tittmoning, Teisendorf] that the world would come to an end on a certain day. The people were so terrified that they dropped their work and ran to the church to make a general confession.[19]

People still commonly had recourse to witchcraft and magic to control the weather, cure sickness, and ward off misfortune.[20] One talisman, a holy card bearing the image of the Virgin Mary, 'which you have deigned to leave behind out of special solace for us,' was in demand as late as 1830.[21]

Not surprisingly, these people considered themselves to be quite religious. Before the Napoleonic Wars Bavarians hardly ever missed church. 'In a thousand there are hardly ten who miss,' wrote a country curate in 1797.[22] Data from the chancery archives of the archdiocese of Munich show that membership did not falter after 1800. On the contrary, there was an actual *per capita* increase in Church affiliation throughout most of the province (see Appendix I). This growth was measured in terms of those fulfilling the Easter duty, rather than the Sunday Church obligation.[23] Since the increase is greater than the growth of the population, we must attribute it to a steady decline of the age at which the youth made their first communion, thereby taking on the Easter duty obligation. This makes sense because precisely during this period children were exposed for the first time to something approaching systematic education, which made their mastery of the necessary catechetical instruction less formidable. It would be better if we had statistical data on Sunday Mass attendance, but there does not seem to be any doubt that the populace was just as dutiful in this respect. The vast amount of correspondence dating from this period between the curates and the Bavarian chanceries that registers bitter complaints about the morality of the rural proletariat makes no mention at all of non-observance of the Lord's Day. The first references to a decrease in Sunday discipline do not occur until the 1840s, and they are uneven even at that late date. The Passau chancery reported that many of the rural proletarian youth either were not attending Sunday services, or did so only to ridicule and make fun of those who did.[24] The Bishop of Munich complained to the Bavarian state ministry that the youth sometimes missed Church, but more commonly came only to take their place in the last pews or in the choir, where they behaved crassly.[25]

These lapses, which happened infrequently before about 1840, astonish us hardly at all when we view them in the perspective of the generally declining European church attendance of the time. It is indeed amazing that while German Protestants in some areas and French Catholics nearly everywhere were neglecting church attendance in ever-increasing numbers, German Catholics were not.[26] Just as remarkable is the persistence of German men in practising religion at a time when their French co-religionists were turning the church over to their wives and daughters.

We may conclude that there is no evidence that disbelief, flagging religious devotion, or enlightened scepticism were conditions that favoured fornication among lower-class Bavarian rustics. On the contrary, during the first decades of the nineteenth century they sought to be both religious and sexually permissive. The youth still regularly attended weekly sessions of catechism, even when they were unable to conceal the promise of new life beneath bulging midriffs.[27] They still sought church weddings, even if their illegitimate children accompanied them to the altar.[28] The Weihmörting parish girls even joined the Sodality of Virgins and proudly carried its banner to church on the appointed Sunday, although the pastor's sharp sermon made them painfully aware of the dichotomy between their religion and their lifestyle, and brought tears to their eyes.[29] It is instructive to remember in this connection that references to the collapse of sexual restraint in the post-1800 correspondence of the Bavarian clergy constitute a *specific* complaint. We hear nothing about a waning of church discipline or even of piety and religious enthusiasm.

Further evidence of Church affiliation among the sexually indulgent proletarian youth is evidenced by society's effort to stem their passions. In June, 1824, an elaborate programme was proposed and partially enacted by the Munich diocese to put a stop to bastardy. When a young woman bore a first illegitimate child she was to be brought to repent in the presence of her parents, and was expected to confess and receive the Eucharist at least once a month for the next three months. With the second illegitimate birth she was to be brought to repentance in the presence of honourable members of the parish, and the period of sacramental probation was increased to six months. If even this proved inefficacious and a third illegitimacy occurred, the entire community was to witness her repentance, and as proof of her amendment she would have to show a confession card during the months to come. A fourth bastard meant banishment from church.[30]

About fifteen years later, when bastardy still had not abated and state authorities had grown ever more apprehensive about the problem, civil authorities initiated another drive to harness the runaway sexual drives of youth. The problem, they felt, had to be dealt with at the familial rather than the bureaucratic level. Consequently, they turned to the Church asking that all seven Bavarian dioceses deal directly with the problem. Accordingly, a Sunday was set aside on which every pastor was to excoriate the rural proletarian youth—the farm hands.[31] This effort proved no more effective than the first, since, as the Passau chancery expressly wrote to its clergy, this very strategy had been tried repeatedly during the last decade to no avail.[32] Since neither the disciplinary programme of the 1820s or 1840s make any sense if the sexually permissive had already apostatised, these actions confirm the statistics on pervasive Church membership. Bavarians practiced their religion regardless of varying sexual behaviour that had begun to differentiate classes.

Another clue to the religious mentality of the German proletariat is the attitude of the Catholic Church towards their newly acquired sexual morality. Established religion found fault with it largely on the score that it was personal. Its roots were sunk into the shifty soil of wilful vanity (*Hoffart*) and shallow faith (*Unglaube*). This, the hierarchy agreed, not weak morals, was causing the flock to stray.[33] In the eyes of religious authorities, sexual permissiveness was immoral, to be sure, but it was basically a crisis of credal belief, not morals. In other words, when the several constraints of the old demographic regime to overt sexuality fell inoperative, the rustics had to be taught in what way sexual morality related to belief. As a matter of fact, this is the basic reason underlying the Church's great interest in popular schooling in France and Germany after 1800. In both countries the Church hoped to stay the *Zeitgeist* by teaching religious truth to youth. A restored faith would then shore up flooding sexual permissiveness.

> For without basic and powerful instruction in eternal truths, youth remains impervious to divine grace, and falls victim to the enticements of immoral desires as well as to the dangers of temptation.[34]

After 1820 school systems were established whose explicit purpose was less to educate than to instil into youth an appreciation of good and upstanding behaviour.[35]

The country rustics found out about their crisis of faith when they got to school and heard about a sexual morality that altogether differed from what they had learned at home. The Church's task was arduous and largely unsuccessful because, while attempting to educate youth about the moral implications of an already acquired life-style, it was, on the other hand, rigorously suppressing superstition, which had remained the single most powerful attraction for European common people to the practice of religion. In Bavaria the clergy had misgivings about the school programme from the very beginning, because they recognised that sexual licence was rooted in a new lower-class culture.[36] A curate wrote to his chancery saying that one thing may be counted on for certain: 'whatever improvement [in morals] is accomplished in the schools, will be spoiled again by domestic upbringing.'[37]

So went the history of the school programme from beginning to end. It was doomed to failure since it was attempting to teach a morality and way of life which the rural proletariat could not or would not understand. By 1838 the Munich chancery admitted the total failure of the school programme, to which it had given its best effort. Youth had eluded them: immorality had only increased. Indeed, girls enrolled in vacation school were coming to class pregnant in increasing numbers.[38] The pastoral letters of the French episcopacy register similar complaints. Pre-school children, who had already learned suggestive songs, acquired a life-style before they left home for school.[39] Immorality had penetrated the lowest social classes and the tiniest country hamlets.[40] Suppressing sexual licence was difficult because, as in Germany, it was part of a lower-class family life-style.[41]

The widespread collapse of Protestant Church membership between 1750 and 1850 makes the question of the relationship between religion and morality more difficult to analyse than in Catholic areas. It is clear that during this time span bastardy increased as church attendance decreased. In Gotha, 50 per cent fewer people were attending services in 1825 than in 1775. Meanwhile, bastardy had quadrupled.[42] The fact that during this fifty-year span the years of greatest bastardy increase, 1808–13, were exactly the years of greatest decrease in church attendance, suggests a correlation.

What was happening in Gotha took place in other Protestant communities. The same trend towards decreased church attendance and increased bastardy is attested by the chronicle of a rural Pomeranian church.[43] In 1709 its congregation numbered 1,608. In 1836 it had declined to 1,136, although the population had grown considerably.[44] During this period the number of annual illegitimacies had tripled, a fact which infers that the rate of bastardy had also increased (number per 100 unmarried fertile women). All these data suggest that those who became sexually more free dropped Church membership.

We ought to be wary, none the less, of asserting this without qualification. The fact that Catholics remained faithful while becoming sexually indulgent gives us cause to be cautious about Protestants. Secondly, none of our data prove that it was the sexually more permissive who abstained from Church. Finally, some evidence, albeit not statistical, is at hand suggesting that some Protestants behaved just like Catholics. In the Pomeranian parish mentioned above, for example, it had been a community practice to disallow the wearing of the bridal wreath if the betrothed was not a virgin. After 1800 this custom abated, signalling less emphasis on sexual morality in the congregation. An unmarried person who was no longer a virgin could attend services, and, indeed be married in church in full regalia.

Later on, in the early 1840s, a religious awakening stirred the Pomeranians. As a result a campaign against gaming, drinking, dancing and so on was started. A Sodality of Virgins also grew out of this

Table 6: Protestant Church Membership in Germany

| Province/City | Year/Population/Membership | | | Year/Population/Membership | | |
|---|---|---|---|---|---|---|
| Hamburg | 1753 | 100,000 | 85,118 | 1853 | 150,000 | 17,647 |
| Bremen | c. 1800 | n.a. | 12,000 | 1853 | n.a. | 6,000 |
| East Prussia (rural) | 1830 | 50% of all communities | | 1853 | 50% of ten communities | |
| Breslau | c. 1750 | n.a. | 40,000 | 1853 | n.a. | 5,000 |
| Nürnberg | 1790 | 31,000 | 29,573 | 1853 | 46,000 | 17,300 |
| Mecklenburg (three rural communities) | 1850 | n.a. | 228 | 1851 | n.a. | 0 |
| Frankenberg (Saxony) | 1783 | n.a. | 7,134 | 1853 | doubled | 5,769 |

Source: Joseph Edmund Jörg, *Geschichte des Protestantismus in seiner neuesten Entwicklung* (Arnheim, 1862), pp. 64-71. Jörg obtained these figures from various Protestant newspapers and from prominent members of the Protestant clergy who revealed them at annual meetings.

movement.[4b] Since it denied membership to the sexually permissive, we may assume that the parish became more strict about these matters. We cannot deduce from this, however, that those not chaste enough to qualify for membership in the Sodality refrained from church attendance altogether. Furthermore, the pastor's chronicle mentions that most people were still much given to superstition, and, like Bavarians and Westphalians, believed in charms and witchcraft. It is highly unlikely that people of this mentality, whatever their sexual behaviour, could sever the bond of Church membership and religion.

Protestant churchmen began weighing the question of morality and faith during the first half of the century. Should a person who is sexually unrestrained be given the sacrament of confirmation? Should a woman who has led a sinful life be given holy communion on her deathbed? An urban pastor wrote about his experience with lower-class children who made their first communion. Since they had to work in factories most of the day, they lacked the education that others enjoyed. Likewise, they had little time or energy for Bible lessons. Consequently, when they received their first communion they did not know how to act. Some returned to their places where they talked and joked among themselves, disturbing others. Upon investigating, the pastor learned that the youthful new communicants—boys and girls together—often talked about sex or told crude stories that they had learned at work when they returned to their pews.[46] The same pastor claimed to know of pregnant girls who attended confirmation class, and even of some who were already working as prostitutes! And, he complained, if one visits the dance halls on Confirmation day, one finds there the same children who had received the sacrament in the morning. They danced away, still dressed in their fine confirmation clothes. (We are to infer that more than dancing took place; see the following chapter.) How could such people seriously and meaningfully renew their baptismal vows during Confirmation he asked?

Another Protestant pastor found himself in a similar predicament. He was called to the sick-bed of a dying Breslau woman who had borne illegitimate children. She requested holy communion. The pastor agonised over whether to give it to her. The lower class, he complained, had lost all moral feeling in recent times, but, superstitiously, believed that 'all's well that ends well.' Hence, they requested the sacrament when dying, even though they did not even belong to any particular church.[47]

These stories suggest that in Protestant Germany, too, some of the more sexually permissive lower class sought to preserve their religion and attended religious services at least as children. Others were no longer active members, but still thought of themselves as Christians. Not surprisingly,therefore, outstanding Prostestant churchmen like Johann Wichern saw their task to be one of reawakening faith rather than stalling off dechristianisation.[48] Thus, declining Protestant church membership came in part from sexually 'respectable' elements of the populace, whose mentality was changing in other respects. While not formally quantifiable, there is simply no neat correlation between promiscuity, proletarianisation and declining religion in the popular culture of Protestant Germany.

Hence, as with the Catholic Church, Protestant piety remained largely traditional during the first part of the nineteenth century. The religious mentality was tenaciously crude and superstitious: 'People think they can atone for breaking the commandments by [performing] mechanical formulas.'[49] But the clergy would no longer tolerate or participate in the more gross forms of superstition that were everywhere in evidence until the Napoleonic era.[50] They now placed more emphasis on education, often in fact taking charge of the administration of rural schools throughout Central and Western Europe. 'It can no longer be concealed,' wrote Johann Michael Sailer, one of Europe's most respected, popular and outstanding religious leaders, 'that ignorance and faulty [religious] instruction cause the pilgrimage places to be so overrun.' [51] Since the clergy actively opposed superstition after 1800, it seems likely that new forms of popular piety would develop to take the place of older, superstitious ones. But there was a hiatus before this process got under way. 'Farmers,' one Bavarian pastor reported, 'don't know what to believe in any more now that they can't believe in ghosts.' [52] Thus, we are dealing with a transitional period during which manifestations of modern trends in popular religion are barely perceptible.

Still, we may single out random traces of vitality, precisely because popular fervour remained intense. For example, the Christmas carol *Silent Night Holy Night* was a product of the folk piety of the early modern period. We may even consider it as a manifestation of proletarian religiosity. Its composer was the son of rural weavers, and its lyricist, the illegitimate son of Anna Schoiberin, a Salzburg pieceworker. The carol was first sung in 1818 in the rural parish church of Oberndorf, which was part of the former Imperial Ecclesiastical Principality of Salzburg, that had been divided between Austria and Bavaria as a result of the Napoleonic Wars and Congress of Vienna. From there—an area with an extremely high incidence of bastardy—the carol spread quickly through both Protestant and Catholic parts of the Continent. [53]

Two points regarding the carol bear emphasis. Firstly, the mental imagery it conjures up, as well as traditional Christmas statuary, approximates the living conditions and physical surroundings of the rural proletariat far more than anything in Palestine during the time of Augustus. Thus, the proletarian social origins of its authors are not surprising. Secondly, the rapid spread of *Silent Night Holy Night* (it was a favourite of Frederick William IV of Prussia!) marked an important first in German popular culture: the triumph of a local folkway over regional and even confessional boundaries.

A parallel if less spectacular case is that of the Oberammergau Passion spectacle. In spite of the fact that the streets of this Alpine village were overrun with the legitimate and illegitimate children of the 'lower class', the people preserved and added to the traditional Passion pageant, while other cities and towns allowed it to atrophy. [54]

Perhaps the single most spectacular manifestation of popular religion in Central Europe during the first half of the nineteenth century was occasioned by the holy veil preserved in the Trier cathedral. This piece of fabric bears an image, said to be that of Christ, who miraculously imprinted it on the cloth when Veronica kindly offered it to Him during the Passion. This relic drew pilgrims to Trier in unprecedented numbers. It is estimated that in the year 1844 alone, 500,000 worshippers from all over Germany sojourned in the provincial capital on the Moselle river to venerate the 'Heiligen Rock'.[55] No other Central European shrine cast a spell as powerful or as wide as the Trier relic.[56]

Unfortunately, quantitative data that would tell us something about the social status of the Trier pilgrims do not exist. Other evidence suggests that the aristocracy and rural proletariat constituted the front line of support for the miraculous veil. This was a typical nineteenth-century social combination in the field of popular culture, as we will see in the case of France, uniting the two traditional elements of society at either end of the social spectrum. Hence, we may speculate that many, perhaps even most, of the feet that trudged along country paths and roads towards Trier belonged to the rural proletariat.

The several manifestations of popular culture we have discussed have one thing in common — each is a Christocentric form of piety. The prevalence of this form probably has some significance, because German Christians, unlike the French, never experienced controversy over religious symbolism. In the first three decades of the nineteenth century there was a rush of popular disorders with religious overtones, but confessional rivalries account for most of these and they may not in any event be viewed as controversy over religious symbols such as the mission crosses in France (see Chapter 7).[57] Thus, we cannot guess from early nineteenth-century evidence along what specific lines the modern German religious mentality will take. No new cults, such as those of the virgins in France, emerge. Rather, there is a persistence of traditional piety and traditional religious aberrations: millenarianism, midnight séances, exorcism, witchcraft, and so on.[58]

In sum, the facts of frequent bastardy and dutiful religious observance with which Central Europe confronts us may appear contradictory, but during the early, transitional period of modernisation they coalesced in a peculiar, proletarian brand of popular religion. Sexuality in the mind of the eighteenth-century rustic had never been perceived as an exclusively or even principally moral issue. As a consequence, when sex suddenly became secularised in Germany, there was no need to choose between it and religion. The common people cherished their folkways and would have practised religion much the way their fathers and grandfathers had before them, had the clergy allowed it. The increase of bastardy notwithstanding, the religious mentality of the nascent lower class changed hardly at all during the first half of the nineteenth century.

The peculiar ability of the proletariat to make the best of two worlds is instructive in several ways. We are put on guard not to read political implications into proletarian 'sexual excess', and to be cautious about the social implications we deduce from it. There is not a shred of evidence to support the notion that sexual non-conformity was an 'acting out' of political discontent. Eventually, late in the *Vormärz*, the right to live in accordance with their desired life-style may have been a politicising factor, as we will see in the following chapter. But this was decades after the lower class had already fallen into the distinctive proletarian pattern of life. Nor do the data on religious observance allow us to impute heavy social implications from the sexual revolution. Although insisting on their sexual freedom while others all around them, both in the city and country, chose to behave more 'respectably', the rural proletariat did not cut adrift from society by severing Church bonds. Indeed, they lingered to savour the vestiges of traditional religious folkways.

Finally, knowing the religious behaviour of the rural proletarian adds a dimension to his composite historical character. In previous chapters we have inevitably exaggerated by singling out and quoting texts from contemporaries which emphasised one or other aspect of the proletarian personality — his sexual looseness, his hard work, his shrewdness as well as his spendthrift ways. If we now add to these a religious quality, the proletarian figure is softened or rounded off by a certain naiveté that we otherwise miss. The following contemptuous characterisation by a rural Bavarian pastor adds the religious element into the character composite as well as other factors that we discuss in the ensuing chapter:

> Towards strangers they are disagreeable, intolerant or deceitful; towards their pastor and church personnel, arrogant, sulky, defiant or even brutal; towards civil personnel, on the other hand, fawning; among themselves they are spiteful, envious, defamatory, and addicted to leisure, begging, indebtedness, voluptuousness, gambling— especially the ruinous lottery, drinking and gluttony—not infrequently to a degree beyond all moral measure; and, at one and the same time, they join an almost complete lack of real religious knowledge and intellectual ability to the crudest manners and most crass superstition: these could serve as the principal characterisations of most of the inhabitants of the parish and especially of Altenmarkt.[59]

**Notes**

1. This appears to hold for Catholic more than Protestant areas of Germany.

2. They very much resemble the Zurich Highlanders in this respect; Braun, pp. 122-56.

3. *Historisch-Politische Blätter,* XVI (1845), pp. 506-8.

4. Christoph Völker, *Aus dem religiösen Volksleben in Fürstbistum Paderborn während des 17. und 18. Jahrhundert* (Paderborn, 1936), pp. 140-3.

5. Hans Müller, *Säkularisation und Öffentlichkeit am Beispiel Westfalen* (Münster, 1971), p. 142.

6. Ibid., p. 183.

7. Ibid., p. 31.

8. *Historisch-Politische Blätter,* XVI (1848), p. 516.

9. Muller, pp. 32-4.

10. *Historisch-Politische Blätter,* XVI, (1848), p. 510.

11. Anita Brittinger, 'Die bayerische Verwaltung und das volksfromme Brauchtum im Zeitalter der Aulklärung' (Diss., Munich, 1938), pp. 8-9.

12. OAM, *Pf. Besch.,* 1784.

13. OAM, *Visitation* Laufen, c. 1796.

14. OAM, *Pf. Besch.* Bogenhausen, 1784.

15. Karl Schornbaum, *Geschichte der Pfarrei Alfred, Quellen und Forschung zur bayerischen Kirchengeschichte,* VI (1922), p. 149.

16. Brittinger, pp. 13ff.

17. Johann Andreas Schmeller, *Tagebücher 1801-52,* Paul Ruf (ed.), *Schriftenreihe zur bayerischen Landesgeschichte,* XLVII, 4 June, 1802.

18. Paul Sieweck, C.S.S.R., *Lothar Anselm Freiherr v. Gebsattel* (Munich, 1955), p. 206.

19. OAM, *Verbotene Bücher,* P. Karl to Vic. General; Laufen, 29 Oct. 1819.

20. OAM, *Vis. Beant.,* Oberwarngau, 1826.

21. OAM, *Verbotene Bucher.*

22. OAM, *Visitation* Laufen.

23. The numbers on which my percentages are based should be accurate as a fairly foolproof method of checking Easter duty fulfilment. During the Easter season a person was given a *Beichtzettel* (confession card), usually a holy card, when he received the sacrament. He then handed the priest the card when he received the Eucharist on Easter Sunday. Consequently, the numbers are based on an actual count rather than on estimates.

24. OAP 07090 Ordinary to parishes, July 1840.

25. *Gen. Samm.* I, pp. 411ff.

26. France and Protestant Germany are discussed below.

27. *Gen. Samm.,* Munich, I (1838), p. 412.

28. Ibid., II (1852), p. 41.

29. OAP 07090 Weihmörting, 1828.

30. *Gen. Samm.,* Munich, I (1824), pp. 84-8.

31. Ibid., I, pp. 443-4.

32. OAP 06766 Ordinary to parishes, July 1840.

33. Pastoral letter of the archbishop of Munich, 1827, in *Gen. Samm.* I pp. 199ff.

34. Ibid., p. 199.

35. M. Doeberl, *Entwicklungs Geschichte Bayerns* (Munich, 1931), III., p. 121.

36. OAM, *Vis. Beant.,* Martinsried, 1833; Garmisch, 1826; Herbertshausen, n.d.; Konigsdorf, 1826; Bayersoien, 1826.

37. OAM, *Vis. Beant.,* Mettenheim, 1833.

38. *Gen. Samm.,* Munich, I (Oct. 1828), p. 412.

39. Lenten letter of Bishop of Marseille in *L'Ami de la Religion,* LXIII (1830), p. 137.

40. Letter of Bishop of Carcassone in ibid., LI (1827), pp. 133-4.

41. See the pastoral letter of the bishops of Orléans, Tours, Bourges, Toulouse and Bordeaux in ibid., CIV (3 and 5 March 1840), pp. 422, 434-7, resp., and of St. Flour, ibid., C (28 Feb. 1839), pp. 405-6.

42. *Evangelische Kirchen-Zeitung,* VII (1 Sep. 1830), c. 560.
43. In *Geschichte des Protestantismus in seiner neusten Entwicklung* (Arnheim, 1862), pp. 64-71, J. E. Jörg mentions that in some places illegitimacy rose as much as Church membership fell.
44. *Evangelische Kirchen-Zeitung,* XXXIV-XXXV 4, 8, 11 and 15 May 1844), c. 287-9. The chronicle makes no mention of a rival church that could have drawn away some of the congregation.
45. Ibid., c. 303.
46. Ibid., XXXVIII-XXXIX (25 Feb. 1846), c. 139-44.
47. Ibid., VI (31 March, 1830), c. 205-6.
48. William O. Shanahan, *German Protestants Face the Social Question* (Notre Dame [Ind.], 1954), p. 345 (footnote).
49. OAM, *Vis. Beant.*, Schliersee, 1828; see also Miessbach, 1826.
50. OAP 07090 Aholming, 1828.
51. Georg Schreiber (ed.), *Wallfahrt und Volkstum in Geschichte und Leben* (Düsseldorf, 1934), p. 80.
52. OAM, *Vis. Beant.*, Kohlgrub, 1826.
53. J. Grassner, *Silent Night Holy Night* (Innsbruck, 1968), pp. 23-30.
54. OAM, *Vis. Beant.* 1826.
55. Wolfgang Schieder, 'Kirche und Revolution', *Archiv für Sozialgeschichte,* XIV (1974), pp. 420-9.
56. It may be questioned whether the holy veil was wholly an evocation of popular religious culture. Political considerations becloud the emergence of its popularity. It has been suggested that the Catholic Church in Germany encouraged devotion to the Trier veil to demonstrate the loyalty and solidarity of Rhineland Church members at the time when conflict with the Prussian state was worsening (*Kölner Wirren*). It is, indeed, remarkable that Church literature of the 1840s upheld the indisputable authenticity of the relic and recounted miracles that had been accomplished through it, even though earlier nineteenth-century bishops of Trier had opposed and even (unsuccessfully) forbade pilgrimages venerating the veil; see Joachim Schiffhauer, 'Das Wallfahrtswesen im Bistum Trier unter Bischof Joseph von Hommer (1824-1836)', *Festschrift fur Alois Thomas* (Trier, 1967), pp. 345-58. But, political motives notwithstanding, the Trier episode represents an impressive show of popular piety.
57. Richard Tilly, 'Popular Disorders in Nineteenth Century Germany: A Preliminary Survey', *Journal of Social History,* IV, I (Fall 1970), pp. 1-40.
58. Alfons Hoffman, 'Aberglaube und religiöse Schwärmerei in der Pfalz in 19. Jahrhundert', *Archiv f. mittelrheinische Kirchengeschichte,* Jahrgang 27 (1975), pp. 203-13.
59. OAM, *Vis. Beant.* Bambury, 1830. It is interesting that the people of Altenmarkt are singled out. As we saw above, the proletariat tended to live in larger villages; they congregated in even greater numbers in villages that had once been subject to a farming landlord (*Gutsherrschaft*) such as Altenmarkt.

# 5 POPULAR CULTURE: DANCING

The insouciant sexual attitudes of the rural proletarian youth pro-
claimed the individualism and affective relationships of modern society.
But by conserving religious traditions they retained communal bonds.
Dancing epitomised this double standard.

How the youth loved to dance! Yet, dancing became a controversial
social issue during the first part of the nineteenth century and the proletariat was the eye of the storm.[1] Modernisation, which had extended
personal freedom to European common people, allowed proletarian
youth to dance in a new and intimate manner. But it also secularised
life in a way that eliminated many traditional occasions for dancing of
which the proletariat was fond. Because of these compound factors,
youth danced during the *Vormärz* under a vicious cross-fire of criticism
—on the one hand, from those who were outraged or scandalised about
*how* they danced; and, on the other, from civil authorities who disliked
*when* they danced. We must now consider how the proletariat got into
this predicament and determine what feelings it aroused in them.

It is not as if dancing had not existed in pre-modern times. Indeed, it
played an integral part of communal life. When an entire village joined
in a dance, the community was physically united. It expressed its unity
through the dance. In Germany trees often served as the focal point of
one type of communal dance which brought all ages together. Peasant
folk danced around the *Dorflinde* for fertility or good crops. In Upper
Franconia there was a special variation of this type of dance called the
*Lindentanz.*[2] In parts of France a type of communal dance known as
the *bourrée* seems to have been common.[3] It is important to note that
these communal dances expressed collectivity. Far from providing a
person with a stage on which to assert individuality, the communal
dance served to give each person the feeling of belonging to the
community.

In the pre-modern dance each movement was closely prescribed by
custom or by the intuition of the group as it enacted a dance which it
knew solely from oral tradition. Judging from descriptions of these
dances, especially those involving the entire community, they were
tedious to the point of boredom.[4] Even in courtship dances nothing
very erotic took place. Since dances often centred around occupational
sub-groups, couples seldom danced with each other and changed

82

partners often when they did. This picture of stylised formality in place
of emotion and spontaneity fits our conceptions of rural engagement
routines such as the *Heimgarten.* The staid, tradition-bound approach
to dancing may have occasionally fallen by the boards at a *Kirchweih*
(parish celebration) or youth dance, but in both civil and episcopal
archives one searches in vain for outraged complaints about wild
dancing before 1800.[5] Baroque preachers, notorious embellishers, were
also subdued on the topic of dancing.[6]

Even the more elaborate and complicated dances performed by
various units in the community such as shepherds, weavers, young men
and so on emphasised the sub-group rather than the individual. Dances
performed by a sub-group usually included but one sex, so dancing sometimes afforded no boy-girl contact at all. The dance itself, although more
elaborate than those performed by young and old alike, was highly stylised. Often the dancers pantomimed the work of their sub-group, so
that the actions of the most accomplished artisans served as a model for
everyone's movements.[7] In Germany the shepherd's 'magic staff', the
*Klingerstock*, played a part in the dance and in community conscious -
ness.[8] In all sub-group dances, individuality is eclipsed. Custom dictates
the motions, movements, and those who can participate.

When dances included both sexes more spontaneity occurred. The
dance of the bonfire on the feast of St John was one of the most
popular among the youth in both France and Germany. Jordan von
Wasserburg, a Baroque preacher, complained that unbridled youth
stoked the fires of passion instead of the bonfire, and he accused young
women of taking part in the dance with breasts half-exposed.[8] He exaggerated, but it was true that the festivities surrounding the midsummer
feast allowed some dancing and other kinds of spontaneity between the
sexes. History records that an occasional pregnancy resulted from the
gaiety.[9]

Another popular dance or ritual involving both sexes was the
*Minneburg.* As in the game 'King of the Mountain', boys 'stormed' a
hill—the 'Chateau d'Amour'—held by the girls. The action was
accompanied by the singing of the round:

> Castle of love, don't you wish to surrender?
> Do you wish to yield or to endure?

The girls eventually succumbed to the bombardment of flowers and
honeyed words of the boys and the hill was taken amidst caresses.[10]
Surely some affective relationships, however limited, must have been

established during these games and dances. In France, mating and courtship dances were common in pre-modern society. Men and women danced together but not in an intimate way.[11] Far from being romantic, these affairs were public and closely regulated by the community.

One occasion for dancing that we have inherited from pre-modern times was the wedding. Both sexes participated and some of these dances even sound erotic. In the German *Brautlauf* the groom danced to woo his bride to undress for him.[12] But weddings in pre-modern times were strictly family and community affairs. The eroticism was not individualistic. Rather, it reflected the community's savouring of an extremely important event—its own propagation by the addition of a new family. In the nineteenth century German farmers in Westphalia, untainted by the new sexual freedom, still celebrated their marriages with pride and elaborate traditions. One of these was 'the Dance of Virginity and Marriage'. At a point in the festivities the men, linking arms, forced a human wall around the bride, dancing around her. The women danced outside the ring, and, as the tempo of the music increased, tried to pummel their way through to capture the bride to signify the change in her life which she was about to experience.[13] In France wedding dances, which 'symbolised the establishment of a new household within the community', adhered to a prescribed ritual which assigned to each a role according to his place in the family and community.[14]

Lusty dancing seems to have taken place during the village and church festivals (*Kermesse* or *Kirchweih*), which bishops and curates regularly bemoaned.[15] Dancing, of course, was only one of a number of diversions—nine-pins, shooting matches, cards, drinking and eating, and so on. Unless the Baroque artists who have captured these scenes on their canvasses exaggerated as much as the Baroque preachers (whose reputations, by the way, were made and measured by preaching on these occasions) inhibitions restrained the dancers as little as anyone else.[16] We must be ready to admit that some sexual contact was involved. And yet we cannot allow imagination to distort fact: the dancing, like other carnival activity, was held in the churchyard, or near it, in broad daylight, and as a community function.

In pre-modern times dancing took place at prescribed times and only at those times. The liturgical cycle functioned as a social event calender as well.[17] Certain times of the year were designated for penance, others for rejoicing. It was within the liturgical cycle that communal celebrations and dancing and the dances of sub-groups took place. Youth rites such as the 'Minneburg' and 'bonfire dance' took place on the first Sunday of May and the Feast of St John (24 June) respectively. On the fifth of February the spinners in Busendorf, a German-speaking settlement in the Lorraine, celebrated the feast of St Agatha with food and dancing on the eve and a pilgrimage on the feast day itself.[18] Every occupational group had its patron and therefore a day set aside for its own celebration. In addition to these, the rites of passage—baptism, confirmation, marriage, death—provided occasions for communal celebrations when dancing took place. In every case, then, the community controlled dancing, not the individual. Dancing itself was not spontaneous but defined in its execution and restrained as to its participants by custom. Instead of being a group of individuals who together constitute what we now call a dance, in pre-modern times it was the dance that absorbed the individuals. In the words of one historian, it 'articulated the existence of a group, defined its membership and celebrated its being'.[19]

Quite suddenly after 1800 the manner and style of dancing changed in Central Europe. Judging from descriptions of 'better-minded' contemporaries, dances abruptly lost their group or sub-group significance. The dancers stamped, whistled, and shouted loudly so that the music itself was drowned out.[20] The movement and music of the group gave place to individual dancing. Dancers no longer acted in unison. The elaborate traditional steps did not disappear overnight, of course, but they now competed with modern dances, which, like the Viennese Waltz, allowed dancers free movement. The contrast of the pre-modern and modern styles demands very little of our imaginations: on the one hand, we see a group of virile young men performing the athletic *Schuh-plattler*, slapping their shoes and *Lederhosen* in perfect unison and letting go now and then with yelps and whoops to delight and excite female onlookers; and, on the other, a man and woman gracefully wheeling about a dance floor locked in each other's embrace and their own little world.[21]

Modern dances distinguished themselves in another way—they became erotic. This may be taken in two senses: couples now danced together at their own choosing, and the dance itself was highly suggestive and sensual. If we may believe the 'better-minded' *curés*, civil servants and respected citizens who reported on these scandalous goings-on, a young proletarian woman went to a dance unescorted in the hope of attracting an admirer with whom she would in all

likelihood make love after the dance.[22] Instead of the formal contact
between dancers of former times, affective relationships were sought
after and secured at the dance. The concupiscent atmosphere of the
dance promoted this. Sex was a topic both of conversation and of the
lyrics of the songs.[23] 'In the country people dance with frantic frivo-
lity; the dancers sing the most shameful and indecent songs [whose
lyrics are] suggested by passionate fantasy *(erhitzte Pfantasie* [sic] )'.[24]

Were it not for the submersion of the rural proletariat in the waters
of sexual permissiveness after 1800, we would be caught completely
off-guard by the sudden reversal in dancing styles. Even so, accounting
for the abrupt transition is not easy. To do so and to know its significance we must discuss what has been called the plebeian culture of
pre-modern society.[25]

In former times the cosmic view of the common people gave life a
set purpose. Single-mindedness was the upshot of pathetic insecurity
felt by a populace that saw its numbers periodically decimated by
famine. Paulus Henrici of the middle Rhine verbalised the pre-modern
mentality when, in the midst of the devastating agricultural collapse of
1770-3, he wrote in his diary: 'We live as always between fear and
hope.'[26] The cosmic view cast a sacral aura around reality which kept
people from distinguishing its various aspects. As a result, life's experiences defied compartmentalisation.[27]

The peculiar one-dimensional view expressed itself on both the
individual and communal level. The farmer's ailing horse or cow was at
once a religious and economic concern, and he never paused to distinguish the two. Friedrich Lütge reckoned that as late as 1800 20,000
Bavarian farmers still annually trekked off on pilgrimages to save livestock or crops.[28] These were spiritual exercises of course, but one
made a day of it by stopping over at road houses to socialise and tipple.
Leisure, business, religion, recreation—everything ran together.[29]

The same jumble of activity is apparent in the life of the community.
About half the calendar year was marked by holy days on which work
was forbidden. In Bavaria the number ran as high as 200.[30] Besides
these community-wide observances, various sub-groups came together
now and then for religious exercises like pilgrimages or processions.
People solemnised holy days with great sincerity because of the ever-
impending threat of plague, famine, and so on. Nevertheless, it would
be a mistake to imagine that they spent half of the year praying in some
church or at some shrine. Religious holy days doubled as holidays providing the community with as many recreational opportunities as
religious rites. On the eve of holy days, which were sprinkled generously

throughout the annual liturgical cycle, church bells rang as early as
3 o' clock in the afternoon to call people in from the field. There would
be vespers that evening and church the following day, but the remaining
time was whiled away in jolly pastimes, including dancing. Church service itself often bore resemblance to a game, a play, or civic exercise.[31]
At times it is difficult to determine what exact significance services
conveyed for common people. It was not unusual for arguments and
fights to erupt in the midst of devotions, and church service itself seems
to have been so casual as to admit of any number of not specifically
religious activities.[32]

It is impossible for us to distinguish between the holy day and
holiday elements in pre-modern communal life because Central Europeans could not themselves distinguish. In urban France the religious
element eroded quite noticeably during the eighteenth century.[33] And
it is thought that in England at this time a materialistic gentry began to
lead common people on to the more carnal and material aspects of holy
days at the expense of the medieval Christian heritage.[34] In Central
Europe, by contrast, this kind of secularisation *only just began* around
the middle of the eighteenth century.

Prodding itself along with the stick of economic progress, German
states dropped the holy days which had occasioned community recreation during Baroque times. During the Enlightenment there were
lively and quite extensive debates on holy days that led to papal,
episcopal and civil decrees which eliminated more than half of them.[35]
Civil authorities generally favoured curtailing them in order to fashion
more productive subjects, and ecclesiastical authorities often co-
operated with them so as to purify religion of the superstitious or the
more secular practices associated with these feasts. The people, however, refused to abandon their folk calendar. Not until after the
Napoleonic Wars in Germany could a secular calendar truly be said to
replace the old liturgical one, and another fifty years elapsed before the
people fully relinquished their traditional feasts.

It is critical to notice that at the time of the reduction of feast
days—the secularisation of the calendar—the religious attachment of
the nascent rural lower class to traditional church-related folkways *had
not yet fallen into decline* as it had in France and England. We may
judge this by observing their reaction to the change of calendar routine.

Because of their superstition, rural Bavarian people wanted to continue to celebrate feast days with church services.[36] In the words of a
country curate, they 'make a to-do over religious ceremony'.[37] But the
nineteenth-century clergy of Central and Western Europe, who found

the 'holy day-holiday' tone of the traditional feast day obnoxious, refused to celebrate them. As a result the religious character of the cancelled feast days quickly subsided after 1800. With this aspect eliminated, they could only be observed by superstitious prattle and by malingering. Since the cancellation of the feast days meant more calendar work days for farm hands, they objected, and could sometimes only be lured into service on the condition that they be allowed the leisure which was traditionally associated with these days.[38] 'The discontinued feast days,' a Bavarian pastor noted, 'which opened the door to idleness and fooling around, are [now observed] neither as holy days for obligatory devotion, nor as workdays for lawful labour.'[39] The proletarian attitude towards the discontinued feast days left them suspended somewhere between a traditional holy day-holiday and a modern work day.

The fact was that common people still enjoyed traditional Baroque community functions and, unlike others, were not yet accustomed to our modern distinction between religious and secular activities. After 1800 we find Westphalian youth playing the old customary communal games: the shooting match for women who parodied as Maria Theresas for a day; the harvest festival with its queen enthroned on a festive harvest wagon; *Fasching* (an extended Mardi Gras); wedding celebrations, and so on.[40]

Similarly, folk customs occupied proletarian youth in the Rhineland as late as mid-century. One traditional game was called the *Maifeier*. On the last Sunday of April young men went around to the homes of women, each calling out the name of the young female he fancied. If she answered she became his *Maifrau*. Then on Trinity Sunday he went to her house and they gathered eggs and ate together. During the premodern era this had been a highly elaborate ritual, but had more recently—under the influence of sexual permissiveness—become the occasion for much more than gathering eggs. Still, it shows the lingering communal mentality of the proletarian youth.[41]

In Bavaria the pious devotions of the Baroque era—holy hours, patronal feasts (of various sub-groups), confraternity days, parish festivals—continued to be enthusiastically feted by the proletariat.[42] The superstitious lower class sought to maintain the spectacles traditionally associated with holy days.[43] Some local business concerns—innkeepers, butchers, bakers, haberdashers—liked to see the spendthrift lower-class youth carry on the holiday spirit of the discontinued holy days because it meant more money in their pockets. Bavarian curates explicitly accused these business people of prostituting religion by exploiting the

superstitious proletariat for their own profit.[44] 'Religion and piety',
they said, 'often serve as a "come on" for business.'[45] Whether or not
it was a case of exploitation we might seriously question, but it is clear
that more than anyone else the 'awestruck proletariat' (*schaulustige
Pöbel*) sought to maintain the spectacles traditionally associated with
holy days.[46]

Since dancing had always been part of communal life it was natural
that it would continue to be a favourite pastime on Sundays and discontinued holy days. In a careful study covering the number and
occasions for public dances in 1852, the Munich chancery determined
that a marriage, church, or guild festival, or one or the other of the long-
suppressed feast days still provided the excuse for holding most of the
4,842 dances in that diocese alone in one year's time (excluding, at that,
the cities of Munich and Landshut!).[47] In their reports to the Munich
and Passau chanceries, the Bavarian clergy make the point again and
again that the former holy days had lately become occasions for
dancing.[48] Thus it was that the rural proletariat, unable to observe
customary religious rites associated with the Baroque liturgical calendar,
retained only the secular aspects of traditional celebrations.

Now no one, we may suppose, would have become much over-
wrought on account of the dances had these been the innocent affairs
of bygone days. In fact, however, it was just at that moment when
communal celebrations associated with the Baroque liturgical calendar
were suppressed that proletarian sexuality had become secularised and
that the dance had become individualistic and intimate. Soon after
1800, as we have seen, dances took on an explicitly erotic aura and
communal overtones gave way to the intimacy of the affective relationship. Rural youth, vibrating to the tempo of 'a free and carefree life',
now got acquainted at dances over which the community at large
exercised no control.[49] Dances became the medium for romantic courtship as it had developed among the rural proletarian youth after 1800.[50]
After celebrating a former holy day by dancing, they sought out their
trysting places to pursue illicit love affairs. In the words of a rural
curate:

> It is striking that it is especially on discontinued feast days that the
> young people often meet and make love in the Alpine meadows in
> summer and in the barns in the winter.[51]

In one area of Franconia, it was said that a fifth of all paternity suits
originated in *Kirchweihen,* the ever-popular church festivals.[52] Thus,

ironically, a traditional, but officially discontinued, feast day became the occasion for proletarian love-making after 1800.

Sporadic efforts were made during the *Vormärz* to curtail dancing. In 1825 Bavarian officials notified all civil servants and diocesan clergy that they must rigidly enforce the fifty-year old law on the reduction of feast days, which, they pointed out, had become occasions for idleness and immorality.[53] Neither this nor other attempts proved very successful.

In Catholic Westphalia, too, proletarian sexual licence showed a pre-ference for former religious holy days, during which the people spent the day dancing and drinking. Some observers looked upon the former feast days as nothing more than an excuse for sexual gratification.[54] No civil or ecclesiastical administrator of a Catholic area doubted the causal relationship between the old holy days and the sexual permissiveness and dancing of the proletariat. German Protestants, however, were less sure. They could not decide if sexual licence was being held in check by church-related socials, or whether these were fanning the fires of con-cupiscence. The Swedish Parliament debated this question in 1829 and finally decided to retain holy days (as a control for immorality).[55] Some German pastors also felt that they should be retained and that socialising should be encouraged, to maintain ties with the youth who had come to see religion as a spoiler of their good times.[56]

In sum, two statements should be made regarding proletarian dancing in early modern times. On the one hand, it had become individualised and affectual, but, on the other, it continued to be as-sociated with traditional community, folk holy days. The rustic who danced by the light of the moon on Saturday night took his place in church with the community on Sunday morning.[57] Dancing (or, for that matter, sexual licence) in Germany did not set itself up in opposi-tion to tradition, but acted itself out within the vestiges of communal rites.

The circumstances surrounding the rise of erotic dancing among proletarian youth are as important as the fact of these behavioural changes. If we had discussed them outside the context of these circum-stances we would have mistakenly concluded that defiance and rebellion motivated lower-class youth to act out their discontent through socially unacceptable behaviour. In fact, the circumstances only reinforce the thesis that the secularisation of sex was not preju-dicial to religion in the mind of the proletariat. It was the Church that was changing, not initially, the hold of religion.

Modernity offered the rural proletariat what the communal society of the Old Regime had often denied them: the opportunity to marry. Their romantic marriages, which contrast vividly with farmers' arranged affairs, are clear testimony to a new modern way of life. But the proletariat did not abandon the community. They did not withdraw like middle-class people into the privacy and seclusion of their homes. This may have been as much out of economic necessity as cultural attachment to communal society. Proletarian marriages were the products of affective relationships and their families generated strong affective ties. But the family economy dictated an early substitution of extra-marital, affective ties for familial bonds.[58] This centrifugal force turned the proletarian family out towards society, opening it up to the life of the community. What they had always enjoyed most about that life—the church and village festivals, the feast day celebrations, and so on, they did not now wish to relinquish. They danced and made love at times when society had always sanctioned conviviality. Far from rebelling either against the old society or against nascent capitalistic society, they sought the best of two worlds.

## Notes

1. Shorter, "La Vie Intim", pp.340ff.
2. W. Gaerte, *Volksglaube und Brauchtum Ostpreussens* (Würzberg, 1956), pp.1-7.
3. Michael R. Marrus, 'Modernisation and Dancing in rural France: From *La Bourée* to *Le Fox-Trot*', p.5. Professor Marrus's insights dealing with dancing in traditional and modern society provided me with a valuable framework within which to deal with the topic of dancing and popular religion and morality around 1830. I am indebted to him for sending me his paper, which is being prepared for publication.
4. Ibid. p.3.
5. Shorter, "La Vie Intim" pp.341-2; I have looked through the 'Visitation' reports for the eighteenth century in the diocese of Munich for complaints of this nature and found none whatsoever.
6. Böck, *Johann Christoph Beer*, p.74.
7. Marrus, p.9.
8. Gaerte, pp.14-15.
9. Shorter, *The Making of the Modern Family*, p.134.
10. Gaerte, p.107.
11. Marrus, p.10.
12. Gaerte, p.1.
13. *Historisch-Politische Blätter*, XVI (1845), pp.594-5.
14. Marrus, p.10.
15. Shorter, *The Making of the Modern Family*, p.135.
16. References to these carnivals are frequent; see, for example, Nikolaus Kyll, 'Zur Geschichte der Kirmes und ihres Brauchtums in Trierer Lande und in Luxemburg', *Rheinisches Jahrbuch für Volkskunde, Jahrgang* XX, pp.93-132; Moser-Rath, pp.358-9. Karl Sigismund Kramer supports the thesis that carnivals and liturgical festivals generally obtained much less in Protestant areas of

# Sexual Liberation and Religion in 19th Century Europe

Germany: 'Eibelstadt und Wilster im 17. Jahrhundert', *Volkskultur und Geschichte,* Dieter Harminung et al. (eds.) (Berlin, 1970), pp. 106-19.

17. See the calendars and annual events in Veit and Lenhart, pp.145ff; Merkelbach-Pinck, pp.85ff; R. Jalby, *Le Folklore de Languedoc* (Paris,1971), *passim.*
18. Merkelbach-Pinck, p.94.
19. Marrus, p.9.
20. Shorter, '"La Vie Intim"', p.340.
21. It would be fascinating if we could determine which people were doing which dance in early modern times; or if we knew which people did modern steps better than traditional ones. It would be facile to suggest that sons of farmers preserved the old *Schuhplattler* while the proletarian youth developed newer steps. Then their situation in the countryside would approximate our inte-grated urban high schools where the predominating race dictates the kind of music and dance step during the mid-day break. While it is likely that the proletariat did pick up the newer steps more quickly after 1800, there is reason to think that they did not scorn the older, traditional steps.
22. Shorter, pp.340-3; OAP 07090 Grafenau, 1828; Waldhof 1828. Virtually all Bavarian curates saw the *Freinächte* (nights on which dances were held) as the occasion of illicit intercourse and rising illegitimacy rates.
23. OAM, *Vis. Beant.,* Reit bei Winkel, 1828; Höslwang, 1827; OAP 07090 Aidenbach, 1828; Kreutzberh, 1828.
24. OAM, *Vis. Beant.,* Reit bei Winkel, 1828.
25. E. P. Thompson, 'Patrician Society, Plebian Culture', *Journal of Social History,* VII, 4 (Summer 1974), pp.382-405.
26. Pfarrarchiv Niederkirchen, *Gedenkbuch.*
27. Karl Abraham, *Der Betrieb als Erziehungsfaktor* (Freiburg im Br., 1957), *passim.*
28. *Die bayerische Grundherrschaft* (Stuttgart, 1949), p.17.
29. Maurice Agulhon treats this extensively and brilliantly in *La Sociabilité Méridionale (confréries et associations dans la vie collective en Provence orien-tale à la fin du XVIIIᵉ siècle)* (Aix, 1966), 2 vols,: see also Möller, Chs. V and VI.
30. Anita Brittinger, 'Die bayerische Verwaltung und das volksfromme Brauchtum im Zeitalter der Aufklärung' (Diss., Munich, 1938), p.49; see also Lütge, p.16.
31. Timothy N. Tackett describes this kind of mentality in a French diocese: 'The Parish priest in the Eighteenth Century Diocese of Gap' (Diss., Stanford, 1973), pp.34-6, 71-5.
32. Hair-pulling seems to have been the most common type of fight. It is one of the most frequent infractions mentioned in *Visitationsbuch* XIV 1ba of the Paderborn diocesan archives.
33. Agulhon, I, pp.127ff., 150-1, 262 3 and *passim.*
34. Thompson, pp.394-5. This is an interesting hypothesis. In Germany the aristo-cracy seems to have been every bit as sybaritic as the English gentry. Yet it has never been suggested that they promoted materialism among lower classes. This has been seen, rather, as a by-product of the liberal reforms of the Napoleonic era.
35. J. Michael (Fintan) Phayer, *Religion und das gewöhnliche Volk in Bayern in der Zeit von 1750 bis 1850, Miscellanea Bavarica Monacensis,* XXI (1970), Ch.IV.
36. OAP 07090 Aholming, 1828.
37. OAM, *Vis. Beant.,* Evenhausen in Pfaffing, 1830; see also OAM, *Vis. Beant.,* Miessbach, 1826.
38. OAM, *Vis. Beant.,* Dietramszell. Copy of letter from the Linden community to

King Ludwig of Bavaria, 1827; see also Engelberg, 1838.

39. OAM. *Vis. Beant.*, Waging 1828.

40. *Historische-Politische Blätter* XVI (1845), p.512.

41. Ibid., XXXVIII (1856), pp.788-91.

42. OAM, *Vis. Beant.*, Baumburg, 1830.

43. Ibid., and OAM, *Vis. Beant.*, Buchbach, 1823.

44. OAM, *Vis. Beant.*, Baumberg, 1830.

45. OAM, *Vis. Beant.*, Trostberg, 1830.

46. OAM, *Vis. Beant.*, Baumburg, 1830.

47. *Gen. Samm.*, II, pp.490-3.

48. OAM, *Vis. Beant.*, Dietramszell, 1822; Königsdorf, 1826; Baumburg, 1830; Buchbach, 1823; OAP 07090 Waldhof, 1828; Zimmermann, 1828.

49. OAM, *Vis. Beant.*, Oberwarngau, 1826.

50. Shorter discusses this in '"La Vie Intim"'.

51. OAM, *Vis. Beant.*, Reit bei Winkel, 1828; see also Höslwang, 1827.

52. Shorter, '"La Vie Intim"', p.542.

53. *Gen. Samm.*, I, p.73 (Aug. 1823); pp.80-1 (Jan. 1824); pp. 91-3 (June 1824); p.94 (June and July 1824); p,95 (July 1824); p.124 (Nov. 1824).

54. Müller, p.32.

55. *Evangelische Kirchen-Zeitung*, V (16 and 19 Sept. 1829), c.585-90 and 593-7 resp.

56. Ibid., XXXII-XXXIII (29 July 1843), c.476-80.

57. It is not until the 1840s that clerical reports begin to note that some proletarian youth absented themselves from church services. Even then the complaints are scattered and unemphatic.

58. This does not mean that bonds with parents were broken. Tilly, Scott and Cohen have shown the permanence of these bonds in the nineteenth century —a carry-over, they think, from pre-modern times.

# 6 PIETY AND PERMISSIVENESS IN FRANCE

Did modernisation produce the same behaviour and mentality in France as in Central Europe? Did the French also remain devout while allowing themselves greater sexual licence? History seldom permits us the luxury of running the same 'experiment' twice and the questions posed here offer no exception. If we are successfully to demonstrate the secularisation of sex in France, we will have to find new ways to ferret out evidence.

France presents a more complex problem at the very outset. It is well known that a process of dechristianisation was both widespread and well advanced by the nineteenth century.[1] Thus, before we can ask if French common people were devout and sexually indulgent, we must first determine if they were even devout. Who had become infected with dechristianisation? Only then—as in the case of the German Protestants—can we ask which party or parties were responsible for sexual permissiveness.

In the last analysis, the rise of new kinds of religious devotion is the factor that will allow us to launch a direct assault on the critical question regarding the secularisation of sex. The new cults had two foci: a Christocentric devotion to the cross, and St Philomena, a virgin and martyr. The latter is a particularly interesting example, since the growth of her cult bucked a trend towards increased bastardy. These, then, are the circumstances that will allow us to resolve the problem of religion and sexual behaviour for France, but let us begin with the question of dechristianisation.

Who was devout and who was not? When it came to Church membership, the usual yardstick of dechristianisation, French Catholics somewhat resembled German Protestants. Easter duty discipline (the canonical requirement of receiving the Eucharist once a year) deteriorated during the eighteenth century and continued to do so during the nineteenth. In the diocese of Orléans only 20 to 30 per cent of the people were fulfilling their Easter duty by mid-century.[2] In the Sedan church attendance remained fairly strong, but in Normandy it collapsed among workers and was spotty in rural areas.[3] In the western part of the diocese of Rouen only about 50 per cent of the people kept up Church membership but elsewhere they were dutiful.[4] In Pouzauges in western France just about everyone took part in a proselytising mission in 1863, but by 1866 only 81 per cent of the people received the sacraments during the Easter season.[5] The Bocage people in the Vendée were faithful, but those who lived in the plains were indifferent.[6] People in north-western France remained dutiful, but in eastern Maine and Anjou religious observance flagged. In Languedoc around Hérault, where there were religious disturbances after the July Revolution, as many as 50 per cent of the people of some parishes no longer fulfilled the Easter duty.[7] By the decade of the forties, the Easter requirement found compliance by, at best, half of the people of the diocese of Bordeaux.[8] Even in Bayonne in the south-western corner of the country— one of the most practising dioceses in all France—Church membership could not match Bavaria's.[9] Obviously France was experiencing a general decline in religious discipline.

For some reason French women resisted the trend towards dechristianisation. Data establish that women were much more likely than men to conform to the Easter duty requirement. Marcilhacy found this to be true everywhere in the department of the Loiret. Table 7 shows a striking discrepancy between male and female conformity at both the adult and adolescent level. During the July Monarchy only 30 to 60 per cent of the people who lived in the eastern (Bray) area of the diocese of Rouen still performed the Easter duty, whereas the practice in the west remained general. In spite of this unevenness, women practised more than men throughout the diocese.[10] In Paris men were gradually losing their fascination for religion and its ritual and services, leaving women and children as the Church's only remaining ties with the people at large.[11] In the diocese of Chartres it was the same. Men had quit going to church at Easter by 1830, but women continued with it.[12] In 1816 in the parish of Gallardon only 40 men made their Easter duty although the total male population ranged in the vicinity of 800. In nearby

Table 7: Easter Discipline Percentages for the Loiret Department, 1852

| Arrondissement | Adult males | Adult females | Adolescent Males | Adolescent Females |
|---|---|---|---|---|
| Pithiviers | 2.1 | 13.9 | 20.5 | 54.9 |
| Montargis | 1.9 | 11.6 | 22.6 | 61.4 |
| Orléans | 6.4 | 31.4 | 28.6 | 88.9 |

Source: Ch. Marcilhacy, *Le diocèse d'Orléans au milieu du XIXe siècle* (Paris, 1964), pp.303, 363, 391. Table shows percentage of *total* male or female population of rural areas (excluding cantonal capitols) who fulfilled the Easter duty (confessed and received the Eucharist).

Ouarville 164 women fulfilled the Easter obligation in 1820 as compared to only 11 men. The bishop, aware of these discrepancies, made
explicit remarks in his Lenten letters concerning the religious
differences separating the sexes. The men, he said, were profoundly
ignorant of and indifferent towards religious matters. But he found
women to be the 'sole consolation of the Church'.[13] In spite of their
husbands' indifference and the sarcasm of their fathers and even their
own sons, women prayed in the morning and evening, went to church,
and, in general, conducted themselves like Christians. In eastern France,
in the departments of Doubs and Haute-Saône, men consistently abandoned the Easter duty in far greater numbers than women during the
second half of the century.[14]

In his studies of religious observance in this century Gabriel Le Bras
has discovered the same trend. In areas where tradition is strong, women
are faithful; in dechristianised areas they are the last to apostatise.[15] So
consistently did Le Bras find this to be the case that he concluded it was
a general rule for France. To explain it he took note of the emotional
and psychological attraction that religious services, including confession,
held for women.

The attachment of women to religion annoyed mid-nineteenth-
century anti-clericals, and led them to dwell upon the discrepancy
between the sexes in matters of religion. They charged that *curés* were
using the confessional to lure French women away from their husbands.[16] The preponderance of religious fidelity, we may conclude, was
shifting towards women in the nineteenth century. The trend was
sufficiently pronounced by the time of the revolution of 1830 to allow
government officials to mention it explicitly in their 1834 dispatches to
the ministry on the state of religion and politics. The report on the
Jura department asserts that women were especially tied to the Church,
even to the extent that they would follow the curés' political opinions
and directives.[17] At mid-century Michelet would characterise French
males as 'Bonapartists', and females as 'Catholics'.[18]

Secondly, statistics on religious vocations offer weighty evidence of
the religious piety of French women. During the nineteenth century
religious vocations among women surpassed those of men for the first
time. In 1831 59 per cent of all religicos were male (priest or non-
ordained members of religious orders). By 1861 the situation had
turned around: women constituted 54.5 per cent of all religious and
men 45.5 per cent. By 1878 the margin in favour of female vocations
had grown even larger. When we view religious vocations of women
alongside female fidelity to the Easter discipline, it is a telling argument

for their religiosity.

The growth rate of French sisterhoods shows that women had become zealous in this respect from the very beginning of the century. From 1808 to 1830 female religious vocations increased at the pace of 4.1 per cent a year, and continued at a pace of 3.5 per cent a year from 1831 to 1860. Not until the last quarter of the century did vocations level off to a zero growth rate.[19] Thus, the nineteenth century was characterised by a consistent expansion of membership in religious congregations of women. For our purposes it is particularly noteworthy that this growth was strong from the very beginning of the century.

At the same time, birth control was an important issue affecting female as well as male attitudes towards religion. No one doubts that fertility declined in western Europe after 1850, or that birth control was largely responsible for this trend.[20] Although there appears to be some correlation between areas of low fertility and areas of dechristianisation, practising Catholics engaged in birth control as well.[21] One bishop reported that women saw no more harm in it than in having intercourse during pregnancy.[22] As the nineteenth century wore on and the practice of birth control became more and more common, reconciling their personal lives with their religion became more and more difficult for Catholics. 'Lord Malthus and Miss Polka' were driving people from the Church, as one mission preacher put it.[23]

The conflict, however, did not confront husband and wife equally. During the first part of the century confessors took a lenient view of the guilt incurred by women who were involved in *coitus interruptus*, which evidently, was the most common way to control birth. The blame was incurred by the husband. Wives were looked upon as being passive to the act, and their confessors counselled them to go on having intercourse with their husbands even though they were reasonably certain of their continuing practice of withdrawal.[24] Thus, women could maintain religious participation in good conscience, but their husbands, who would be treated as recidivists, could not. In the second half of the century the Church's discipline became more strict. Confessors were not to leave female penitents in 'good faith' concerning birth control, but were to treat it insistently as a mortal sin and press them about their co-operation in *coitus interruptus*. Thus, the moral position of the wife became more questionable. But she remained a more passive agent in the act than her husband, and therefore less guilty than he. The pastoral theology of the day makes it easy to understand why, especially for the first half of the century, men shied away from confession, and, consequently, failed to make their Easter duty, but women did not. The birth control controversy forced French males to choose between religion and life-style, but allowed French women to temporise and to blend secular with religious ideals.

A final more general clue to popular belief concerns the pattern of growth of the cult of the Virgin Mary. Instead of following along the usual lines which differentiate religious fidelity and dechristianisation, early nineteenth-century Marian devotion largely redraws the map of religious observance (see below, pp.141-2). If, as seems certain, women were slower to dechristianise than men, then we may speculate that it was they who supported such new Marian devotions as the Immaculate Conception Archconfraternity. Thus, female piety offers a plausible explanation for the rise of new religious devotion in dechristianised areas.

Taking all the evidence together—Easter discipline, religious vocations, birth control, Marian devotion—leads us to conclude that early in the nineteenth century French women became more distinguished for their religious fidelity and piety than men. We may safely assume that dechristianisation in France ran along sexual, as well as geographical, lines.[25] Indeed, one historian goes so far as to speak of a 'progressive feminisation of the permanent institutions of religion'.[26]

We are now in a position to enquire about the secularisation of sex. Did this occur only among the dechristianised? Or were French common people both religious and sexually permissive? Even more to the point, were the still devout women allowing themselves greater sexual latitude? If so, we may assume that, as in Germany, the proletariat had not yet learned to co-ordinate their sexual habits with the teaching of their religion.

As a matter of fact, there is evidence of this mentality in France much earlier than in Germany. French people celebrated church festivals and feast days with an abandon that belied the religious origin of these events long before it ever occurred to Central Europeans to do so. These occasions had become, as Maurice Agulhon has written, expressions of popular religion but more 'folklorique' than pious.[27] Dancing and sexual licence came to be associated with Sundays and feast days, especially in cities.[28] Generally, however, it seems clear that the observance of religious duties such as Sunday mass and vespers did not suffer as a consequence of increased socialising and intimacy. Although dancing on Sunday was proscribed, it went on anyway, but not in a manner that prejudiced either religious services or the liturgical calendar. In southern France the people of Auch danced on Sunday afternoons in summer time after vespers until nightfall . They held dances during winter as well, but not during Advent or Lent.[29] Thus, during the eighteenth century the French drifted into an easy coexistence between religious and sexual pursuits, whereas the emergence of this state and mentality did not occur in Germany until around 1800.

Sonnely in Sologne (central France) reveals the French situation. Even before the Revolution of 1789 the people of Sonnely joined sexual licence and religious fervour in a remarkable combination.[30] Their not infrequent bastardy has been attributed to loose parental control over adolescent sexuality. One eighteenth-century writer claims to have known cases of intercourse between seven-year-old children, but Enlightenment writers are not reliable sources for popular morality. Still, we may assert that sex became freer. Pre-nuptial pregnancies increased from 10 to 14 per cent between 1675 and 1779, as it became more common for girls to extract marriage proposals by bargaining with sexual favours.[31] Nevertheless, Sonnely people were religious zealots and still markedly superstitious. They practised witchcraft and nurtured countless local superstitions such as the *'l' ouef codrille'*, an egg laid by a rooster which hatched a snake through which details about death could be learned. The village's religious culture completely overran its daily life. Church attendance was remarkable and reception of the sacraments regular. As for the non-essentials of religion—the processions, pilgrimages, Marian devotions—the people simply could not get their fill of them, imbued, as they were, with a fascination for ceremony and liturgical regalia. Religion in Sonnely was anthropomorphised to such an extent that its control by ecclesiastical authorities became questionable and the line distinguishing it from folklore largely blurred.

Under these circumstances it is hardly surprising that religion and morality were not closely co-ordinated. The manner in which Sonnely people practised the sacrament of penance leaves no doubt that this was the case. When they went to confession, which was not often since the priest could not get them to remember the time of their last absolution, the people did everything but confess their sins. They complained about life, the wretchedness of existence, their great poverty, the perversity of their neighbours, and so on, but could not be brought to recall any wrongdoing on their own at all![32] Perhaps some casuistic sleight of hand allowed them this moral latitude; possibly this is conduct fairly representative of the pre-modern mentality. In either event, it is clear that moral behaviour in general and sexual behaviour in particular posed no deterrent to the enthusiastic practice of religion.

Neither time nor the French Revolution of 1789 did much to change the nature of belief and behaviour in Sonnely. Unlike many other Frenchmen, the villagers did not become edgy towards the Church or clergy during the Restoration or in 1830. Content with religion as they knew it, the people still used their amulets and talismen. Pious folklore still intermingled inextricably with religious service. At midnight mass on Christmas shepherdesses, often accused of being without rival in both superstition and sexual licence, filed before a sacrificial lamb, attaching colourful hair ribbons around its neck in preparation for the curé's blessing and the procession. While continuing with these accustomed devotions and observing Church prescriptions such as the duty to attend mass on Sunday more zealously than anyone in the Loiret department, they showed no interest in moral reform. If anything they became more indulgent in both sex and drink. And, in the meantime, they picked up the reputation of being inveterate and incurable thieves.[33]

How typical of France is Sonnely? There are two facets to this question: *what* was happening (increased bastardy) and *why* it was happening. First of all, Sonnely's pattern of illegitimacy seems rather normal for France. Bastardy was everywhere on the rise between 1750 and 1850 in France just as it was in other western countries.[34] Illegitimacy hovered around the 7 per cent level.[35] Actually, the ratio was much higher than this because there were annually almost as many foundlings as bastards.[36] Since it cannot be determined how many of these babies were born out of wedlock, it is obvious that illegitimacy percentages are low and very imprecise. Thus, bastardy steadily rose during the eighteenth and nineteenth centuries, rather than jumping suddenly around 1800 as in Germany. Finally, although some rural French settlements supported an incidence of bastardy to rival Bavaria's, the moderate ratio of Sonnely is more characteristic of France.[37]

We come to the second, more difficult question: why was bastardy increasing? Was it, as some assert, because of dechristianisation?[38] While not ruling this out as a contributing factor in some areas, we must unequivocally eliminate dechristianisation as a sole or principal cause of illegitimacy. The study of certain new manifestations of popular piety will allow us to demonstrate this. Since the nature of the new devotions is discussed in the following chapter, we need only briefly identify them here. First, a Christocentric cult found widespread favour throughout France until 1830 and, thereafter, until about mid-century in some areas, notably northern France. Christocentrism manifested itself in the erection of monumental crosses in public streets or squares. Second, popular enthusiasm for a certain virgin and martyr—thought to be Philomena, a third-century Greek princess—flashed across France in the decade of the thirties and triggered a meteoric rise in her popularity. Let us begin with this sensational new saint.

Using the number of Philomena namesakes as a yardstick, it may be determined which *arrondissements* favoured the new saint in the department of the Loiret, which straddles the Loire river about a hundred kilometres south of Paris. This, in turn, will provide us with a fairly accurate index to dechristianisation in those parts.

As it happens, Philomena never achieved as great a success in the Loiret as in some other parts of France.[39] On average only about two children in a thousand were given her name between 1837 and 1842. But this meagre rate could be greatly altered depending upon where and to whom one was born. Let us first discuss place.

Being born in the country rather than the city increased the likelihood of receiving the saint's name. This is not surprising since the department had remained overwhelmingly rural and agricultural in its constitution. Orléans, the departmental capital, maintained a rate which at better than four per 1,000 was much greater than the departmental average and considerably higher than that of many rural cantons. We will have occasion to see, however, that this figure is not a true representation of urban-rural attraction to Philomena.

Secondly, one stood little chance of being baptised into the new Philomena cult if one's place of birth was in the eastern half of the department (see Figure 4). Montargis, the *chef-lieu* of the region, has the distinction of being the only city which produced no 'Philomenas' at all. Marcilhacy has insisted on the influence of the bourgeoisie in the process of dechristianisation in the Loiret.[40] The area around Montargis strongly bears out her assertion. No communes thereabouts, in fact, no communes in the entire canton of Montargis produced a new citizen named 'Philomena'. No fewer than four parishes in the Gatinais, the area immediately to the north, enlisted schismatic Chatel priests after the July Revolution. Montargis' liberal attitudes had influenced them. Similarly, Gien, a much smaller cantonal seat in the southernmost part of the *arrondissement*, counted a very moderate rate of one 'Philomena' per 1,000 births.

Just as strong and important as the bourgeois influence in the east was that of the nobility in the western half of the department. In the Sologne, which Marcilhacy described as an island of Christianity in the Loiret, their presence was constantly felt, for the chateau still served as a harbour from troubled waters for the sick, unemployed and indigent. However, religious practice was a condition of finding employment or charity from the aristocracy, who also took active and regular interest in the religious education of the people. Partly as a result of this

influence, the people of the Sologne remained steeped in traditional
piety and folklore. It is to be expected then that they would readily
pick up the cult of St Philomena. The canton Jargeau, the heartland of
religious and political traditionalism in the department, counted almost
six 'Philomenas' per 1,000 births, one of the highest rates in the entire
department.[41] The neighbouring canton, Ouzover-sur-Loire, also maintained a high rate of five per 1,000.

To sum up, the evidence discloses three fairly distinct areas of support for the Philomena cult. Orléans was strongest; Montargis weakest;
Pithiviers was roughly in between (see Figure 4). If we now compare

Figure 4:   The Philomena Cult in the Loiret Department

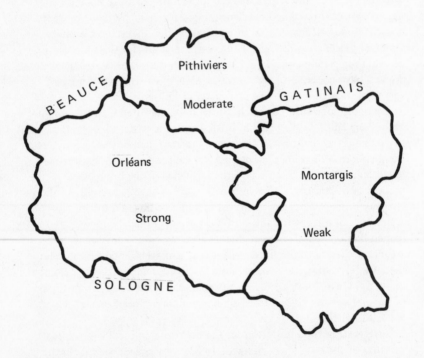

Source: *A. D. Loiret Etat-Civil, Naissances, 1833-1854*

bastardy statistics with these findings, it turns out that they correlate
negatively: Montargis—10.8 per cent; Pithiviers—6.8 per cent; and
Orléans—3.9 per cent (1846-51). Thus, the pattern in the Loiret runs
just the opposite of Germany's Westphalia where illegitimacy ran

highest where religion thrived. On the basis of these figures for illegitimacy, Marcilhacy felt justified in using bastardy as a measure of
religious vitality in the Loiret.[42] Superficially, it seems justified then to
posit dechristianisation as a cause of bastardy in the Loiret.

But we have only considered the geography of Philomena nomenclature. If we now enquire as to whom 'Philomena babies' were born, we
will discover that the dechristianisation hypothesis does not stand up.
Admittedly, the sociological factor bearing on Philomena nomenclature
—to whom one was born—was less important than the factor of
region. Whether bourgeois, farmer, skilled artisan or proletarian
counted little enough if home was in the *arrondissement* of Montargis.
But in other parts it counted a great deal. If a young man or woman
was fortunate enough to be the son or daughter of a wealthy farmer of
the Beauce, where the average standard of living was higher than anywhere else in the department, it can be said categorically that he or she
did not answer to the name 'Philomena'. These farmers, whose estates
were described as 'les foyers de la plus affreuse corruption', affected
bourgeois attitudes towards religion and disdained Church services
although not religious folklore.[43] They were noted for remarks such as,
'I don't want to go to heaven—it's too high; I'd rather go to hell,' at a
time when most rural Frenchmen were steeped in superstition. This
attitude did not necessarily hold true of other large but less wealthy
farmers of the western *arrondissement*. About 6 per cent of the 'Philomena' children were born to these farmers, who, along with the
*fermiers,* constituted an estimated 9 per cent of the total population.

None of these farmers, however, lived in the Beauce. The combination of large property holdings and residency in the Beauce ruled out
support of the Philomena cult. Small farmers, who accounted for
roughly a quarter of the total population, also slightly undersubscribed
to the Philomena cult in the two western *arrondissement*. About 14
per cent of the 'Philomena' babies were born to them. Here, again,
regional differences protrude; almost all of the small farmers who supported the cult of the virgin-martyr came from Pithiviers and the
Gatinais. In itself there may be nothing unusual about this since the
area had a small farm economy promoting this type of property-owner.
But this leaves open the question of the hesitancy of the small farmers
elsewhere to support the cult. Perhaps in the Sologne they sought to
display their superiority over the day labourers or their independence
from the aristocracy by disdaining Philomena.

Interestingly enough, the haughty attitude of the Beauceron farmers
did not rub off on to the people of neighbouring small towns. This is

especially true of the northern cantons in the Beauce where the Philomena cult enjoyed moderate success. One of the cantons, Patay, maintained a higher rate of 'Philomenas'—12 per 1,000—than any other in the entire department. Largely because of these people, small town support of the Philomena cult on a departmental scale was far from minimal. Small townsmen—unskilled and skilled artisans, domestics, small merchants or shopkeepers—accounted for 30 per cent of the department's Philomena namesakes. It was the skilled artisans of the Beauce who especially supported the new saint. In fact, throughout the department it is only there that artisanal support is stronger than that of the neighbouring agrarian people. For whatever reason, this points to clear lines of cultural distinction separating the *fermiers* and artisans in the Beauce.

Who it was in rural Loiret that took up the slack in the Philomena cult is by now obvious—the proletariat. This group, among whom are included cotters, day labourers, vine-dressers, carters, woodcutters, etc., constituted roughly 65 per cent of the population, yet 80 per cent of the 'Philomena' babies were born to them. The heaviest concentration of devotees to the new cult fell within this class in the Sologne region. Here it was that the aristocratic property holdings dominated the economy, giving the area greater imbalance in property distribution than obtained elsewhere, and allowing them to maintain great influence over the common mentality, so vividly described by Marcilhacy.[44] The annual budget of these proletarian families could be as much as 50 per cent lower than the average in the Beauce, a fact which in hard years left them at the patriarchal mercy of the religiously conscientious rural aristocracy. The latter strove to cultivate a traditional cosmic view among the proletariat and the relatively high number of 'Philomenas' among the rural poor testifies to their success. This group more than any other in the Loiret nurtured a hierarchical view of society with the king at the summit, which, in reality, was nothing more than an extension of their own immediate world. This hierarchical social structure, the mortar for which was provided by religion—and Philomena was one agent through which the day labourer integrated himself into the hierarchy—gave way gradually during the nineteenth century in both town and country, allowing other ideologies to seep in, but the mortar was slow to crumble among the poorest classes in agriculture.[45]

Now it was also precisely this class who maintained the pattern of religious affiliation and loose sexual morality that we found typical of the German rural proletariat.[46] Young men and women, it was said, kept no secrets from each other regarding sex. As in Germany, farm

hands were accused of being particularly lusty. They frequently
engaged in pre-marital sex while tending their flocks. This was so much
a part of local life that when a girl engaged too often or indiscriminately in sex and became pregnant, the boys composed a song about her
and went about the village singing it until they reached her door![47]
Thus, the same class who retained religious bonds enjoyed sexual
permissiveness.

Figure 5: Philomena Namesakes by Occupation in the Loiret
Department

Source: *A. D. Loiret Etat-Civil Naissances, 1833 1854.*

The point may be made statistically as well. A study of Orléans'
'Philomena babies' between the years 1834 and 1852 shows that only
88 children were named after the saint in the city itself. These babies
were so thinly dispersed among working-class and clerical families that
no one group of citizens could be said to support the cult fanatically.

The most interesting aspect of the cult in Orléans lies in the fact that an extraordinary number of 'Philomena babies' were either illegitimate or foundlings. An incredible 33 per cent fell into this category. More than any class or sub-group within the city, parents of illegitimate children supported the Philomena cult.

Some, but certainly not all, of Orléans' illegitimate 'Philomenas' may be attributed to domestics and other citizens of the city itself. The remainder were children of young, probably unmarried, rural women, who, finding themselves pregnant, took advantage of the convenient foundling hospital in Orléans. The peasant girls of certain areas in the Loiret were known for using this outlet, and we may assume a correlation with nomenclature because, in comparison with other areas, relatively few of the department's rural illegitimate children were named Philomena.[48] The balance of them was thus recorded as foundlings in the Orléans hospital.

It cannot be determined exactly how many foundlings were assigned their names by attendants of hospitals or institutions, but it is clear that parents of foundlings often took special care to see that their children would be Philomena namesakes. In 1850 a note attached to the dress of an Orléans foundling read, 'This child was born the fifth of March at a very early hour in the morning. She is not baptised. It is hoped that she'll be given the name Emma Philomène. . . so that one day she will find her mother'.[49] Thus, parents of foundlings not only chose the popular new saint as patroness of their children but made special efforts to insure them with the good fortune associated with Philomena.

The illegitimate Philomenas demonstrate that exactly the same people who were pious were also sexually indulgent. During some years, as a matter of fact, a baby was more likely to be named Philomena if she were illegitimate! In Orléans at mid-century, 0.5 per cent of all legitimate babies were named after the saint, whereas 0.8 per cent of bastards or foundling children became her namesake. Even if we consider the long run of Philomena's popularity in Orléans, 1835-50, we find negligible difference between a legitimate child's chances of receiving the name (0.4 per cent) and that of foundlings and other children (0.3 per cent).

There is nothing exceptional about the Loiret department in this regard, nor does the phenomenon apply to the rural proletariat alone. In 1839 2.9 per cent of Marseille's legitimate babies were named Philomena, but 3.1 per cent of the foundlings and bastard children were given her name. Book Five alone of Marseille's registers for 1840 shows four foundlings whose names—all Philomena—were pinned to their clothing. In Arras between 1837 and 1842 31 per cent of the Philomena namesakes were foundlings or bastards and in Marseille (1835-50) and St Omer (1837-42) 9 per cent and 5 per cent, respectively, fell into these categories. Obviously, many devout and sincere believers bore illegitimate children in France.

Our study of the Philomena cult in the Loiret department conclusively demonstrates that dechristianisation did not everywhere cause bastardy. Although there is no reason to disallow its causal role in Montargis, which fostered no Philomena cult, it is clear that for most people religious belief and sexual licence coalesced easily and mindlessly.

Another test of the relationship between religious belief and sexual behaviour concerns France's cross cult. During the Restoration years it had been common throughout France to erect large public crosses to memorialise 'missions' or religious revivals. Between 1830 and 1832 these monuments became controversial. Most of them were removed or destroyed. In the wake of these widespread disorders it only became possible for the cult of the cross to thrive in areas where the overwhelming majority of the populace fervently practised their religion. The regions that most distinguished themselves in this regard were Picardy and Nord in northernmost France.

Within this area there were several foci of the cross cult but that of the Nord department is of particular interest here because we can compare religious enthusiasm there with regional bastardy statistics. The only area of the department where religious conditions generated a revival of the cross cult during the decade of the thirties was in the south. With only one exception all the new cross erections took place in this concentrated area defined by the three southernmost arrondissements. This was one of the few places in all of France where the cult of the cross strongly revived after the July Revolution. This fact establishes it as one of France's most tenaciously religious cultures.

A study of Nord's incidence of bastardy, however, would hardly lead us to guess which area was foremost in religious strength. Illegitimacy increased from arrondissement to arrondissement as one moves southward from Dunkerque to Cambrai.[50] The four southern arrondissements —precisely the ones that were promoting the cross cult— sustained the most bastardy. Again, it is hardly possible to use illegitimacy as a measure of religiosity. Next to the southern arrondissements of the Nord, Lille sustained the highest ratio of illegitimacy in the department. But of what import was this for popular religion? Devotion seems to have been growing until sometime in the second half of the century: in 1847 there were 86 wayside statues of the Virgin

Mary in the streets of Lille; in 1863, 94; but in 1888, only 74.[51] Thus the city was simultaneously experiencing increased religious fervour and illegitimacy. A study of the city's Philomena cult would undoubtedly reveal that the same people were contributing to both.

Figure 6:  Bastardy And Popular Religion in the Department of the Nord

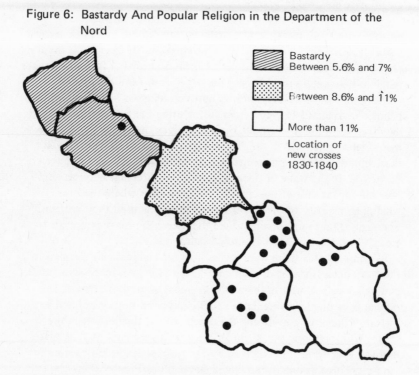

Source for Illegitimacy (1885), Claude-Hélene Dewaepenaere, 'L'Enfance Illegitime dans le département du Nord au XIX siècle', *'L'homme, la vie et la mort dans le Nord au 19$^e$ siècle* (Paris, 1972), 172; for crosses, *L'Ami de la Religion*, 1834-40.

The Philomena and cross cults in nineteenth-century France allow us to avoid some common errors. Most importantly, the cults warn us not to equate bastardy with dechristianisation. If dechristianisation is a factor contributing to illegitimacy in some areas, *it was demonstratively not a factor in many other areas.* Secondly, the cults warn us not to look for one set of causes or one pattern to explain all bastardy. Lille's illegitimacy has been attributed to urbanisation—industry, housing, and so on.[52] We may presume that the reasons for illegitimacy in neighbouring rural Cambrésis were different. Similarly, what caused bastardy in Montargis, an industrial and shipping centre in the Loiret department, and in neighbouring rural Sologne, is not the same, and in the latter case it had nothing whatsoever to do with dechristianisation.

The Philomena babies of unwed or uncertain parents make it obvious that sexual permissiveness was no more of an impediment to religious belief in France than it was in Germany. If anything, France accentuates the dichotomy. Both men and women, especially those of the lower class, as we will see, cherished the cult of the cross during the Restoration. This same piety exploded for a second time during the first half of the nineteenth century, propelling Philomena to fame. Thus, we are not dealing with a stagnant and moribund religious situation in France. In dechristianised areas such circumstances obviously obtained, but we have dealt with those whose credal belief had remained unshaken.

The evidence forces us to accept the imponderable: lower-class French women enlisted in the cult of the virgins (Philomena and Mary) even though they were not themselves able to sustain the virginal ideal.[53] Indeed, we might question whether they were interested in doing so. Sexually permissive girls—*filles scandaleuses*—not only went to church, but thought nothing of carrying the banner of the Blessed Virgin in parish processions![54] The non-discriminating mentality of early modern lower-class people allowed religion and sexual licence to run together in a manner which more educated and reflective people found discomforting or even repulsive.[55]

## Notes

1. The term 'dechristianisation' enjoys wide currency among French historians. I use it with the mental reservations expressed by Gabriel LeBras to the effect that during the Old Regime religious practice was not unanimous nor was virtue exemplary. 'Social constraint, the political regime, the local conditions required or countenanced the observance of canon law.' (See Ch. Marcilhacy, *Le diocèse d' Orléans au milieu du XIXe siècle* [Paris, 1964], preface.) Dechristianisation was an on-going process with roots extending back into the eighteenth century. What we have to say about popular religion in this chapter and about mission crosses in the following chapter is part of the unfolding process. The reader should not think of dechristianisation as a blanket term covering a finished historical process. For geographical details on dechristianisation see F. Boulard and J. Remy, *Pratique Religieuse urbaine et régions culturelles* (Paris, 1968).
2. Marcilhacy, *Le diocèse d' Orléans*, pp.303-4 and 363-5. Marcilhacy's figures show the percentage of church members in relation to total population, rather than to only those who were old enough to make their first communion. Her figures are lower as a consequence than normally would be the case.
3. F. A. Isambert, *Christianisme et classe ouvrière* (Paris, 1961), pp.187-8.
4. N. J. Chaline, 'Une image du diocèse de Rouen sous l' épiscopat de Mgr. de

Croy (1823-1844)', *Revue d' histoire de l' église de France* CLX (Jan-June 1972), p.69.

5. Auguste Billaud, *Histoire religieuse de Pouzauges* (Luçon, 1967), pp.166-7.
6. Charles Tilly, *The Vendée* (Cambridge, Mass., 1964), pp.101-3.
7. Gérard Cholvy, 'Le legs religieux de l' Ancien Régime au département de l' Hérault', *Annales du Midi*, LXXXV, p.113 (July Sept. 1973), pp.307-11.
8. V. Wright, 'Religion et politique dans les Basses-Pyrénées pendant la deuxième république et le second empire', *Annales du Midi*, CXXXI, p.94 (Oct. 1969), p.409.
9. Ibid., pp.409-14.
10. Chaline, p.64.
11. Isambert, p.245.
12. E. Sevrin, 'La pratique des sacrements et des observances au diocèse de Chartres sous l' épiscopat de Mgr. Clausel (1824-1852)', *RHEF*, XXV (1939), p.333.
13. Ibid., p.320.
14. Paul Huot-Pleuroux, 'La Vie Chrétienne dans le Doubs et la Haute-Soane de 1860-1900' (Diss., n.d.), pp.43, 49, 54, 62, 66, 72.
15. Gabriel Le Bras, *Etudes de Sociologie Religeuse* (Paris, 1955-56), I, pp.356ff; see the statistics and data in Appendix I, I, pp.120-94, and in 'Notes de statistique et d' histoire religieuses', *RHEF*, XXIV (1938), pp.307-30.
16. Theodore Zeldin, 'The Conflict of Moralities', *Conflicts in French Society*, T. Zeldin (ed.) (London, 1970), pp.13-50. Popular culture mirrored the curé-husband-wife triangle:

> A qui je donnerai la trique?
> Co co co, se dira la, la!
> A qui je donnerai la trique?
> A ma femme ou a mon chat?
>
> Si je donn' la trique a ma femme,
> Co, co co, se dira la, la!
> Si je donn' la trique a ma femme,
> Le curé me grondera.

The poem is taken from Desrousseau, *Moeurs Populaires de la Flandre Française* (Lille, 1889), I, p.12.

17. A. N. F[19] 5601; see the entire box, especially the report on the department of Jura, 28 June 1834.
18. Trenard, p.413.
19. Claude Langlois, 'Les effectives des congrégations féminines au XIXe siècle', *RHEF*, LX (1974), p.62.
20. Shorter, 'Female Emancipation', pp.605-40.
21. John T. Noonan, *Contraception* (Cambridge [Mass.], 1965), Ch.XIII, 'The Spread of Birth Control: the Responses of the Bishops and the Pope'.
22. J. C. Flandrin, *L' Eglise et le controle des naissances* (Paris, 1970), p.81.
23. Y. -M. Hilaire, 'Les missions intérieures face à la déchristianisation pendant la second moitié du XIXe siècle dans la région du Nord', *Revue du Nord*, 46 (1964), p.59.
24. Flandrin, loc. cit.; see also Zeldin, *The Conflict of Moralities*, pp.34-5.
25. Adeline Daumard, *La Bourgeoisie Parisienne de 1815 à 1848* (Paris, 1963), p.366. Daumard notes that what little religion was imparted to Parisian children came to them from their mothers.
26. Langlois, 'Les effectives des congrégations féminines', pp.63-4.
27. Maurice Agulhon, *La sociabilité meridionale* (Aix; la Pensée Universitaire,

1966), I, pp.117, 125, 150-3, 165, 231.

28. Ibid., p.616; J. Eich, *Histoire religieuse du département de la Moselle pendant la Révolution* (Metz, 1964) I p.58.

29. H. Polge, 'Le Dimanche et le Lundi', *Annales du Midi*, 87, I (1975), p.16.

30. Gérard Bouchard, *Le Village Immobile: Sennely-en-Sologne au XVIII<sup>e</sup> siècle* (Paris, 1972), pp.233-8.

31. Ibid., pp.324-5.

32. Ibid., p.292.

33. Marcilhacy, *Le diocèse d' Orléans*, pp.376-405.

34. Shorter, *The Making of the Modern Family*, pp.80-98.

35. Claude Hélene Dewaepenaere, 'L' enfance illégitime dans le département du Nord au XIX<sup>e</sup> siècle', *L' homme, la vie et la mort dans le Nord au 19<sup>e</sup>siècle* (Paris, 1972), p.147.

36. Y. Turin, 'Enfants trouvés, colonisation et utopie. Etude d' un comportement sociale au XIX<sup>e</sup> siècle', *Revue Historique*, CCXLIV, p.496 (Oct.-Dec. 1970), pp.330-2.

37. Shorter, 'Illegitimacy, Sexual Revolution. . .', see charts.

38. P. Chaunu, 'Malthusianisme démographique et malthusianisme économique', *Annales, Economies, Sociétés, Civilisations*, XXVII, 1 (Jan.-Feb. 1972), p.18; J. Depauw, 'Amour illégitime et société à Nantes au XVIII siecle', *Annales, E. S. C.*, XXVII, pp.4-5 (July-Oct. 1972), pp.1155-82.

39. All of the data on the Philomena cult in the department of Loiret is based on an analysis of the birth registers in the departmental archives in Orléans. These records are kept in the 'Naissances' books of the *Etat Civil* collection.

40. Marcilhacy, pp.202ff.

41. Ibid., p.396.

42. Ibid., pp.90-7.

43. Ibid., p.213.

44. Ibid., pp.181ff.

45. Pierre Barral, *Les Agrariens Francais de Méline à Pisani* (Paris, 1968), Ch.II, 'Types de Sociétés Rural', and William B. Sewell, 'Social Change and the Rise of Working-Class Politics in Nineteenth Century Marseille', *Past and Present*, LXIV (Nov. 1974), pp.75-109.

46. E. Sevrin, 'Croyances populaires et médicine supranaturelle en Eure-et-Loire au XIX<sup>e</sup> siècle', *RHEF*, XXXII (1946), pp.265-308. Marcel Lachiver, *La population de Meulan du XVII<sup>e</sup> au XIX<sup>e</sup> siècle (vers 1600-1870)* (Paris, 1969), pp.67-9.

47. Marcilhacy, *Le diocèse d' Orléans*, pp.283-5. Just as priests in Bavaria blamed the immorality of the Vormärz on the Napoleonic era, so French curés saw in the Revolution the roots of the collapse in morality between 1815 and 1848; see Maurice Agulhon, *La Vie sociale en Provence intérieure au lendemain de la Révolution* (Paris, 1970), p.409.

48. Ibid., pp.324-5.

49. A. D. Loiret Orléans, *Etat-Civil*, 1850, *Naissances*, no.81.

50. Dewaepenaere, p.171.

51. A. J. Desrousseaux, *Moeurs populaire de la Flandre française* (Lille, 1889), p.291.

52. Dewaepenaere, pp.141-76.

53. Although it was not possible to correlate tax and parish records for France to determine class differences in sexual behaviour, the état-civil (birth) records do

give the occupations of unwed mothers. These show, without exception, that bastards were children of working-class mothers. I doubt, however, that any such sharp distinction could be established for rural France.

54. Marcilhacy, *Le diocèse d' Orléans,* p.318.

55. The bourgeoisie objected to the confusion of activity that took place around or in the vicinity of the mission cross; by day, loitering, by night, prostitution. See Maurice Agulhon, *République au village* (n.p., 1970), p.169 (footnote).

# 7 POPULAR RELIGION AT A CROSSROAD

Towards the middle of the third decade of the nineteenth century popular religion in France reached a major crossroad. After having steadily drifted towards a Christocentric cult of the cross for more than a dozen years, it suddenly stopped dead in its tracks and then moved off in a new direction. The cult of the virgins—St Philomena and the Blessed Virgin—supplanted Christocentrism in popular piety. To describe these very distinct cults would exceed the thematic limits of this book, but understanding the reason for the shift in popular devotion provides an insight into the proletarian religious mentality that Germany did not afford us.[1] What forces, we may ask, drove popular piety along its erratic path during the first half of the century?[2]

French common people picked up Christocentric devotion during the Restoration through the mission movement.[3] The immediate success of the French mission, which consisted of sermons, prayers, services and hymns, should rank alongside other great nineteenth-century mass movements.[4] In the second decade, when the mission preachers got out on the circuit, they discovered the abysmal ignorance of French people about the simplest truths of their religion. This dismal circumstance proved to be lucky for the laity as it precluded all possibility of indoctrinating them with the current obtuse theology. Instead, the missionaries schooled them in the fundamentals of religion, got them to frequent the sacraments, warned them repeatedly not to have truck with Enlightenment literature, reviewed all the sins and sacrileges of the Revolution—a touchy point since many a man in the pew had come to property at the expense of the Church or aristocracy—and finally, upbraided them for their immorality, especially for their excessive dancing.[5] But none of this conveyed a devotional feeling for the suffering Christ, the substance of the mission message. To this end the missionaries engaged action and emotion more than words and the mind, and therein lay the secret of their not inconsiderable success.

When the mission came to town it created a sensation. Not one preacher, but six, eight or ten worked a city at once, preaching simultaneously in the several major churches. Well financed and organised, effective propagandists, great orators in an age of oratory, the missionaries knew how to rivet attention on themselves in such a way as to create a public spectacle of religion for the duration of the mission—a period of up to two weeks. Although the missionaries forbade the balls and carnival atmosphere that once accompanied a revival, they managed everything—large receptions upon arrival, greeting with civic authorities, receiving faculties from the bishop, processions, devotions—to make religion a public spectacle.

The single technique which proved most effective in engaging the people emotionally, and in building rapport between them and the missionaries, and between the different classes of people, was the singing of canticles. The incredible effect of these songs resulted when traditional lyrics were put to new popular tunes, or, conversely, new lyrics to favourite old melodies. As some of the tunes were stolen from the revolutionary era, liberal newspapers like the *Constitutionnel,* fuming at the success of the canticles, found themselves in the awkard spot of having to accuse the Church of prostituting religion, a process which, in any other circumstances, they would have applauded. The canticles, which could have as many as twenty or thirty verses, were sometimes printed on a broadside, called a *complainte,* which pictured, in somewhat comic strip fashion, the action described by the lyrics.[6] As these sheets cost next to nothing, they circulated readily amongst the lower class, who could not sing enough of the canticles. Nothing could have been better suited to sustain enthusiasm and emotion during the mission.

After religious enthusiasm and fervour wound itself up over a period of a week or more, it finally released in a flood of emotion with the erection of a cross, terminating the mission. These spectacular crosses awed the masses, who came in droves to see them erected: 14,000 in Blois, 25,000 in Cherbourg, 40,000 in Avignon![7] The crosses—actually crucifixes—were usually gigantic, measuring up to 20 metres in height and costing thousands of francs. When they were made of iron, the logistics of carrying them in the processions was a major operation in itself. In Clermont—home of one of the most famous missions—12,000 men in divisions of 100 each took turns under the cross' weight On 21 April 1825, 12,000 people jammed into the *Grand Place* of Arras in northern France to see the mission cross that had been constructed at a cost of 8,000 francs.[8]

For these occasions the entire city, public as well as private buildings, was decorated with banners, flowers, garlands, crosses, and the like, and all Church and civil officials, including the band and national guard, wore their colourful uniforms. The procession itself could count thousands of participants, each of whom carried a small cross in his or her hand, or wore a lapel cross. As the entourage wound

its way through the narrow streets, the city echoed with the mighty
sound of the canticles and the chant, 'Vive la croix!'. When the cross
was finally erected in the public square, the enclosure resounded with
shouts of 'Vive la croix! Vive Jésus! Vive la religion!' As a youth, Marseille native Victor Gelu thrilled to the sound of 80,000 chanting voices
while church bells pealed, the militia played martial airs, and the
artillery roared, all in salute to the mission cross. Gelu, who remembered
this scene all his life, likened the missionary preacher abbé Guyon to
the great American showman, P. T. Barnum.[9] The erection of the cross
was the final spectacular event of the mission, and, like the mission
cross itself, it was calculated to transfix the people with the emotional
conviction that Christ had taken the city by storm.

Over the course of the Restoration years the missionaries had a
tremendous impact on French consciousness. Certainly, for them the
cross had been the heart of the mission. Their sermons and devotions,
centred on the suffering Christ, had moved consciences; the mission
cross would stay on in the midst of the people in a public square to
inspire an enduring cult of the cross and of Christ.[10] There it would
remain throughout the Restoration, a monument for which most
French common people nurtured attitudes of affection since the missionaries had awakened in them by word and song an appreciation for
the cult of the suffering Christ. Deeply religious feelings sank tenacious
roots among a people who never imagined that one day the political
and religious significances of the cross would become irreconcilable.

The same mission crosses that stirred sentiments of piety among
French common people provoked bourgeois contempt. The latter's
attitude was rooted in two considerations, one political and one cultural. On the one hand, they objected to the identification of
Christocentrism with Bourbon legitimacy, and, on the other to the
missionaries' censure of modern dancing. Let us briefly review these
grievances.

Before common people adopted it, Christocentric devotion was
espoused by the aristocracy. A cult of the suffering Christ, which originated in the writings of the great seventeenth-century mystic, Margaret
Mary Alacoque, was revived by French royalty and the aristocracy
around the time of the Revolution of 1789.[11] Louis XVI took up
devotion to the Sacred Heart in 1791 or early 1792, as the day drew
nigh when France would break with the monarchical principle and sac-
rifice its king.[12] Two months after his execution the royalist army of
the Vendée marched to battle against the revolution to the tune of
*Vexilla regis prodeunt* ('Let the standards of the King go forth. . .'), a

liturgical hymn which exalts the suffering yet triumphant Christ in his Davidic royalty.[13] Thus, the Christocentric devotion of Louis XVIII, who entered Paris in 1815 on the feast of the Finding of the Holy Cross to reclaim the Bourbon throne, was no accident.

Mission societies were the agents that carried Christocentrism from the aristocracy to the people. Although the societies were independent of the government, nothing did more for royal legitimacy during the Restoration than the mission movement. Not only was this so because the mission preachers were former non-jurors and ultra-royalists by conviction, but, still more importantly, because of their total identification with the accepted theology of the Restoration, whose key point insisted on the kingship of Christ in His human as well as divine nature. For them it followed that the authority of the king of France, derived from God through Christ, was indivisible.[14] The King must try to rule both his private life as well as France's public affairs according to Christian principles. And, in turn, it meant that the Church could exercise power in temporal affairs. To deny either's authority in *res publica* was tantamount to affirming that Christ is God as King and as Word, but not as man.

Turgid as this reasoning sounds, it contained serious consequences for the values of the revolution. Liberty had to be regulated by the law of God. Talk of the 'rights' of man was dangerous. M. Coste, administrator of the diocese of Tulle and author of the extremely popular *Manual for Missionaries,* urged preachers to make the people see the error of ideas holding, for example, that a person could resist authority when oppressed, or that insurrection was healthier than obedience. Rather, the people should be instructed that the authority of society's leaders is like an emanation of the creator's supreme power. The political corollary of this Christocentric theology insisted on the authority of both Church and legitimate monarch in French public life. In practice the missionaries, as a matter of course and without thinking themselves dabbling in politics, preached obedience and submission to the legitimate monarchs of France—the Bourbons.[15] In the minds of the French people the mission became inextricably identified with legitimacy.

This legitimist colouration of Christocentrism sparked hostile bourgeois feelings against the crosses. After the July Revolution, from the autumn of 1830 to the summer of 1832, liberal factions attacked mission crosses throughout most parts of France.[16] They defaced, destroyed or removed over a hundred of them—perhaps as many as several hundred.[17] This onslaught was led by liberal political activists who swept into power after the July Revolution. When crosses were simply removed, newly appointed departmental prefects usually played a key role; when they were destroyed, the national guard or bourgeois youth usually proved to be the activists.[18]

What happened to the canticles after the July Revolution illustrates the political nature of bourgeois hostility towards the mission crosses. During the missions, the missionaries had come equipped with whole books of the canticles, one of the most famous and popular of which juxtaposed religion and legitimacy in the familiar verse:

> Vive la France!
> Vive le Roi!
> Toujours en France
> Les Bourbon et la Foi!

The thoroughness with which the government of Louis Philippe supressed the canticles after the July Revolution testifies to their tremendous propaganda potential. Instructions went out from Paris to the prefects, and from them to the mayors and *gendarmerie* to seek out all collections of canticles—in libraries, churches, bookstores, and among hawkers—and rip out those judged hostile to the new regime, especially the canticle 'Les Bourbon et la Foi!' These orders were followed up throughout the country.[19]

Changing cultural values provided a second spur goading on bourgeois hostility against Christocentrism. In this case the issue that exposed conflicting social values in French society was dancing. During the Restoration, when the religious awakening that we have identified with the mission movement came over France, opposition to dancing intensified significantly. There are two reasons for this: the introduction of a new dance step, the waltz, and dancing on Sundays during church services.

It was, in fact, the missionaries who had spearheaded the attack against dancing. Next to 'bad literature' (writings of the Enlightenment), no issue provoked greater pulpit denunciation than dancing. Since serious reading concerned adults for the most part, the missionaries directed the attack against dancing at the youth. All through the 1820s they relentlessly excoriated the youth about their life-style and morality, or lack of it. Since it was their incessant dances that displayed their supposed wantonness at best, the missionaries zeroed in on these. Falling victim to that curious human foible which permits one to see other countries as, alternately, morally worse or as having more fun than one's own, the French mission preachers in 1818 began lambasting the dangerously corrupt new method of dancing invented in Germany called the Viennese Waltz![20] It was sweeping westward across Europe, and was now, the missionaries feared, about to strip the last vestiges of decency from French life.

We are tempted to pass lightly over these monumental struggles our ancestors had with morality. Humorous or inconsequential as they may seem to us, they were matters of grave concern to youth and a point of great community conflict during the Restoration. Why had the mission preachers become so exercised over waltzing? They correctly judged that the new style of twirling round and round with a chosen partner bespoke a modern era and a new society. For the waltz was a couple dance that permitted 'the kind of sexual contact that had heretofore been unthinkable'.[21] In the waltz one danced intimately, danced where one chose, and danced to catch the eye of another.[22] It was personal, sentimental and emotional. In a word, it was everything that the communal dances of the Old Regime had not been. The waltz, a bourgeois dance, proclaimed the advent of a new kind of society which would bask in a new culture. It was revolutionary. Thus, although at first sight it appears that the missionaries fretted foolishly over the waltz, they had good reason to inveigh against the new dance. It personified a lifestyle that threatened and, indeed, helped terminate their cherished society of the Old Regime.

Secondly, the controversy around dancing escalated during the Restoration because dances interfered with church services. French curés, taking their cue from the missionaries, kept up the attack on dancing. As in Germany, communal dancing had been one way to observe Sundays and feast days in the France of the Old Regime. The curés complained about the growing secularity with which these occasions were celebrated. Thus, in spite of the law of 18 November 1814, which sought to preserve religious tradition and the Sabbath, the balance was beginning to tip towards dancing as leisure and away from dancing as a communal feast day activity.[23]

Furthermore, the secularisation already afoot in larger cities, now began to infiltrate the countryside. In 1826 on the feast of the patronal saint of the village of Meys, near Lyon, cabaret music was so loud that it drowned out the prayers of the people in church. The curé tried to get the mayor to stop the dance music but he refused.[24] In Treport in northern France, 500 people refused to make their Easter duty in 1828 because the curé had spoken out too harshly against their dances.[25] Two young men of bourgeois families were found guilty of disturbing the peace (by dancing during religious services) in the town of St Martin-la-Campagne near Dieppe.[26] Their case was appealed to Rouen but the court upheld the verdict. Dancing on patronal feasts occasioned repeated controversies in Alsace during the 1820s. The curé of Bergheim was incensed over a 'petit bal de société' that was sponsored by 'Jacobins' at which the mayor and municipal council members danced.[27] In Canton Seltz the curés preached incessantly against dancing and refused absolution both to youths who danced and to their parents as well. Other curés were accused of striking youths who went to dances. The curé of Niedersteinbach made four young women who had taken part in the dance on the feast of St Charles do public penance by kneeling before the altar in front of the congregation. In Brittany, the controversy surrounding dancing was less heated than in Alsace, but dancing, especially on Sunday, was a common complaint of the curates.[28] The Church 'warned the faithful against these pitfalls [dances]; forbade them to the devout; [and] refused access to the church for those who danced.'[29] In southern and north-western France dancing was seen as a principal factor contributing to the alarming rate of apostasy.[30] Thus, throughout the nation, in town and country alike, tempers flared during the Restoration over the dancing issue.

No one reacted more hotly than the youth. A number of incidents occurred in connection with the mission cross disorders which suggest that the missionaries' and curés' challenge to their life-style and their dancing was a key factor in their politicisation. In Monsart the mission cross occupied an open square in the village. During the nights of the 15 and 16 September 1832, the youth held candle-light dances in the square under the mission cross. They surely meant this as an affront to the values of the mission, and to those villagers who held with these values, since, to provide light, they profaned the cross itself by setting their candles on its arms, scorching them as they burned down in the course of the evening's gaiety.[31] A bizarre, almost macabre, scene— dancers in dim light under a smoking cross.

We may suppose that the incident in Monsart indicates scorn and disregard on the part of the youth for the mission and its values. In other cases, we know exactly what motivated them. One of the most vicious attacks on a mission cross in all of France came about because the youth of Ferté-sous-Jouare wanted a dance hall. They argued that the place occupied by the mission cross offered the best prospect for a locale (or platform). The curé, giving way to mounting pressure and fearing insults to the cross, agreed to its removal. What happened after that shows that there was more at stake than a simple matter of real estate. On 23 August 1830, when the cross was removed, the youth came out to jeer at it, and the next day, while the curé was saying mass in the church to which the mission cross had been transferred, they took the cross outside and battered it it pieces.[32] Clearly, it was not enough to win the dancing issue; the youth venomously destroyed the Restoration's symbol of cultural oppression.

The wrath of French youth vented itself on many other crosses after the July Revolution. Prefect Thomas specifically blamed them for the Marseille riot of 16 August 1831.[33] On 4 October 1831 the youth of Le Mans attempted to attack that city's mission cross.[34] A similar situation developed during February 1831 in Limoges. Serious disorders took place there for several days, after the youth uprooted the mission cross.[35] A bitter dispute ensued during which the youth, beside themselves with rage, attacked the bishop's residence, forcing him to leave the city. The prefect acknowledged in his report to Paris that the bourgeois youth caused the disorders.

When a prefectural report or newspaper article implicated the youth in mission cross controversies, it was generally understood that this meant bourgeois or liberal youth. There was no question about this in the case of the Marseille riot. It was also the 'liberal youth' of that city who caused the mission cross trouble of November 1830, outside St Martin's Church.[36] In Villeneuve-les-Maguelonne some medical students of Montpellier University, out on a botany field trip, tipped over some crosses, and were violently set upon by the locals.[37] Bourgeois youth caused mission cross disturbances in Montargis, whose cross they dumped in the river. 'Middle-class' youth was specifically blamed for the vicious destruction of the Ferté-sous-Jouare mission cross.[38] Finally, we should note that a common theme running through litigation between mayors and curés after the July Revolution was the right of the youth to more liberal dancing privileges.[39]

It is true that the youth had been politically and economically frustrated during the Restoration, and we must allow for grievances other than dancing to account for their anti-cross activism. But the evidence also allows us to be specific about dancing. Since the missionaries' attack on 'bad literature' was primarily directed at adults, no single mission sermon lashed out at the youth harder than the denunciation of dancing. The identification of the missions with the Bourbons and the presence in the larger French cities of the mission cross reminded the youth of an old, unsettled score. What would be more natural than to tear the crosses down? Finally, although other factors may have contributed to politicisation, we cannot dismiss the fact that whenever a

*specific* reason for the anti-cross activity of the youth is given, it turns
out to be dancing.

As a result of strong emotional ties on the part of French common
people to the mission cross and of equally strong emotions against it
on the part of liberals, heated controversy swirled around the public
crosses in the months following the July Revolution.[40] Bourgeois
elements, as we noted, attacked the cross; common people, on the
other hand, defended it. The lower class may be said to have reacted in
this way throughout France.[41] But they did not everywhere display the
same fanaticism and in some areas, notably central France, there are
exceptions and contradictions. Let us begin with the zealots.

The strongest opposition to interference with the cross occurred in
southern France, where the efforts of the *gens du peuple* often succeeded in maintaining the mission monuments. In Belgencier near
Toulon on the southern littoral, paper-mill workers rescued the cross
from would-be bourgeois arsonists.[42] On the evening of 16 August
1831, the common people of Marseille's 'Old Quarter', near the dock-
yards, armed themselves with clubs, knives and fish hooks and fought
off liberal youth from the great port city's bourgeois sector. This riot
took place directly beneath the mission cross in the Place de Calvaire.[43]
There were also serious riots in Nîmes, where the women of the city
attempted to defend the cross. They failed, but demonstrated their
fanaticism with loss of life and injury.[44] In Montauban, as we will see,
the common people were successful in their defence of the cross. Other
cities in the *Midi* where the *gens du peuple* exhibited strong sentiment
in favour of the crosses include Toulouse, Avignon and Carcasson.[45]

A less extreme way to indicate displeasure over anti-mission cross
activity was to refuse to be party to their dismantlings. We know that
in about half of the recorded cases of trouble, mission crosses were
destroyed by violence.[46] The remainder were not defaced but removed
from public property and transferred to churches. In these cases a
mayor, sub-prefect or prefect were the agents of removal. In pursuing
this policy they not infrequently ran up against the impetuosity of the
common people. In Riom, for example, no workers could be found
who were willing to dismantle the cross. When strangers were imported
by the mayor to dismantle it, they were dispersed by the Riom people.
At this point, the mayor had the monument surrounded with horse and
bayonet so that the work could proceed. However, the visiting
labourers lacked the necessary tools for the job, and local workers
would not lend them theirs, and, in fact, hid them in spite of threatening messages from the mayor. Other cities in which resistance took this

form include Carpentras in the south and Noyon in northern France.[47] These examples indicate that the *gens du peuple* often acted sponta- neously on behalf of the mission cross, and that, not infrequently, they could not even be finagled into acting against it at the bidding of others.

Displeasure or disapproval of anti-mission cross activity could also be expressed via the petition. The civil authorities of Noyon, Besançon and Toulon ordered their mission crosses removed in the face of widely cir- culating petitions in favour of them.[48] It is clear in these cases that a bourgeois minority acted unilaterally, challenging the popular cult of the majority. Toulon is a case in point; not only did the mayor order the dismantling of the mission cross, but he called out the national guard to play patriotic tunes of the revolution as the work was carried out. No one missed his message: the removal of the cross meant the end of the legitimist era. But as far as most common people were concerned, it was more religious than political sensibilities that suffered when Christocentrism was attacked.

The religious temperature of the *gens du peuple* also provides a guide to the pattern and intensity of mission cross trouble across France. Generally speaking, anti-cross disturbances were least frequent all around the country's perimeter and both more frequent and more violent in central and north central France. In the *Midi* common people were described as 'bigoted' and 'superstitious' by a prefect and another government official who toured the area a year after the July Revolu- tion and lamented, 'We must make do with patriots who are Carlists.'[49] Marseille itself was described as a hotbed of religious organisations (it was, indeed, a great mission centre). Thus, Christocentric piety in the *Midi* accounts for the paucity of anti-cross disturbances and for the fact that many demonstrations in favour of the cross occurred there. These demonstrations were frequent because, as the prefect of Bouches du Rhône put it, threats to the cross alarmed 'the ignorant, weak of con- science and superstitious all of whom abound in this department'.[50]

The situation in north-western France, which experienced relatively few mission cross troubles, resembles that of the *Midi*. The population was devout, a fact that caused civil authorities to respect the crosses. Timidly, they sought only to remove the *fleur-de-lys* from the mission monuments.[51] It is a safe assumption that violence seldom befell a mission cross in Brittany and Normandy because of the reprisals com- mon people would have taken. The same may be said of northern France, where the cult of the cross flourished even after the July Revolution (see below, p. 140 ).[52]

In central France, on the other hand, mission cross troubles were both frequent and violent. This was hardly happenstance since the urban lower classes had become politicised in these parts. United bourgeois opinion and politicisation of the working class was the combination that produced anti-cross violence. Cities with these tandem forces where violence erupted, leading to the destruction of the cross include Montargis, St Dizier, Blois, St Calais, Chalon-sur-Saône and Beaune, where the Christ figure was removed from the cross and defaced and indecently defamed.[53]

Elsewhere in central France the common people displayed little interest in the fate of the cross, neither attacking nor defending it. This attitude allowed bourgeois elements to pressure successfully for the cross's transferral from public grounds to the privacy of the church walls. Orléans is one example among dozens of this kind of pattern.[54] Sometimes the common people opposed tampering with the cross, but remained passive. This happened in Le Mans, where the lower population' by the prefect's own admission opposed the removal of the cross [55] and in many an *arrondissement*, like that of Pontalier whose *chef-lieu* bourgeoisie had become liberal, while the *gens du peuple* remained attached to the cult of the cross.[56]

It is clear, in sum, that French common people generally supported or defended the mission cross. Even in central France, the area of exception, there were instances of support (Blois, Noyon, Le Mans) where the lower class had not cultivated liberal attitudes. Of course, it would be simple-minded to assert that common people alone assured benign treatment of the crosses. After visiting Montpellier, Nîmes, Avignon, Carcasson, Marseille and Toulouse, a government agent made note of the unholy alliance in those parts between people whose interests sometimes clashed: the clergy, the old nobility, part of the commercial people and almost all of the 'people'.[57] In popular religious matters this meant that moderate bourgeois elements looked upon the fanaticism and superstition of some of the lower class with a certain lassitude. In Marseille Prefect Thomas wisely refrained from tampering with the cross because he correctly analysed the attitude of benign amusement that many middle-class citizens nurtured towards excessive popular piety.[58] The same situation prevailed in north-western France.[59]

We may conclude that to varying degrees and with some notable exceptions—Paris, above all—the common people of urban France supported the mission crosses. One may presume that this support was even stronger among rural folk. In fact, an analysis of the nature and extent of mission cross troubles reveals that religious controversy was of far greater importance in the aftermath of the July Revolution than we have imagined.[60] Thus, the social impact of pious common people must be emphasised. It was they who anchored support for the crosses, and, when push came to shove, it was they who got out into the streets and defended them. If bourgeois youth were the protagonists in the mission cross disturbances, the common people were the antagonists.

Now that we know the role of common people in the mission cross troubles, we may ask a more perplexing question. Why were they reluctant to side with the predominant political position of the bourgeoisie? Was it for political or religious reasons? Lower-class youth obviously enjoyed dancing quite as much as anyone else; so why did they not side with bourgeois youth in this matter? If we are to grasp the proletarian mentality, it is important to address these questions concerning their motive for supporting Christocentrism.

Among French common people religious superstition blended with political *naïveté* in a remarkable way. Because of this they could not sharply distinguish between political and religious aspects of Christocentrism. Consequently, unlike the bourgeoisie, it seldom occurred to lower class people to demonstrate against the cross when aggravation over food prices, taxation, or even clericalism arose. The situation in Montauban after the July Revolution illustrates the utter confusion of religious superstition and political preference.

On 25 August 1830, the rumour began circulating in Montauban that the city's mission cross would be uprooted during the night. By evening the rumour of the threat to the cross had fermented, causing great unrest among the common people. That night a large vigilante group was formed among the *gens du peuple* to protect the cross.[61] They camped out all night, sleeping on the pavement beneath the cross. Particularly interesting is the fact that these people disguised themselves, evidently so that their employers would not recognise them. This bizarre scene of strange-looking vigilantes bivouacked beneath the mission cross repeated itself for five nights running before the people could be convinced that no harm would befall their cross. But they remained disturbed in the weeks that followed. In December a mob of 300 people reportedly ran through the streets yelling, 'The Prussians are in Paris! Charles X is coming to Montauban.'[62]

A final incident occurred in February 1831 which provides us with a glimpse of the mentality of the Montauban common people. On the eleventh a white pigeon, flying around the cathedral square, landed on top of a statue (possibly of Joan of Arc) which surmounted the church edifice. Many people were in the square and saw this, which gave rise to the rumour that the pigeon signified the return of Charles X to the throne. When the pigeon repeated its performance the following day for the benefit of a great many more onlookers in the square, who had gathered because of the rumour, it was deemed definite confirmation of Charles's return.[63]

The missionaries had fused Christocentrism with a traditional political view and there is no doubt that most common people, like the citizens of Montauban, harboured Carlist sympathies. While conceding this, we must insist that when people demonstrated in favour of the cross or moved to protect it, they did so not because of their politics, but because of their piety. The mission cross trouble in Marseille, for which excellent records exist, illustrates this point.

Tumultuous events took place in France's great southern port city on 15 and 16 August 1831, which classically dramatised the roles of activists after the July Revolution. Liberal youth attacked a procession on the Feast of the Assumption, and, on the following day, attacked the mission cross itself, precipitating a riot. Lower-class vigilantes from the city's Old Quarter successfully defended the beleaguered cross, and, fortunately, we know what motivated them. Although the prefect harboured political reasons for wanting to cancel the procession on the fifteenth, there is no doubt that it was the religious, not political, fanaticism of the common people that prevented his doing so:

> The 'Old Quarter' of the city is filled with a devout—
> even superstitious—population. The cult of the Virgin
> is particularly strong. As far as they are concerned, it is
> an attack on religion to suppress a procession. They
> represent a considerable part of the population, and if
> one deprives them of their fanaticism, they will become
> enemies of the government.[64]

Similarly, although Marseille working classes, like Montauban's, confused their Christocentric piety with political legitimacy, the only specific motive attributed to them in their defence of the mission cross was religious fanaticism.[65] As they rallied around the cross on the night of the sixteenth and then, recklessly, rioted against the national guard, no one heard cries of 'Vivent les Bourbon!' but only 'Vive la croix!'[66]

Many aspects of the Marseille mission cross troubles were typical of what happened in other French cities. In one respect this may be asserted without reservation: bourgeois elements, not the *gens du peuple*, initiated mission cross troubles. We have it on the authority of the prefect that they were *wholly* responsible for the outbreak of the August riot in Marseille.[67] This is of primary importance because if liberal fanatics had not made an issue of the cross by attacking it, the politically naïve lower classes would not have been disturbed. Two considerations underpin this assertion: seldom did the lower class initiate mission cross trouble, *and in almost no mission cross controversy did they demonstrate politically.* Thus, there is no cause to think that a transition to Christocentrism without legitimacy raised problems for the common people. In fact, the government of Louis Philippe wisely helped its own shaky cause by disclaiming responsibility for the attacks on the crosses.

The political flexibility of the common people may be documented by the conduct of lower-class Nîmes women who defended the city's mission cross. When they gathered to protect the monument, they cried out: 'Strike! We are without arms! We have only come to die for the cross!' But they also exclaimed, 'Long live [Louis] Philippe, if he saves our cross!'[68] Nîmes was the site of the most hysterical mission cross disturbances in the entire country. The pious and courageous Nîmes women were unparalleled in religious zeal. They sacrificed their lives and sustained serious injury on behalf of the cross. Yet, astonishingly, they would forfeit legitimacy for Christocentrism! We may conclude from their example that for the politically naïve it really did not matter who was king so long as popular piety was left undisturbed and that the political implications of the theology of Christocentrism never much bothered the gens du peuple.

If Christocentric piety precluded lower-class support of liberal action against the cross, why did they not at least side with the liberal cultural position? Why did they not back bourgeois youth for wider dancing privileges? To be sure, lower-class youth loved to dance, but other considerations intervened causing them to withhold support. It is obvious at the very outset that if pious proletarian women had no scruples about pre-marital sexual indulgence, they would hardly be likely to quibble about the limited sexual contact of the waltz.

Yet it will be recalled that a second aggravation about dancing arose during the Restoration over disputes concerning the playing of music and dancing during church services (vespers and other afternoon devotions).[69] In other words, a public dance was in question. In the mind of the curé, and doubtlessly many others in the community, dancing was a communal activity and therefore could not compete with communal prayers, much less disrupt it. At stake in this aspect of the dancing controversy is the question about the nature of the activity: is it individual and secular or is it communal? May one dance when he or she wishes or only on Sundays and feast days when the community authorised it?

After the July Revolution bourgeois youth hoped to settle this question. Lower-class youth, we may speculate, withheld their co-operation for two reasons. First, it is doubtful that they made the distinction between dancing as a communal or secular activity. It is one thing to be disappointed about curtailed dancing hours, quite another to retaliate by moving to free dancing from communal control. As in Germany, custom provided the occasions for community recreation and dancing on holy days and Sundays. This traditional attitude still lingered among lower-class youth. Communal celebrations—patronal feasts, *Corpus Christi* celebrations, certain locally favoured feast days, the 'Bravades' —still enjoyed immense popularity in France in 1835.[70] There was little likelihood that lower-class youth would disassociate themselves from these communal activities by violating the accepted code governing dancing. The Loiret youth illustrated this attitude when they dutifully attended May devotions to Mary before going off to dance.[71]

The traditional outlook found lower-class acceptance through a second factor. As we have seen, curés fussed and railed about dancing during the Restoration for several reasons. Not all of their grievances applied equally to the entire populace and one concerned only bourgeois families. These people dared to hold dances in the privacy of their homes.[72] This flew right in the teeth of tradition. But the private chaperoned dance was clearly not a lower-class activity, nor was it likely to become one.[73] The issue therefore provided no cause for lower-class youth to join with bourgeois youth in attacking the mission cross, that symbol of socio-religious values preached by the missionaries.

In 1830 society was suspended somewhere between eighteenth-century communal dances and the dance hall of the turn-of-the-century era. Although the bourgeois attack on the mission cross may be seen as an important juncture in changing social values, it effected no sudden reversals. True, dancing of the modern variety became more common after 1830. Judging from clerical complaints this type of dance became frequent during the July Monarchy, when no effort was made to enforce the repressive law of 18 November 1814.[74] Sometime after 1830 dances could legally be held at any time (i.e. during church services) in cities with a population of 5,000 or more, which included most of France's 600 *chef-lieux.* [75] In other places authorities tolerated it. So dancing went on just as in Germany, where the efforts or rhetoric of German authorities to enforce curfew laws failed to curb the dances of the rural proletariat. But, although the quantity of the dances increased their quality remained much the same. As late as the 1840s, youth were intermingling the traditional styles of communal dancing with the newer steps, sometimes, in fact, giving the former a place of honour.[76] This means that the common people, if not the bourgeoisie, still held dances in the spirit of communal celebrations. Neither in France nor Germany, therefore, did communal dancing suddenly give way to the modern dance hall during the July Monarchy and Vormärz.

In sum, we must carefully distinguish between class and issues in attempting to grasp the crux of the cross controversy. All the evidence points to the fact that bourgeois and liberal elements wanted the crosses removed for political and cultural, not religious, reasons.[77] While pressing for the removal of the crosses from public grounds, they insisted that the prayer for the king be said during church services. In other words, they supported institutional religion even though we might question their religious sincerity and find entirely practical reasons for this support. The problem resided in the fact that in their utter naïveté, the gens du peuple did not understand what the liberals sought to achieve by acting against the cross. For them, to assault the cross was to assault religion—nothing less and nothing more. Thus the political actions of one class injured the religious sensibilities of another. When this occurred popular religion in France reached an impasse.

### The Virginal Cults

A fortnight before the July Revolution the Blessed Virgin Mary appeared to Catharine Labouré in the chapel of the Paris community of the Sisters of Charity of St Vincent of Paul in the Rue de Bac. This was the first of a series of spectacular apparitions of the Virgin in France during the nineteenth century of which the most important were those of La Salette (1846) and Lourdes (1858). Subsequent apparitions in the Rue de Bac convent led to the striking of a medal honouring the Immaculate Conception of Mary the Mother of God.* In 1842 Grignon de Montfort's 1712 tract on 'The True Devotion to the Blessed Virgin' was discovered and published in France, where it found an immense following.[78] Although the Virgin Mary has enjoyed a centuries-long Christian tradition of veneration, Mariologists look upon the events of the nineteenth century, beginning with the 1830 Rue de Bac apparitions, as the origin of the contemporary Marian movement.[79]

The ineluctable momentum which Marian piety ultimately attained could not yet be clearly discerned in France during the 1830s. The seed

---

* This doctrine teaches that Mary, alone among all human beings, did not carry the stain of Original Sin on her soul when she was conceived.

from which the devotion to the Virgin Mother was to spring was planted
in the Rue de Bac before the July Revolution which was shortly to bring
down the mission crosses, but the new Marian cult did not immediately
germinate. The vehement anti-clerical sentiment engendered in Paris by
the revolution was a hostile environment for a pious movement which
was itself slightly tainted with political overtones. In the very first
apparition it had been revealed to Catherine Labouré that, in her own
clumsy phrases, 'the Times are Very evil, misfortunes are going to fall on
france the throne will be overthrown...'[79] The prophecy was ambiguous since it was taken to refer both to the events of 1830 and those of
1870, but, in either case, the royalist prejudice is clear. This may possibly explain the initial slow growth of the Marian movement.

Also, the 1832 Immaculate Conception medal did not shun identification with the suffering Christ. On its reverse side it pictured a large
capital 'M' surmounted by a cross with two 'suffering' hearts beneath,
that of Mary, pierced, and that of Christ, wrapped in a crown of thorns.
At any rate, it was not until four years later that the cult of the Virgin
began to gain some momentum. In 1836 the mystical curé of a Parisian
parish, *Notre Dame des Victoires*, received an inspiration to dedicate
his church to the Immaculate Heart of Mary, and to found a confraternity in her honour. After some delays and opposition this congregation
finally became by an 1838 papal decree the 'Archconfraternity of the
Most Holy and Immaculate Heart of Mary'. It was entitled to subscribe
members from all of France and Christendom but it did not really
become nationally active until the fourth decade.

Precisely in the mid-thirties Philomena burst upon the scene, filling
the hiatus in the Marian cult. The Philomena fad began to catch on immediately after the mission cross débâcle. Birth records of several
French departments allow us to be quite exact about the timing of the
movement. Before 1834 'Philomena' as a given name was unheard of.
Then, within a matter of a few years, it became one of the more popular
names in the country. Late in 1834 the first Marseille child to be given
the name was born. Four years later it had become the ninth most
popular name in the great city, having surpassed dozens of other traditional Christian names (see Appendix 2, graph 1). The same thing
happened in tiny rural Liettres at the other extremity of the country
where four out of five girls born in 1838 were named 'Philomena'.
The timing of the fad in Marseille and Liettres seems to be typical of
other French cities. It experienced an enormous spurt of growth around
the mid-1830s, varying a year or so from place to place. During the
latter years of the decade it crests, holding its attraction for several

years (see Appendix 2, graph 2). Then its influence quickly wanes
during the early 1840s, although the saint's popularity does not die out
by any means. Philomena takes her place, as it were, amidst a bank of
other favoured saints.[81]

The Philomena cult presents the social historian with a unique and
rare combination. Unlike other Christian heroes and heroines, Philomena was a completely new personality set in the context of a
centuries-old Christian tradition.[82] Those whom she attracted have
recourse to her for the same reasons Christians have always besought the
favours of saints, but because Philomena was only just 'discovered' in
1802, her devotees, unlike all others, took up their devotion afresh.
Those who flocked to her did so because they had not severed themselves from the traditional Christian mentality, apart from which
Philomena made no sense. Those who refused to take up her cult had
already become alienated, or were being alienated from the traditional
concept of man, society and the world.

We have already had occasion to discuss Philomena's progress in the
Loiret department. The distinctly rural flavour of the cult and its
equally distinct acceptance among the rural proletariat disclose important characteristics about the new enthusiasm.

The situation in the Loiret was closely approximated in northern
France. In Pas de Calais the Philomena cult found the same backers:
rural rather than urban people and the proletariat rather than land-
owners. Data covering four of the department's six cantonal seats
indicate strong support of the cult in St Omer, no support in the seaside
city of Calais, and only very moderate support in Montreuil and Arras,
the prefectural city (see Appendix 2, graph 3).[83] Preachers who worked
the missions in these areas during the second half of the nineteenth century reported that Calais became dechristianised after 1830.[84] Whether
that was the critical year or not may be questioned, but the city's
complete lack of support for Philomena at the end of the decade
indicates that they were not greatly mistaken.[85] St Omer does not contradict the pattern as much as it would appear, because roughly half of
the parents there who named their children Philomena worked in
agriculture.

Although cultural change and modernisation may have been afoot in
some northern cities, much of the surrounding countryside remained
untouched by these intruders. One did not have to search long in rural
Pas de Calais to find traditional celebrations and 'old ways' of thinking
about life and death.[86] Nevertheless, just as in rural Loiret, considerable diversity attended the reception given to Philomena by the country

people of northern France. Farmers in Vimy, the canton bordering
Arras to the north, paid scant attention to the new saint.[87] But just
north of Vimy lies the canton of Norrent Fontes, centre of the strongest
Philomena cult in the entire department. Far away as the names of these
cantons may sound to us, Vimy and Norrent Fontes are within 25 kilometres of each other. In nineteenth-century rural France one had only
to travel a little way to discover a completely different cultural milieu.
The cult of Philomena in Lièttres accounts for much of the strong
showing of the cult in Norrent Fontes.[88]

Houdain, the canton separating Vimy and Norrent Fontes, presents
an interesting case. Religious observance had slacked off in Houdain,
so that by the end of the century it was one of the most dechristianised
areas in the department's mid-eastern region. Most non-observing of all
the communes in Houdain was Bruay, where less than 15 per cent of
the population still fulfilled their Easter duty. Yet, earlier Bruay gave
Philomena an enthusiastic reception. Between 1837 and 1842 about
20 babies in 1,000 were named Philomena. Thus, dechristianisation
occurred precipitously sometime after 1842.

Support for the Philomena cult in other rural areas in the department seems to follow the same chequered pattern we have already
discovered elsewhere in rural Loiret. The 23 communes in the canton of
Montreuil gave Philomena a cool reception. Missionaries complained of
dechristianisation in this area in the second half of the century, but we
can be sure it had already experienced a cultural change by 1840. On
the other hand, Bapaume in the southernmost part of the department
showed considerable interest in Philomena.

Although regional religious discipline is important in tracing cultural
change in nineteenth-century Pas de Calais, a study of religious observance by social class appears to be even more instructive. For no matter
what area we choose, we find again that agricultural workers were
providing the support for the Philomena cult. In general, there is
nothing very surprising about this, but lack of support for her by other
groups, especially artisans, is difficult to explain. Vocations to the priesthood—a common measure of religiosity—were of about average strength
in Pas de Calais compared with the rest of France.[89] Many of the vocations came from the homes of rural artisans. Yet, for some reason, neither
artisans nor people in commercial or service occupations showed as much
interest in the Philomena cult as they did in directing their sons towards the priesthood. In pre-revolutionary France large farmers and
the bourgeoisie had provided Arras with its vocations. In the nineteenth
century the *classes aisées* disappeared from the religious vocational

scene. After 1830 their role was increasingly assumed by rural artisans.[90]
In the 1820s agricultural people had furnished their share of vocations
(50 per cent), but by the 1840s they had slipped back. But, curiously,
during exactly this time they became great supporters of Philomena.
Eighty per cent of all 'Philomenas' came from their families, although
they constituted at most 60 per cent of the rural population. If we look
closer at the agricultural sector, an answer to this riddle emerges. Only
one type of person—the rural proletarian—was providing all the support for the Philomena cult. Not one farmer of medium to large
property holdings named his child Philomena. Rather, domestics, day
labourers and cotters shared support of the new saint in almost equal

Table 8:  Social Origins of Philomena Babies and Vocations to the
Priesthood in the Diocese of Arras

|  | Philomena Cult (1837-42) | Vocations to Priesthood (1842-7) |
|---|---|---|
| Agriculture | 80% | 47% |
| Artisan | 11% | 32% |
| Commerce | 5% | 8% |
| Service | 4% | 13% |
| Bourgeoisie | 0% | 0% |

Source: (for vocation statistics) Y. M. Hilaire, 'Le recrutement ecclésiastique dans
la première moitie du XIXe siècle: Le diocèse d' Arras represente-t-il un cas
original?' *Bulletin de la Société d' histoire Moderne*, LXVII année, 6, pp.13-19.

proportions. These were the people—the former propertyless, the latter
two the most wretchedly housed families in the entire department—
who flocked to Philomena.[91] Thus, in areas where traditional community functions—patronal feasts, May Day celebrations, etc.—
remained popular, the poorest and most illiterate segment of the
population was culturally the least affected by modern ideologies that
threatened this world.

Pas de Calais resembles Loiret in one other respect. In both departments the local nobility played a hand in keeping the hierarchical view
of society intact.[92] In Liettres Baron d' Halwyn arranged to have a
life-sized statue of Philomena made and procured a relic of the saint
which he had encased in a precious reliquary. On Saturday 5 July 1837,

the entire parish and many people of the surrounding Norrent Fontes canton turned out for the inauguration of the new cult. Along with many parish priests and other ecclesiastics, including the bishop of Arras, they processed from the church to the chateau of the Baron, where the bishop blessed the statue. A procession was formed to accompany it back to the church. While the people sang psalms, the statue was carried by young girls dressed in white, the reliquary 'by four young virgins'. Once inside the village church a mass was said in honour of the saint; her relics were exposed on the altar, and a special sermon recounting her life was delivered. Finally, after mass, the statue was installed in a new chapel dedicated to Philomena in the Liettres church. A novena to her was begun that same day which attracted a great number of sick and handicapped people from the surrounding countryside. All of this made a tremendous impression on the people, who, it must be understood, were by no means passive agents in getting the new cult started, even if an aristocratic family was instrumental.[93] We noted above that the aristocracy played a very active role in the religious life of Sologne in the Loiret department. Their ability to foster this kind of traditional religious outlook among the rural proletariat earmarks their continued political influence in the nineteenth century and deserves attention particularly in the light of efforts by subsequent historians (and contempory socialists) to blame the new middle class for the promotion of a religious opiate.[94]

Very little about the Philomena phenomenon in central and northern France resembled the cult in Marseille, a fact which prevents us from rushing into generalisations about rural—urban and class distinctions. In spite of urbanity—Marseille was the second-largest city of the country and one of the world's leading ports at the time—Philomena had a sensational impact there. In the course of just one year, 1836, her name was given to so many children that it surpassed literally dozens of traditional names in popularity. In spite of the fact that no one had ever even heard of Philomena before the 1830s, the name became the ninth most popular given name in Marseille during the latter years of the decade. During this time about 2,500 to 2,800 female babies were born each year in Marseille. One out of every 16 to 20 of them was named 'Philomena'. Then, rather abruptly during the early 1840s the name fell from favour, but remained a common given name for Marseille children.[95] The dramatic rise and fall of the Marseille 'Philomenas' testifies to the sensational manner in which the cult of the saint swept the city.

No less striking than the differing general reception afforded

Philomena in the south was the pattern of behaviour of the city's bourgeoisie. In Orleáns they showed total disinterest, but in Marseille they picked up the cult with astonishing celerity (see Appendix 2, graph 4).[96] In 1836—really only the second year of the cult—the bourgeoisie named their children after the new saint at the highest rate the name would achieve among any class at any time during its decade of popularity (see Appendix 2, graph 5).

Among other Marseille classes Philomena's name caught on more slowly, reaching a peak in 1838, 1839 or 1840 (among unskilled workers). But when these groups did begin to pick up the fad they followed the same pattern as that established by the bourgeoisie. This means that no matter to what kind of working-class family a girl was born she was less likely to be named Philomena than if she had been born to either the upper or petty bourgeoisie (see Appendix 2, graph 6). The regularity of the pattern is even more extraordinary if we consider the component groups within the bourgeoisie and working class. Only farm workers, not a small group even in a port city like Marseille, do not fit the pattern of descent by social level. Because of their working environment in a still strongly practising Catholic region, this is not in the least surprising.[97] If we consider only city occupations, support for

Table 9: Percentage of All Babies Named Philomena by Class in
         Marseille, 1835-50*

| | |
|---|---|
| *Haute* Bourgeoisie and *Rentiers* | 2.25 |
| Small Business and Clerical | 1.95 |
| Agricultural Workers | 1.9 |
| Skilled Workers | 1.7 |
| Unskilled Workers | 1.4 |
| Service/Maritime Workers | 1.15 |

*   For the social structure of Marseille's population, as well as for the classification of Marseille occupations, I am indebted to William H. Sewell, Jr., who has studied these matters intensely and has generously allowed me the use of the manuscript on Marseille society which he is preparing for publication.

Philomena decreases as one descends the social ladder. Among the petty bourgeoisie, small business and clerical families were twice as likely to add a 'Philomena' to their families than were working-class people, while service/maritime people picked up the name more slowly still. In 1835 and 1836 alone, agricultural workers fit the descending stair pattern as well, ranking above only the service/maritime category in their adoption of the name. Obviously, then, the new cult was not imported from the country into the city.

But we must beware of fabricating rural and urban cultural differences in the first part of the nineteenth century for the lower classes particularly. In both Central and Western Europe a mobile population shifted residency back and forth between town and country as job opportunities and other factors dictated.[98] Religious identity in general and the cult of Philomena in particular facilitated the acclimatisation of these footloose people. Marseille illustrates this point. Although indigenous elements provided the initial boost for the Philomena cult, rural immigrants readily picked it up. By mid-century 50 per cent of Marseille's artisans were immigrants. Much of Philomena's more durable support came from skilled or unskilled first-generation city dwellers. We may surmise that for country people, flooding into Marseille in the 1830s and 1840s to take advantage of the job market in the booming port city, the Philomena cult constituted one aspect of urban life that did not seem strange and totally new.

Sooner or later during the nineteenth century rival ideologies emerged in town and country to compete with the traditional, hierarchical view of society of which Philomena was a part and manifestation. When this happened, and it would vary from city to city and from region to region, Philomena's fortunes fluctuated. Both Marseille and in northern France, St Omer demonstrate this. Let us first consider the former city for which much more data are available.

Skilled workers constituted Marseille's largest occupational group. Filling 31 per cent of all occupations, including dockers, they were nearly twice as numerous as their nearest rival, unskilled workers.[99] In the data on the Philomena cult which was drawn from birth rather than marriage registers, they make their presence felt even more strongly: in 1839 artisans accounted for 41 per cent of all Marseille births. But it is their politics as much as their numbers that make skilled workers interesting. Exhaustive studies have led to their sub-categorisation into two groups—those belonging to exclusive as opposed to open trades.[100] The former—longshoremen, coopers, packers, tanners, packagers, shipbuilders, maritime artisans and masons—constituted a labour aristocracy. All artisans enjoyed much better annual incomes than non-skilled workers, but those in the so-called exclusive trades were able to control membership much better than others, keeping at bay the steady influx of immigrants who annually flooded the city, thereby easing the labour scarcity in the growing economy. As dilution of native Marseille stock advanced apace among non-skilled workers and

open trade artisans, differences in social and political behaviour began
to set them apart from exclusive tradesman. The latter, disdaining new-
comers, nurtured their traditional socio-religious subculture. Open trade
artisans, by contrast, awash in the flood of immigrants, lost theirs and
became a fertile seedbed for new socialist and republican ideologies. In
the decade beginning with 1848 a native working in an open trade was
four times more likely to be politically radical than his counterpart in
a closed trade. One does not make the metamorphosis from a traditional Christian tradesman to a socialist or republican radical overnight.
Since native Marseille stock was still relatively undiluted during the
Restoration, the watershed years for open trade artisans who switched
to political radicalism after 1848 must lie in the decades of the 1830s
and 1840s.[101]

We may observe this process by using the Philomena cult as an index
to the growing division between open and exclusive tradesmen. During
the earlier years of the 1840s the open trades continued their support.
As late as 1846, 1.4 per cent of their children were named after Philomena, a higher rate than any other group except agricultural workers,
who stood also at 1.4 per cent. But 1848 was the crucial year, in which
the ambiguous politico-religious posture of the open tradesmen began
to give way to something like a profile. The revolution of 1848 clearly
indicates a correlation between the Philomena cult and the everyday
political feelings and experience of French people. The year was not a
good one for Philomena. People still sufficiently captivated by Philomena to name their children after her refrained from doing so until the
nature and implications of the revolution were clear to them. Few
people dared use the saint's name during the time of trouble. However,
during this year the rate of decrease among the upper classes did not
quicken, but in fact held steady (bourgeoisie) or even declined (clerical
and small business). Among the working classes—with the significant
exception of the exclusive trades—support for Philomena fell off
noticeably in 1848, and, among them, most noticeably in the open and
unskilled trades and agriculture (see Appendix 2, graph 8). Alone
amidst the working class, the exclusive trades in 1848 buck the trend
and actually increase their support of Philomena. Furthermore, agricultural workers rebound strongly by 1850, surpassing their 1846 rate
of support, and non-skilled and service workers hold their ground.
Alone among all the people of Marseille, the open tradesmen abandoned
Philomena in 1848 and were unable to regroup behind the cult
thereafter.

In St Omer in northern France, much of Philomena's support came from skilled artisans and agricultural workers, who together account for 90 per cent of working-class 'Philomena babies'. Missionaries who worked in the city later in the century complained that the parish of St Denis in particular had suffered a collapse in religious observance.

Figure 7: Philomena Namesakes in Marseille, 1848

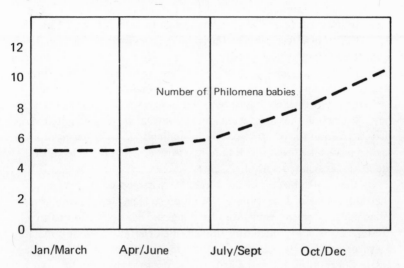

Source: *A. D. Bouches du Rhône Etat Civil, Naissances.*

By comparing the baptismal registry of this parish to the birth registry of the city we can test the strengths of the cult in this neighbourhood with the rest of the city (see Appendix 2, graph 3). It is clear that the missionaries knew what they were talking about. The trend away from religious practice had already begun by the time of the Philomena fad. The mission preachers singled out shoemakers and pipe-makers as the residents of St Denis who had become dechristianised.[102] Since artisans in general strongly supported Philomena, we must ask why two or three particular trades abstained from the movement. Neither pipe-makers nor shoemakers, with one exception, named their children after Philomena between 1837 and 1842. Other artisans, meanwhile, were adopting the new name: four 'Philomenas' each were born into butchers' and masons' families during this same period and most other trades were represented in the new cult by at least two 'Philomenas' by 1842. Thus, we may speculate that it was the unskilled workers and artisans of perhaps as few as only two or three trades, whose dwellings were concentrated in St Denis parish, who held aloof from the Philomena fad.

We have, then, in Marseille and St Omer a sure sign of the disengage-
ment of certain tradesmen from past customs and a hierarchical,
Christian view of society. But did not St Simonians also believe in God?
Even as the Philomena cult captured France was not the abbé Lamennais making Jesus Christ a champion and hero of the working class?
This must be granted. Isambert has pointed out that the working-class
radicals esteemed Jesus Christ right through the revolution of 1848.[103]
Their Christ, however, was the Christ of the cleansing of the Temple—
a wrathful activist who wrought justice now. In contrast, the Philomena
devotees could accept the order of things more or less as they were
without needing to be rigid about them. They could be either Orléanists
or Carlists, but they could not be revolutionaries or activists. This is the
basic distinction that must be made. Philomena, we may conclude, bore
little attraction for those who were beginning to think in terms of social
justice in this life, even if still in religious modes, and in terms of the
ideologies associated with this goal.

By the 1840s the cult of the Virgin Mary had edged Philomena off
the centre stage of French piety. Devotion to Mary defies ready quantifiable measurement, since, for one thing, she has been a fixture in
Western Christianity since time immemorial. Her most recent popularity,
however, was largely occasioned by the medal in honour of the Immaculate Conception. Everyone had easy access to it through the
Archconfraternity of the Immaculate Conception since nothing more
was required for membership than inscribing and promising to say the
'Hail Mary' along with the short prayer, 'Mary, refuge of sinners, pray
for us'. From 1840 to 1860 the Archconfraternity enjoyed a spectacular growth period during which it enlisted 800,000 members who
ranged geographically over large parts of France.[104]

The success of the Marian movement in France sharply contrasts
with the experience of Central Europe. No doubt the Virgin Mary was
popularly acclaimed by German Catholics. Of the 285 pilgrimages
made by parishes in the diocese of Trier in 1827, 99 were specifically
of Marian character.[105] But, as these figures suggest, there was nothing
exclusive about this Marian devotion. We may assume that all or most
of these pilgrimages were traditional affairs carried over from pre-
modern times.

If a budding Marian cult had been emerging in nineteenth-century
Germany, we might expect to find an increase of Marian namesakes.
But, to date, nothing suggests this. In fact, the number of female
infants christened Mary in Oberwinter, a rural middle Rhineland village,

has declined rather steadily ever since the middle of the eighteenth
century (see Appendix 3).[106] This may be explained by the fact that
in modern times, despite the persistent piety in the culture of the rural
proletariat, political and secular figures rival Biblical personalities as
namesakes. Even so, the fact that Mary was not even as popular as the
namesake Anne suggests that no Marian cult was stealthily taking form
from within the amorphous religious mentality of Central Europeans.

The German reaction to the cult in France further substantiates this
estimate. We would naturally expect German Protestants to be sceptical
and critical of the Marian cult. But it also rocked German Catholics
back on their heels a bit. In 1855, the *Historisch-Politische Blätter*
noted that Frenchmen

> not only treat [Mary] as the first princess of the Church but as
> actually French and as the protectress and leader of their army,
> and as patroness of their fame, so that from the Ardennes to the
> Pyrenees. . . the church of Notre Dame des Victoires is the most
> popular in all of France—possibly because of a misunderstanding
> regarding the true meaning of this title.[107]

Clearly, the Germans saw something different and perhaps suspicious
in the Marian devotion of Frenchmen. Even German Catholics stood
back in awe of the apotheosis of Mary by Frenchmen.

Finally, it is indisputable that the impetus for the proclamation of
the dogma of the Immaculate Conception by Pope Pius IX in 1854
came from France. Pius's predecessor, Gregory XVI, had held back on
the matter because of the cool reception given it by the episcopacy of
England, Ireland and especially Germany.[108] The dogma was finally
proclaimed under unusual circumstances: the doctrine, which was without scriptural foundation, was defined on the authority of a pope
whose own infallibility was not yet an article of faith. In addition,
non-French bishops, especially the Germans who were not satisfied
with the wording of the proposed text of the dogma, caused a two-
week delay in its solemn proclamation—much to the embarrassment of
Pius.[109] Thus, in the course of just two decades the explosion of
virginal devotion in France had supplanted popular Christocentrism and
led to a new article of faith for all Catholics everywhere.

More than anything else, it was the fortunes of virginal and Christocentric cults after 1830 that proclaimed the triumph of the former over
the latter. After 1830 Christocentrism fell back to provincial or local
importance, giving place on the national level to the cult of the virgins.

A brief survey of the geography of popular devotion will confirm this.

During the latter years of the thirties, after the mission cross controversy had subsided, Christocentrism attempted a comeback. With the ebb tide of revolution a rash of new public crosses, called *calvaires*, dotted the countryside. Almost as many new crosses were erected between 1834 and the end of the decade as had been knocked down or removed in the wake of the July Revolution. Once again thousands of people swarmed around the cross. Once again the cries of 'Vive la croix!' and the singing of canticles were to be heard. Often the mayor and municipal council even took part in the proceedings surrounding the erection of a new cross, while the national guard, resplendent in its uniform and led by its officers, would carry the cross to the designated site, or would act as an honour guard![110]

However familiar these scenes may have seemed to someone who had taken part in the mission cross erections during the 1820s, they were in fact quite different. The *calvaire* after all was no mission cross; it did not culminate a mission. Many may have thought of them as replacing the mission cross, and, indeed, many were erected to right the insults that had befallen the mission crosses, but the great emotional tie between the cross and legitimacy that the missionaries had instilled in the people had evaporated and could not be resurrected. Both the Bourbons and the old-style missions were gone. The *fleur-de-lys* did not adorn the *calvaire*, nor was the famous couplet 'Les Bourbon et la Foi!' heard beneath it.

Even more importantly, it was not the same mayor nor the same guardsmen who toppled crosses in 1830-2 that helped erect them a few years later. A comparison of new cross sites with mission cross troubles (i.e. old cross sites) reveals very conspicuous geographical differences. *Calvaires* were few and far between in most parts of France. A great preponderance of them, something approaching 47 per cent, were to be found in France's northernmost departments, Picardy and Nord, and Normandy accounts for a good portion of the remainder. The mission cross monuments, on the other hand, had been sprinkled indiscriminately throughout France, the only possible exception being the department of Aquitaine in the south-west corner of the country. Clearly, *calvaires* did not enjoy the nation-wide enthusiasm lavished on mission crosses during the 1820s.

Of equal significance is the urban quality of the crosses which sharply contrasts with the rural flavour of Christocentrism after 1834. The great majority (83 per cent) of the mission cross troubles occurred in the *chef-lieu* of a canton or capital of an *arrondissement*, whereas, on the other hand, the great majority (74 per cent) of the *calvaires* were erected in smaller settlements.[111] When crosses were erected in *chef-lieux* and other cities during the Restoration, so many country people came into town for the ceremony that a city's population could temporarily double. But the reverse did not happen during the July Monarchy: city people did not flock to the countryside for calvaire ceremonies.

Furthermore, if a city removed its cross in one way or another during the mission cross troubles, it almost never erected a *calvaire*. When the people of Charroux petitioned their mayor in April, 1834, asking that the cross be replaced at their expense and without any religious ceremony where it had originally stood, he refused and the issue was dropped.[112] The bourgeoisie stood their ground in other cities as well, indicating that, although during the cholera epidemic they may have become more tolerant of various pious practices, they did not themselves engage in the revival of the cult of the cross. Thus, geographical and social restrictions confined Christocentrism after 1834.

Meanwhile the cults of the virgins had begun their conquest of French popular piety, in this case rural and urban alike. Although devotion to Philomena was finely attuned to local cultural conditions, unmistakable traces of her cult can be found in widely scattered areas and in both town and country. The sudden, widespread and simultaneous growth of her cult in several areas—1835, Paris; 1836, Poitiers, Brittany; 1837, Bordeaux, Amiens, Nevers, Marseille—emphatically suggest its national scope.[113]

Even more extraordinary was the growth pattern of Marian devotion which largely redraws the map of religious observance in nineteenth-century France.[114] The northern half of the country, which was generally thought to be less religious than the south, picked up the devotion quickly. Even more astonishing are the areas in the north that took to it. Brittany and Normandy showed little interest whereas the country around Paris, the departments in central France, and the departments to the east of the 'Siegfried line'—a dechristianised area—backed the Marian cult strongly during its very first years of growth between 1838 and 1843![115]

The growth of the virginal cults can also be demonstrated by nineteenth-century marriage patterns. In traditional society there had been a taboo against marriage during the Advent season, a period of penitential preparation for Christmas. During the nineteenth century Frenchmen disregarded this custom in increasing numbers so that it had become only vestigial by the twentieth century. On the other hand, the custom of respecting Mary by not marrying in May, 'the month of the Virgin', grew during the nineteenth century even though it did not have the weight of tradition behind it. In 1810 only a few departments honoured Mary in this way but by 1837 15 departments had picked up this pious custom, and it 'continued to spread in the nineteenth and twentieth centuries, the two foci being the Loire valley and the Mediterranean littoral'.[116] Again, it is cause for some amazement that the new practice would catch on first in central France, a region not distinguished by its religiosity.

In sum, the cults of the virgins, Philomena and Mary, enjoyed widespread, indeed national, popularity, whereas the resurgence of Christocentrism after 1834 was markedly regional.

French popular piety sprouted a new branch in the third decade of the nineteenth century when an old one, Christocentrism, was cut off. Common people opposed the amputation because their still traditional mentality kept them from discerning and appreciating liberal motives in attacking the cross. The most ready explanation for the change in popular religious tastes is that society felt oppressed by the cross cult because of its ambiguous politico-religious symbolism. The cult of the virgins either lacked political overtones from the very beginning (Philomena) or sloughed them soon enough (Mary).

But the demise of one devotion cannot explain the rise of another. In the last analysis, the cults of the virgins arose because of the piety of the French common people, which was both widespread and irrepressible. Was it the piety of common people alone? Or was it the exclusive piety of French women? These tantalising questions remain to be solved. But the broad outlines have come into focus: French piety insisted on a national cult after the debacle over Christocentrism; against the odds of increasing sexual licence, the cult of the virgins triumphed; and, finally, wide segments of the French population supported or at least tolerated the new cults.

## Notes

1. The mission cross troubles are analysed in 'The July Revolution and the Mission Cross Troubles', a paper which I delivered at the Bicentennial Meeting of the American Catholic Historical Association, March 1976. The analysis will appear in a forthcoming issue of the *Catholic Historical Review*.
2. It is undoubtedly true that expressions of piety at this time were still quite local rather than national, as Michael Marrus affirms in his paper, 'Cultures on the Move: Pilgrims and Pilgrimages in Nineteenth Century France', which he generously allowed me to read. Local saints, patron saints and universal saints made local (one thinks of the innumerable local shrines to the Blessed Virgin) undoubtedly still exercised their attraction. But various forces were working

to break down particularised, local piety. It is not surprising, then, that popular religion began taking on national contours early in the century. It is these, rather than local piety, that we will deal with to understand the religious mentality of common people.

3. The mission successes are chronicled in *L' Ami de la Religion.* A wealth of information and accounts of individual missions (but no systematic account of the movement) is contained in E. Sevrin's two-volume study, *Les missions religieuses en France sous la Restoration,* I (St Mandé [Seine], 1948), II (Paris, 1959).

4. In his valuable study of Marseille, Fernand Charpin found that the mission had an immediate, not enduring, impact on the practice of religion. *Practique religieuse et formation d' une grande ville: le geste du baptême et la signification en sociologie religieuse, Marseille, 1806-1958* (Paris, 1964), p.189. Although I do not think the time lapse between birth and baptism is always sensitive to political developments, Charpin shows that it fluctuated because of the disturbances of the liberal youth in July 1831.

5. Sevrin, I, pp.130-260.

6. Several have been preserved in the *Musée des Beaux-Arts,* Orléans. See display A. 6705.

7. These are by no means isolated cases. Sevrin, I, *passim,* refers to many others.

8. Georges Lacroix, *Charles de la Tour d' Auvergne* (Lens [Pas de Calais], n.d.), p.189.

9. Voctor Gelu, *Marseille au XIX^e siècle,* L. Gaillard and J. Reboul (eds.) (Paris, 1971), pp.103-5.

10. Sevrin, I, pp.314-29. The cross may not have been the only way by which a cult of the suffering Christ was maintained. The aristocracy kept up its devotion to the Sacred Heart, and confraternities of the Sacred Heart were established in parishes which enrolled the common people. However, it is not yet known how widespread these movements were. See J. M. Mayeur, 'Catholicisme intransigeant, catholicisme social, democratie chrétienne', *Annales,* XXXVII, 2 (March-April 1972), p.489; and Auguste Billaud, *Histoire religieuse de Pouzauges* (Lucon, 1967), pp.143ff. See the comments on M. de Janson's sermon on the cross during the 1818 Riems mission: *L' Ami de la Religion,* XVII (15 Aug. 1818), p.24.

11. Jacques Le Brun, 'Politics and Spirituality: the Devotion to the Sacred Heart', *Concilium,* IX, 7 (Nov. 1971), pp.29-43.

12. Ibid., p.41.

13. Bernard Plongeron, 'Théologie et politique (1770-1880)', *Annales Historiques de la Révolution Francaise,* LLXIII (July-Sept. 1973), p.448.

14. Bernard Plongeron, *Théologie et Politique au siècle des Lumières (1770-1820)* (Geneva, 1973), pp.305-10. See as well the first chapter of Nora E. Hudson's *Ultra-royalism and the French Revolution* (New York, 1973).

15. Sevrin, II, p.83.

16. After 1832 there were sporadic troubles for about 18 months.

17. Phayer, 'The July Revolution and the Mission Cross Troubles'. I have documented 110 cases.

18. Ibid. The roles of the lower classes and bourgeoisie in the mission cross troubles are analysed in this paper.

19. A. N. In the F^19 series see 5722, 5728, 5748, 5749, 5752. See also the *Constitutionnel,* 13 August 1832.

20. Sevrin, I, pp.272-88; II, pp.66-7.

21. Ruth Katz, 'The Egalitarian Waltz', *Comparative Studies in Society and History,* XV, 3 (Nov.-June 1973), p.371.

22. Marrus, pp.14-15.

23. Polge, pp.18-9.
24. *L' Ami de la Religion*, XXXIX (1826), p.189.
25. N. J. Chalin, 'Une image de diocèse de Rouen sous l' épiscopate de Mgr. de Croy (1823-44)', *RHEF*, LVIII, 160 (Jan.-June 1972), p.65.
26. *L' Ami de la Religion*, LX (16 May 1829), p.24.
27. Paul Leuilliot, *L' Alsace au début de XIXᵉ siècle* (Paris, 1960), p.141.
28. Langlois, pp.502-3.
29. Le Bras, *Sociologie religieuse*, II, p.659; see also *Introduction*, II, pp.35-6.
30. B. Peyrous, 'La pratique religieuse dans le diocèse de Bordeaux au XIXᵉ sièlce', *Annales du Midi*, 87, 4 (1975), p.454: Claude Langlois, *Le diocese de Vannes au XIXᵉ siècle, 1800-1830* (Paris, 1974), p.502.
31. *L'Ami de la Religion*, LXXIII (13 Oct. 1832), pp. 504-5.
32. Sevrin, I., 3/6; *L'Ami de la Religion*, LXV (4 Sept.1830), pp. 227-8.
33. A. D. Bouches du Rhône, 28. V. 1. Thomas to Min. of Cult.; Marseille, 18 August 1831.
34. *L'Ami de la Religion*, LXVIII (5 Oct. 1831), p.56.
35. A. N. F¹⁹ 5601 Report of 18 March 1831.
36. *Gazette du Midi*, 4 Feb. 1831.
37. *L' Ami de la Religion*, LXII (9 June 1832), p.294.
38. The account given by Sevrin is that of a contemporary mission preacher; I, p.316.
39. The best example is the letter of the mayor of Douces, 20 May 1831, to the prefect: A. N. F¹⁹ 5712.
40. The violence often done to the Christ figures of the mission crosses indicates an emotional attitude on the part of the bourgeoisie.
41. For a more complete account see Phayer, 'The July Revolution and the Mission Cross Troubles'.
42. *Gazette du Midi*, 15 May 1831.
43. This was a bizarre scene to say the least. A contingent of army troops had been dispatched by the prefect to guard the mission cross. Taking their orders literally, they stood by and watched the riot taking place under their noses.
44. *Orléanais*, 20 March 1831. See also accounts in the *Berruyer*, 23 March 1831; the *Gazette du Midi*, 15 and 18 March 1831; *L' Ami de la Religion*, LXVII (4 April 1831), pp.472-3. Newspaper accounts set the number of injured at about fifty.
45. A. N. F¹⁹ 5601 Report from Marseille; Aug. 1831.
46. Phayer, 'The July Revolution and the Mission Cross Troubles'.
47. Gaxette du Midi, 3 April 1831; *L' Ami de la Religion*, LXVI (20 Nov. 1830), 135 and LXVI (30 Dec. 1830), pp.407-8.
48. *L' Ami de la Religion*, loc. cit.
49. A. N. F¹⁹ 5601 Report from Marseille; Aug 1831 and A. D. Bouches du Rhône, Prefect to Min. of Cult, 23 Nov. 1830.
50. Quote is from the same report from the prefect as cited immediately above.
51. A. N. F¹⁹ 5734 Prefect to Min. of Cult; 9 Feb. 1831.
52. There are some striking discrepancies: southern Languedoc and, above all, in south-western France the departments to the north and south of the Garonne river. For a discussion of religious conditions in this area see B. Peyrous, 'La Pratique religieuse dans le diocèse de Bordeaux au XIXᵉ siècle (1838-1909)', *Annales du Midi*, 87, 4 (1975), pp.443-68.
53. Edgar Leon Newman, 'The Blouse and the Frock Coat: the Alliance of the Common People of Paris with the Liberal Leadership and the Middle Class during the Last Years of the Bourbon Restoration', *JMH*, XXXXVI, 1 (March 1974), p.44. *L' Ami de la Religion*, LXVII (12 Feb. 1831), p.91; LXV (24 Aug. 1830), p.144; LXV (16 Sept. 1830), p.306; LXVII (16 April 1831), pp.504-5; *L' Avenir*, 4 Nov. 1830; *Berruyer*, 29 Sept. 1830.

54. A. N. F¹⁹ 5742 Copy of letter of prefect to Bishop; Orléans, 3 Sept. 1830; prefect to Min. of Cult., Orléans, 13 Sept. 1830.
55. A. N. F¹⁹ 5736 prefect of Sarthe to Min. of Cult.; Le Mans, 17 Sept. 1830.
56. A. N. F¹⁹ 5601 Brief on state of ecclesiastical affairs; Paris, June 1831 (cf. 'Besancon'); P. Huot-Pleuroux, *Le Recrutment sacerdotal dans le diocèse de Besancon de 1801 à 1860* (Besancon, 1965), pp.289-90.
57. A. N. F¹⁹ 5601 Report from Marseille; August 1831.
58. A. D. Bouches du Rhône prefect to Min. of Cult., Marseille, 14 March 1831.
59. A. N. F¹⁹ 5601 Brief on state of ecclesiastical affairs in the Vendee; 17 June 1834.
60. Phayer, 'The July Revolution and the Mission Cross Troubles'.
61. A. N. F¹⁹ 5601 prefect to Min. of Cult.; Montauban, 28 Sept 1830.
62. *Journal de Loiret,* 16 Dec. 1830.
63. A. N. F¹⁹ 5739 Sec. of War, 22 Feb. 1831.
64. A. D. Bouches du Rhône 28.V.1. Thomas to Min. of Cult., Marseille, 18 Aug. 1831.
65. A.N.F.¹⁹ 5601 Report from Marseilles; August 1931.
66. One of the vigilantes who refused to stop crying 'Vive la croix!' was killed by the national guard.
67. Prefect Thomas makes this point explicitly in his report on the riot to Paris.
68. There are a number of accounts of the Nîmes mission cross riots. See footnote 44.
69. See above and Claude Langlois, *Le diocèse de Vannes au XIXᵉ siècle, 1800-1830* (Paris, 1974), p.502.
70. Agulhon, *La vie sociale,* p.367; Fortin, p.28.
71. Marcilhacy, p.369.
72. A. N. F¹⁹ Mayor of Douces to prefect, 20 May 1831.
73. Shorter, 'Difference', pp.1046-7.
74. Polge, pp.20-2. and 74.
75. *L'Ami de la Religion,* CLXXX (29 April 1858), p.262.
76. Marrus, pp.17-8.
77. I discussed this matter in 'The July Revolution and the Mission Cross Troubles'.
78. André Rayez, 'De la revolution au début de 20 siècle', *Histoire spirituelle de la France* (Paris, 1964), pp.287-358.
79. René Lauretin, *The Question of Mary,* trans. I. G. Pidoux (New York, 1964), pp.42-3.
80. Madame Louis-Lefebvre, *The Silence of St. Catherine Labouré,* trans. The Earl of Wicklow (Dublin, 1953), p.48. The exact French text is given on pp.49-50.
81. Some cities, like Orléans, do not fit this pattern. The growth of the cult there coincides with the experiences of other areas, but it lacks the sensational quality in evidence elsewhere and it maintains its relative strength much longer.
82. On Philomena see the *Dictionnaire d'Archeologie et de Liturgie,* V, 2. 'Filomena', c. 1600-1606 and the bibliography cited there. Particularly important for the spread of devotion to Philomena was the book *La vie et miracles de Ste. Philomène* (Amiens, 1835), which was printed in several cities and reprinted repeatedly during the 1830s and for the rest of the nineteenth century.
83. The other two cantonal cities, one of which was a mining area of advanced dechristianisation, would probably complement this study in contrasts. See Y. M. Hilaire, 'Remarques sur la pratique religieuse dans le bassin houiller du Pas-de-Calais dans la deuxième moitié du XIXᵉ siècle', *Communication de M. Hilaire du colloque Charbon et Sciences humaines* (n.p., n.d.), pp.265-79.
84. Y. M. Hilaire, 'Les missions intérieures face à la déchristianisation pendant la second moitié du XIXᵉ siècle dans la region du Nord', *Revue du Nord,*

XLVI (1964), p.65.

85. Ibid., p.64.

86. Hilaire, 'Remarques', pp.266, 274.

87. A study of their Easter duty discipline later on in the century shows great differences in religious affiliation within Vimy itself. It has been suggested that the coolness of some Vimy farmers towards religion stemmed from the fact that their families had bought nationalised Church or aristocratic property during the French Revolution (see ibid., p.274). This would account for their indifference towards Philomena as well, since, during the Restoration the missionaries' sermons had fostered bad consciences in those who had made profitable deals out of the Secularisation.

88. But other communities in the canton were involved as well: Cauchy-à-la-Tour, Ligny, Rombly, Rely, Mazinghen, and so on. The strength of the cult in Norrent Fontes is hardly surprising since the entire northern part of the Béthune *arrondissement* preserved religious discipline throughout the nineteenth century (Hilaire, 'Les missions intérieurs', p.56).

89. Emmanuel Le Roy Ladurie, *Le territoire de l' histoiren* (n.p., 1973), p.65.

90. Y. M. Hilaire, 'Le recrutement ecclésiastique dans la première moitie du XIXᵉ siècle: Le diocèse d' Arras représente-t-il un cas original?' *Bulletin de la Société d' Histoire Moderne*, 67ᵉ Année, 14 series, no. 6, pp.15-6.

91. André Fortin, 'Aspects de la vie sociale du Pas-de-Calais durant le second empire', *Revue du Nord*, CCIV (Jan.-Feb. 1970), pp.17-32.

92. Pierre Barral, *Les Agrariens Francais de Méline à Pisani* (Paris, 1968), pp.42-3.

93. *L' Ami de la Religion*, XIVC (18 July 1837), p.120.

94. Claude Fohlen (ed.), *Histoire de Besancon* (Paris, 1965), p.330.

95. Today the name seems to be unheard of in Marseille. I do not know when it fell from use altogether. Information for all the graphs on Marseille are derived from the *Etat-Civil* births registers from 1833 to 1850 in the departmental archives of Bouches du Rhône.

96. Statistical evidence has established that during the same decade of the Philomena sensation, Marseille people in general and the bourgeoisie in particular became less dutiful in religious discipline. The lapse of time from birth to baptism, the initiatory rite which gives membership in the Church and eligibility for salvation, increased, and no one became more lackadaisical about it than the bourgeoisie (Charpin, 122). This class lived in the parishes south of Canebière and precisely these were the ones that showed the least discipline in 1841. St Joseph's church, sponsor of the Philomena cult, was one of the city's least rigorous regarding baptismal discipline and to its immediate east lay St Victor's, the most lax area of the entire city (ibid., p.103). Thus one and the same class exhibit fervour and laxity. There is no solution to this riddle, short of conceding that considerable diversity among bourgeois people was hidden beneath a cloak of social homegeneity. Prefect Thomas alluded to this dichotomy during the mission cross troubles, when he divided the bourgeoisie into 'hostile' and 'tolerant' groups vis-a-vis religious practice. One explanation is that bourgeois immigrants to Marseille—a group that was less stable than some of the working classes according to William H. Sewell, Jr., 'La classe ouvrière de Marseille sous la Seconde République: structure sociale et comportement politique', *Le Movement Social*, LXXVI (July-Sept. 1971), p.32— were cool towards Philomena while the indigenous bourgeoisie were fervent.

97. Charpin's study of baptismal discipline shows that the rural area surrounding the city of Marseille remained dutiful after it had begun to slip in urban parishes. See pages 103ff.

98. Statistics on residency in Bavarian parishes indicate a massive turnover in the population on a year by year basis. Jobs, marriage licence possibilities,

inclination and other factors seemed to have played a role in this population movement.

99. William H. Sewell, Jr., 'The Occupational Structure', Ch.3 of the manuscript which is being prepared for publication; see Table 11.

100. See William B. Sewell, 'La classe ouvrière', and 'Social Change and the Rise of Working-Class Politics in Nineteenth Century Marseille', *Past and Present*, LXIV (Nov. 1974), p.75-109.

101. It was during that Victor Gelu noticed the collapse of the traditional mutual aid societies; Gelu, p.99. However, no decline in artisanal baptismal discipline for this decade has been determined; Charpin, pp.102-4. Unlikely as it may sound, it could be that the radicalising open tradesmen clung to some traditional religious practices. There are places in modern Italy where Communist municipal governments have taken over the rites of community (celebrations, holidays, etc.) but the Church still controls rites of passage (sacraments), and the people share in both! (David I. Kertzer, 'Participation of Italian Communists in Catholic Rituals: A Case Study', *Journal for the Scientific Study of Religion*, XIV, 1 [March 1975], pp.1-11). We should not forget that late in the nineteenth century the daughter of that most distinguished of French socialists, Jean Jaures, was baptised— even if it was somewhat embarrassing for him!

102. Hilaire, 'Les mission intérieures', p.60.

103. F. A. Isambert, *Christianisme et classe ouvrière* (Paris, 1961), pp.170-2.

104. C. Savart, 'Pour une sociologie de la ferveur religieuse: L' Archconfrérie de N.-D.-des Victoires', *Revue d' Histoire Ecclésiastique*, LIX, 3-4 (1964), pp.828 and 840.

105. Wolfgang Schieder, 'Kirche und Revolution', *Archiv für Sozialgeschichte*, XIV (1974), pp.436-9.

106. Eva Ammermüller, 'Meckenheim-Merl: Konfessionelle Unterschiede der Taufnamen?',*Rheinisches Jahrbuch für Volkskunde*, XXI (1973), pp.102-33.

107. XXXIV (1855), p.466.

108. R. Aubert, *Le pontificat de Pie IX (1846-1878), Histoire de l' église*, XXI, pp.278-9.

109. Loc. cit.

110. See, for examples, *L' Ami de la Religion*, LXXVII (3 Oct. 1833), p.438; (24 Oct. 1833), p.584; LXXVIII (2 Nov. 1833), p.5; (14 Nov. 1833), p.87; (19 Nov. 1833), p.136; LXXI (18 Oct. 1834), p.566; LXXVI (9 July 1833), p.470.

111. Phayer, 'The July Revolution and the Mission Cross Troubles'.

112. *L' Ami de la Religion*, LXXIX (10 April 1834), pp.504-5.

113. Ibid., XC (17 Sept. 1836), p. 537; XIC (1 Nov. 1836), p. 213; XVC (7 Oct. 1837), pp. 37-8; XIVC (17 Aug. 1837), p. 325 and (29 Aug. 1837), p. 406 and (28 Sept. 1837), p. 616.

114. Le Roy Ladurie, *Le Territoire*, pp.45-6 and 65. Gabriel Le Bras, 'La Religion dans la société francaise', *Aspects de la société francaise*, (ed.) Andre Siegfried (Paris, 1954), pp.221-40. See as well the maps in F. Boulard and J. Remy, *Pratique Religieuse urbaine et regions culturelles* (Paris, 1968).

115. André Siegfried, *Tableau Politique de la France de l' Ouest sous la Troisième République* (Paris, 1913), pp.390-400. How might we account for this extraordinary growth pattern? It is likely that in areas where traditional culture had remained relatively undisturbed by the 1840s, people were satisfied with their customary cycle of liturgical celebrations. Devotion to the Blessed Virgin continued within the scope of the traditional liturgical calendar and pilgrimage routine. In dechristianised areas, however, religious and folk ties with the past had been broken or had

become slack. The fact that women remained more devout than men in these areas suggests that they seized upon the Immaculate Conception Archconfraternity and other Marian devotions to express their piety in a new and particularly feminine manner. It has not yet been established that membership in the Archconfraternity was sexually biased in favour of women, but the pattern of its growth signals that this may well be the case.

116.    Wesley D. Camp, *Marriage and the Family in France Since the Revolution* (New York, 1961), pp.41-2.

# 8 CONCLUSION: RELIGION AND CHANGE

By a process which historians of institutions have called the Secularisation enormous tracts of property in Western and Central Europe changed from ecclesiastical to capitalistic ownership in the course of the French Revolution and Napoleonic era. It is now time for the social historian to ask if people underwent a process of secularisation. If they experienced transformations that were equally massive and epochal, should we not be more interested in these than in real estate transactions? Was society secularised? Did people begin to think about themselves and life in new ways?[1]

To proceed along this line of questioning it is necessary to rearrange the furniture in our minds. Institutional history has cast the secularisation of Church property as the last act of a drama. The Secularisation terminated Church ownership. The curtain falls, ending an era. But it is by now obvious that the Secularisation did not terminate the religiosity and piety of common people. To say that people became sexually indulgent because they were secularised from religion (i.e. the *termination* of religious influence) is historically incorrect. The legacy of the term Secularisation disposes us to look for terminal social implications, but when we search in the obvious places none are to be found.

To make headway in social history we must think of the Secularisation as a beginning. People began to exercise greater individual control over their lives and they began to distinguish between the various activities of life which transpired in their midst. We have seen that individual people, rather than the community, began to decide whom they would marry, and, simultaneously, common people steadfastly resisted attempts to relate sexual activity with religious precepts as had been done in traditional society. These were new attitudes. They set the early nineteenth-century German proletariat off from other classes and from farmers and clearly distinguished them from their pre-modern ancestors.

It must be emphasised that around 1800 this process had only just begun. As a consequence, it is much easier to identify areas that had remained untouched by it than those that were affected. French common people still confused politics and Christocentrism (religion) and in neither France nor Germany were they able to treat dancing as a wholly secular pastime. Thus, the proletariat of the Restoration and

Vormärz is not fully disentangled from the pre-modern holy day-holiday, community-centred view of life. But important breaks in the old pattern had been made. When common people seized (France) or were given (Germany) personal freedom, autonomous proletarian family units emerged that did not recognise the authority of the community in matters that pertained to the familial life-style. Once that stage had been reached, additional unravelling was inevitable.[2]

Viewing the secularisation as a force that ushers in new social development provides us with an historical perspective that we otherwise miss. While avoiding casting the proletarian as a penniless rebel, it allows us to recognise his distinctive and tenacious life-style and to deduce something about how he or she viewed life. We have long trumpeted the great freedoms which the Declaration of the Rights of Man and the Citizen and, to a lesser extent, the reform constitutions of Germanic states introduced. It gives pause for thought to imagine what many of these reforms might have meant to the bigoted, illiterate proletariat. But the freedom to marry at one's will and choosing and the release from communal penalties for bastardy were values understood and cherished.

Secondly, this approach allows us to understand the continuing importance of religion in the life of common people, particularly on the Continent. Too often we have been tempted to minimise this aspect if for no other reason than because it ill prepares us for the transition of the proletariat to socialism in the latter half of the century. If we refuse to ignore the role of religion and attempt to understand what it meant to the proletariat, we will not be forced to think of the new prophets of socialism as irresistible magnets which pulled the proletariat out of the orbit of Christianity and a traditional view of life. For it was not Marx but the Church itself that paved the road for the exodus.

There are two reasons for this. At every turn the Church rebuffed the fascination of the proletariat with the externals of religion or with outright superstition. (The episode surrounding the sacred veil of Trier—itself incomparably less crass than pre-modern forms of superstition—cannot be taken as typical of Church discipline.) As a result, the practice of religion changed enormously between 1750 and 1850. Gone were the feast days that dotted the months of the year, affording occasion for the faithful to engage in local devotions and bizarre superstitious rites. A standard, universal liturgical calendar began to emerge which gave precedence to Sundays and demoted many feast days that had great but local significance.

Philomena herself illustrates this process. As an evocation of popular piety she presented the Church with a golden opportunity to create a major attraction by establishing her as an important saint. Instead, she was assigned a bottom rung on the liturgical ladder and her feast day was placed just a few days before that of the Assumption of the Blessed Virgin, whose popularity was so established that Philomena could not hope to rise above mere satellite importance. (In 1968 the Church removed Philomena from the liturgical calendar altogether, declaring the archeological evidence of her existence insufficient.)

Marx and Freud expressed themselves in remarkably similar terms when one called religion an opiate and the other an illusion.[3] Decades before their time it had become clear to enlightened leaders that common people, as a matter of course, used religion as a vehicle of wish fulfilment to escape nature's capriciousness. Since enlightened classes infiltrated the decision-making positions of both Church and State, these agencies joined forces to suppress superstition. When they had finished eliminating the more sensational aspects from traditional religion, what remained seemed effete and abstract to the proletariat.

A second factor in the alienation of the proletariat from religion revolves around the sexual question. Ironically, everyone looked to institutional religion to bridle the animal instincts of the common people after traditional restraints were removed. Even Voltaire sought to turn the religious instinct to the public good by 'yoking the violent passions of the masses with the "noble lie" of an eternal hell'.[4] But the subterfuge did not work. When the various props of sexual control in traditional society collapsed, governments everywhere gave control of primary education to the churches in the hope that moral discipline could be instilled in the common people. The task of teaching a Christian code of sexual morality proved arduous. For those types of families that fostered sexual restraint the lessons made sense, but among the proletariat, who had already acquired a disposition for sexual indulgence, few inroads could be made. Eventually it dawned on them that the differences between moral codes were irreconcilable and that alternatives would have to be chosen. The proletariat, which constituted the Church's most recent and enthusiastic supporters, slowly departed.[5]

But all of this lay in the future. For the time being, 1800 to 1850, religion continued to play an important role in society at large and in the lives of the proletariat. It provided both a cement for a society that was breaking up into classes and a balm for those who found themselves uprooted by urbanisation. Let us review these internalising factors.

We have discussed French popular religion during the July Monarchy at length. When we think of this era the names of Lamennais and Lacordaire come readily to mind. However, neither the publicist nor the orator could rival the mission cross and the virginal cults in religious significance so far as most Frenchmen were concerned. But, what, precisely, is the significance of these occurrences? How are we to relate them to French history in general during the two decades following the Three Glorious Days?

The events surrounding the mission cross troubles and the rise of the Philomena and Marian cults may appear to run off in opposite directions. It is time now to put these matters in balance. True, demonstrations against the crosses had often been bitter, sometimes downright venomous. Granting that heavy political overtones surrounded the controversy, we cannot overlook the fact that most simple-minded people, unable to grasp this, were greatly scandalised by the anti-cross movement. Nor can it be denied that the Church itself looked upon the mission cross débâcle as a great setback. These facts must be contended with; they have even led some historians to assert that 1830 was a more momentous year in the process of dechristianisation than 1789.[6] It may well be that in the long run the July Revolution of 1830 was a great milestone. But in the short run, let us say for the duration of the July Monarchy, the ebb tide waters soon rushed back in, washing away the scars left by uprooted crosses.

Several considerations lead to this judgement. In the first place, there never would have been any mission cross trouble had not many Frenchmen—probably most, if the truth were known—supported them. Secondly, the mission cross troubles were basically urban disputes brought on by the bourgeoisie at a time when France was overwhelmingly rural and peasant. Thus, even though mission cross riots appear spectacular or even cataclysmic, they did not directly concern most Frenchmen, some of whom, it will be recalled, responded by putting up a rash of crosses in the countryside all through the latter 1830s. Thirdly, no matter if the victory of bourgeois forces over the crosses was real, the government was by no means anxious to cash in on the rewards. On the contrary, by 1835 it had assumed a quite conciliatory attitude towards religion and the Church, as a great groundswell of spiritual fervour embraced the French.[7] Philomena and Mary were the marrow of this religious renewal.

By 1848 their cults had sufficiently matured to bind up the fissures in French society and to underwrite the religious equanimity of the revolution of that year which contrasts so conspicuously with the violent anti-Christocentrism following the July Revolution of 1830. That the Philomena and Marian cults could spontaneously arise and sweep through France allows us to measure the strength of the traditional view of life, religion, and society that most French people still entertained at mid-century. By the end of the July Monarchy at the time of the Revolution of 1848 'the vital link', as one historian has written, 'between those relatively wealthy, relatively well informed, influential opinion leaders and the mass of the population was Catholicism'.[8] The experience of the mission cross controversy and the rise of the Philomena and Marian cults comprised the substance of that link.

In Germany the absence of any basic, pivotal conflict surrounding popular devotion makes it more difficult to analyse the ongoing importance of religion in Central European society.[9] The prevailing particularism of German states afforded each of them an internal cultural unity and cohesiveness that was supplied by religion in France. Yet, the Napoleonic era and the Vienna Congress had so completely redrawn the map of Germany as to eliminate the confessional exclusiveness of many states. Prussia's Catholic population burgeoned, as did Bavaria's Protestant. The irreconcilable differences between the confessions and within Protestantism itself make it difficult to imagine how religion could have acted as a societal cement except at the local level. When cross-confessional efforts towards national unity finally developed (supported by men such as Julius Rupp and Richard Ronge), they were both feeble and tardy.[10]

At regional level, however, the importance of religion in German Vormärz society surpassed its status in France. This estimate is ventured on the strength of religious observance which approached unanimity in Catholic areas and remained vital in Protestant zones. The religious discipline of Catholics, which cut across class and sex lines, testifies to the continuing attraction which liturgical and pious services held for common people. Protestant piety, which also cut cleanly across class lines, produced such movements as the Great Awakening and Wichern's Inner Mission.[11] Although there is no proof that German pietism broke down class boundaries, it cannot be doubted that people from all ranks came together to pray as pietists.[12] Movements related to pietism gushed up like springs both inside and outside of the official Church throughout the nineteenth century.[13] Some of these religious movements, such as the Friends of Light, transmitted political consciousness to the people at large.[14] Not until the second half of the century did it become clear that the failure of the Church to side with the people in 1848 would lead to their alienation from Protestantism.[15]

If religion reflects ongoing rural traditionalism, it was equally vital in providing the uprooted proletariat with social orientation. In this it resembles the family, which has also been assigned a premature demise. The young German proletarian set moved about from country town to city and back frequently during the Vormärz. When the price of bread dipped, young marrieds, not needing the dole of the *Heimat,* picked up and set off for the big city. A rural labour vacuum developed which was filled by single people who returned from the city to bargain for marriage licences from the *Heimat* with their much needed brawn. When bread prices rose again, as they did every decade, the two groups switched places again.[16] These, and possibly other circumstances, kept the proletariat on the move. Yet, remarkably, the religious devotion of these sexually indulgent, mobile people did not flag. Wherever they found themselves, they joined in the traditional spiritual exercises of religion. This means that the proletariat, which did not yet have a class consciousness, found continuing identity with the community, from one place to the other (rural or urban), through religion and religious services. This was of enormous importance to them. Hankering for the pre-modern holy day-holiday communal life-style that the feast days had formally anchored and not yet settled into an urban lower-class pattern of their own, the proletariat found in their religion a remaining link with the community.[17] Small wonder that common people hesitated to relinquish the vestiges of Baroque communal folkways and even sometimes did the modern dance steps in this context.

Philomena's cult makes it easy to document this process in France. Her popularity became established in cities as well as in the country, and she found her devotees among every class (through this varied enormously from place to place). Of course, dechristianisation and advanced politicisation came too soon for Philomena in some cities and regions and among certain factions of the working class, so that we often find lacunae in her support. But most of the rural proletariat were still pious, if superstitious, believers. As urbanisation slowly absorbed them, they felt themselves cut adrift from local traditions and found in the cult of the virgins a happy surrogate for lost folkways.

The social effects of a secularisation, that was in fact both gradual and partial, played an important and unique role in the process of modernisation. While releasing proletarian sexuality from communal and cosmic control, it allowed religion to provide the lower classes with a safe harbour until such time as they felt prepared to stand alone. Independent and pluralistic in their families and private lives, the proletariat still felt the need of security and protection that the local community had always offered and which neither state nor class could provide during the first half of the nineteenth century. Like fledglings, the proletariat thrashed about in the nest before winging off on their own.

## Notes

1. On the Secularisation see the essay by Martin Marty, 'Secularization in the American Public Order', *Religion and the Public Order* (Ithaca,1969), V, pp.3-26; and Harvey Cox, *The Secular City* (London, 1966).
2. For the psychodynamics of this process see Gerald Platt and Fred Weinstein, *The Wish to be Free* (Los Angeles, 1969), and *Psychoanalytic Sociology* (Baltimore, 1973).
3. See the discussion of this by Leslie Dewart, *The Future of Belief* (New York, 1966), pp.20ff.
4. H. C. Payne, 'The French Philosophes and the People: A Study in Enlightenment Social Vision' (Diss., Yale, 1973), p.90.
5. Claude Fohlen (ed.), *Histoire de Besancon* (Paris, 1965), II, p.330.
6. L. Trenard, 'Aux origines de la deChristianization: le doicèse de Cambrai de 1830 à 1848', *Revue du Nord*, 47 (1965), p.409.
7. Agulhon, *La République au village* (n.p., 1970), p.154.
8. Roger Price, *The Second French Republic: A Social History* (Ithaca, 1972), p.286.
9. Inspite of contemporary expectations the *Deutschkatholiken* never materialised into a middle-class Catholic movement; see Schieder, p.429.
10. Walter Hubatsch, *Geschichte der Evangelische Kirche Ostpreussens* (Göttingen, 1968), I, pp.298ff.
11. Shanahan, pp.340ff, and *passim;* Robert M. Bigler, *The Politics of German Protestantism* (Berkeley, 1972), pp.128-9.
12. P. Toon, E. Weis, and H. Lehmann, 'Religion-Politik-Gesellschaft im 17 und 18 Jahrhundert, Ein Versuch in vergleichender Sozialgeschichte', *Historische Zeitschrift*, 214, 1, p.85.
13. Hubatsch, p.306.
14. Bigler, Ch.6.
15. Ibid., Epilogue.
16. See Phayer, *Religion und das gewöhnliche Volk,* appendix. It is not possible to say if this fascinating picture of rural migration obtained for all Germany; the situtation did, I believe, although the particulars may have varied from state to state.
17. Compare E. P. Thompson, *The Making of the English Working Class* (New York, 1964), pp.379-80. It does not appear that either Continental Catholicism or Protestantism served to internalise middle-class values such as work among the lower class as did Methodism in England.

# APPENDIX 1

Church Membership in the Catholic Diocese of Munich [München-Freising], Bavaria, 1822-1852

| Deanery | Percentage Increase of Population | Percentage Increase of Church Membership |
|---|---|---|
| Abens | 15.2 | 15.5 |
| Babensham | 3.9 | 12.5 |
| Bad Aibling (1822-44) | 8.6 | 14.8 |
| Bad Töltz (1827-52) | 4.0 | 6.1 |
| Berchtesgaden | 7.6 | 12.4 |
| Dachau | 9.9 | 12.0 |
| Dorfen (1822-41) | 6.2 | 8.9 |
| Egenhofen | 13.4 | 15.4 |
| Erding | 12.9 | 12.8 |
| Gündelkofen | 36.9 | 37.7 |
| Freising | 13.7 | 14.5 |
| Haslach | 3.8 | 7.9 |
| Höslwang | 3.8 | −1.0 |
| Landshut (1827-52) | 11.1 | 13.7 |
| Laufen | 3.8 | 8.3 |
| Miesbach | 5.9 | 9.4 |
| Mühldorf | 8.9 | 9.4 |
| Oberbergkirchen | 3.5 | 6.2 |
| Oberföhring | 26.0 | 27.0 |
| Peterskirchen | 10.5 | 13.5 |
| Raitenbuch (Rottenbuch) | 6.3 | 12.1 |
| Reichenhall | 10.4 | 11.3 |
| Schwaben | 38.7 | 37.7 |
| Sittenbach (1822-33) | 3.4 | 5.3 |
| Sölhaben (1822-43) | 4.3 | 7.0 |
| Steinhering | 22.0 | 25.0 |
| Teisendorf | 2.0 | 3.8 |
| Tittmoning | 1.6 | 3.7 |
| Wasserburg (1833-52) | 3.0 | −4.5 |
| Werdenfels | 22.7 | 25.0 |
| Wolfratshausen (1827-52) | 3.4 | 6.4 |

These figures derive from one of the best statistical records for early modern Europe that I have seen, the *Seelenstandbeschreibung* in the Munich diocesan archives In the first part of the nineteenth century the clergy were pressed into state service in the capacity of bureaucratic record-keepers. Each parish pastor was obliged to submit statistics on his community. Besides church membership these records kept data on number of marriages, legitimate and illegitimate births, deaths, suicide, insanity, absence from the parish (the number who had residency in the parish but were away), and so on.

In the above table I have omitted data on the city of Munich itself because I suspect that it is not as reliable as those for smaller communities. It will be noticed that with only a few exceptions (where membership declined ever so slightly), the entire diocese experienced increased membership. There is the possibility of a small margin of error in the statistics due to the fact that they do not take into consideration change of age at the time of First Communion (the tally actually reflects the number who have made the First Communion rather than all of those who have been baptised). Thus, if in 1822 the average age was 14 but in 1852 10, much of the increase may be accounted for by this discrepancy. In all probability, membership remained unchanged: virtually 100 per cent in 1822 and in 1852.

# APPENDIX 2: THE PHILOMENA CULT

## Graph 1: Given Names for Females in Marseille

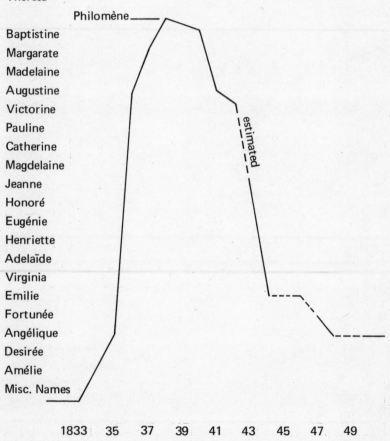

Marie
Joséphine
Rose
Anne
Françoise
Antoinette
Elizabeth
Théresa
Philomène
Baptistine
Margarate
Madelaine
Augustine
Victorine
Pauline
Catherine
Magdelaine
Jeanne
Honoré
Eugénie
Henriette
Adelaïde
Virginia
Emilie
Fortunée
Angélique
Desirée
Amélie
Misc. Names

estimated

1833   35   37   39   41   43   45   47   49

Since none of the other saints' names were experiencing a sensational rise in popularity, I used the year 1839 as a standard to sample their frequencies.

It is important to notice how quickly the Philomena namesake fad spread in Marseille in 1836, 1837 and 1838. In spite of the fact that this namesake had surpassed literally dozens of others in popularity, only a rather small percentage of parents chose the name for their new-born babies. As subsequent graphs show, even a rate of 20 Philomena namesakes per 1,000 infants is high. The enormous variety of names from which to choose obviously explains the seemingly low rate. Thus, even names more popular than Philomena (with the exception of Mary) would not have enjoyed a popularity of more than 30 or 40 per 1,000.

Graph 2:  The Philomena Namesake Fad: Four Cities

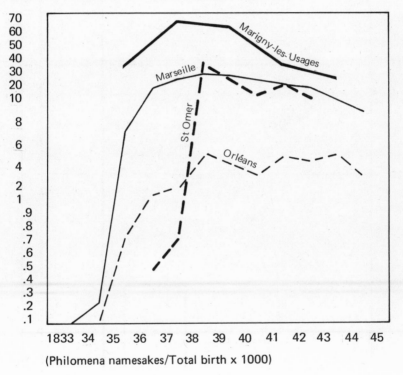

(Philomena namesakes/Total birth x 1000)

It is obvious that by using nomenclature as a yardstick we are only measuring a relatively small segment of the population—those who are most fertile. But we need not be sceptical on this score, since the literature on the Philomena cult shows she was even more popular with other segments of the population—the sick, handicapped and aged.

Graph 3:  The Philomena Cult in Four Pas de Calais Cities

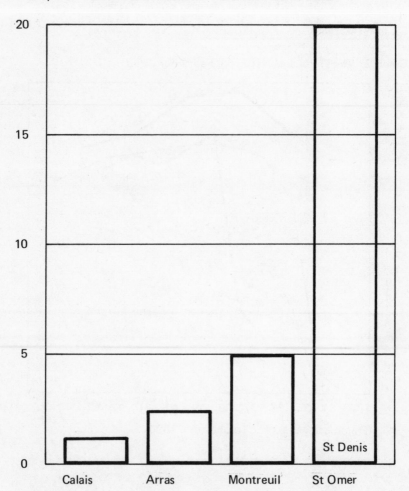

(Babies named Philomena/Total number of births x 1000)

Source:  A. D. Pas de Calais Etat Civil Naissances, 1837-42; Livre de Baptême, St Denis, 1837-42.

Graph 4: The Philomena Namesake Fad by Class in Two Cities

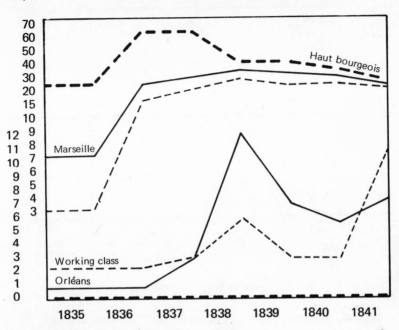

(Philomena namesakes/Total births x 1000)

The rate for the city of Orléans is higher than both other groups during certain years because of the many illegitimate children who were named after Philomena. In the case of both cities the graph measures legitimate children of the bourgeoisie and working class.

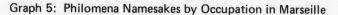

Graph 5:  Philomena Namesakes by Occupation in Marseille

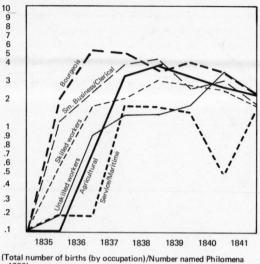

(Total number of births (by occupation)/Number named Philomena x 1000)

Source:  A. D. Bouches du Rhône Etat Civil Naissances.

Graph 6:  Marseille's Upper and Lower Class Philomena Babies

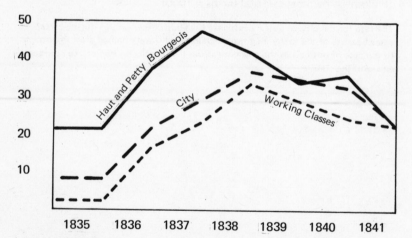

(Philomena namesakes/Total births (excluding foundlings and bastards) x 1000)

Source:  A. D. Bouches du Rhône, Etat Civil Naissances

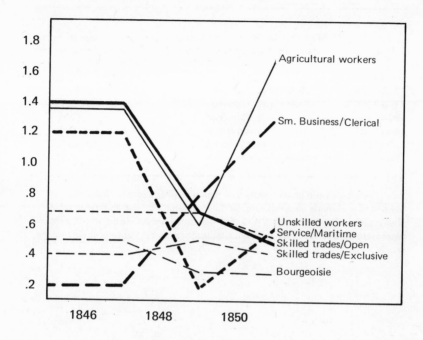

Source: *A. D. Etat Civil Naissances*

The meagre rate of the Philomena namesake among all classes makes it obvious
that by the latter years of the decade of the forties the fad had run its course.
Such a low rate means that actually only a few people from each class named
their children Philomena during the years 1846 to 1850. This creates an obvious
weakness in the sample. Nevertheless, the steady erosion of support for the saint
among the open trades is striking.

# APPENDIX 3

Mary as Namesake in Oberwinter, Middle Rheinland

| Year | Most Popular Names for Female Infants (in order of preference) | Percentage of Female Infants Christened Mary |
|---|---|---|
| 1686-1705 | | 0.7 |
| 1706-1755 | Mary, Anne, Margarete | 14.2 |
| 1756-1805 | Anne, Mary, Catherine | 19.1 |
| 1806-1855 | Anne, Mary, Catherine | 12.6 |
| 1856-1905 | Anne, Mary, Catherine | 9.4 |
| 1906-1955 | Mary, Anne, Catherine | 9.3 |
| 1956- | Mary, Elizabeth, Anne | n.a. |

These data have been gleaned from Eva Ammermüller's article, 'Meckenhiem-Merl: Konfessionelle Unterschiede der Taufnamen?', *Rheinisches Jahrbuch für Volkskunde,* XXI (1973), pp.9-113. For baptismal names see pp.102-3; percentages were derived from her numerous tables throughout the second part of the article.

# BIBLIOGRAPHY

## I.    Archives

### 1. Archives nationales de France

$F^{19}$ 5440: suppressed canticles.

$F^{19}$ 5601: attitude of clergy toward government of Louis Philippe.

$F^{19}$ 5709-5767: these boxes contain prefectural-ministerial correspondence on mission crosses and a variety of other socio-religious topics.

### 2. Archives départementales de France

Pas de Calais: Etat-Civil *Naissances,* 1837-1842.

Loiret: Etat-Civil *Naissances,* 1835-1858.

    50 J 420: correspondence on mission crosses.

Bouches du Rhône: Etat-Civil *Naissances,* 1833-1850.

    28.V.1: correspondence on mission crosses.

### 3. Staatsarchiv für Oberbayern

K Wolfratshausen 10d: tax records for Dietramszell.

K Linden 25D: tax records for Dietramszell.

K Wolfratshausen 16D: tax records for Dietramszell.

K Tölz 11d: tax records for Dietramszell.

### 4. Ordinariatsarchiv Müchen

*Geburts-, Trauungs-u. Sterbebücher:* Dietramszell, 1809-1827.

*Pfarrbeschreibung:* parish reports for eighteenth and nineteenth centuries.

*Visitation Beantwortungen:* extensive parish-chancery correspondence, 1820-1840.

*Relatio Synodalis* Gars, 1721-1800: statistics on births, marriages, etc.

*Seelenstandbeschreibung:* extensive population statistics for diocese of Munich, 1822-52.

*Verboten Bücher,* 1800-1850: superstitious literature.

### 5. Bistumsarchiv Münster

*Taufbücher:* Werne, 1823-32; Herzfeld, 1820-30; Appelhüsen, 1822-45; Dülmen, 1825-34.

6. *Bistumsarchiv Paderborn*

*Visitationbuch* XIV 1ba: reports on parish communities, 1650-1775.

7. Ordinariatsarchiv *Passau*

07090 *Sittenverfall*, 1828-30: extensive correspondence between parishes and chancery on bastardy, dancing, etc.

8. *Bistumsarchiv Trier*

*Visitation* Piesport: reports on the community, 1715-50.

9. *Landeskirchenarchiv der Evang. Kirche von Westfalen* (Bielefeld)

*Taufbücher:* Elsey, 1820-50; Iserlohn, 1820-50; Lüdenscheid, 1820-50.

10 *Various parish archives*

Niederkirchen: *Gedenkbuch*, 1750-1811.
Pirmasens: *Gedenkbuch*, 1800-1900.
Korbach: *Taufbuch*, 1826-35.
Rüthen: *Taufbuch*, 1826-35.
Arolsen: *Taufbuch*, 1826-35.

**II. Newspapers and Periodicals**

*L' Ami de la Religion* (Paris), 1815-60.
*L' Avenir*, F. Lamennais (ed.), 1830-2.
*Le Berruyer* (Bourges), 1830-4.
*Christliche Zeitschrift für Christen* (Nürnberg), 1806-32.
*Le Constitutionnel* (Paris), 1830-4.
*Evangelische Kirchen-Zeitung* (Berlin), W. Hengstenberg (ed.), 1827-36 and 1843-6.
*La Gazette du Midi* (Marseille), 1830-2.
*Historisch-Politische Blätter* (Munich), J. Görres (ed.), 1838-70.
*Journal du Loiret* (Orléans), 1830-4.
*L' Orleanais* (Orléans), 1831-2.
*Semaphore* (Marseille), 1830-2.
*L' Univers*, 1830-2.

**III Other Printed Sources**

Aigremont. *Volkserotik und Pflanzenwelt*, Halle, n.d. 2 vols.
Alexis, W. *Volkskalender*. Berlin, 1854-7.
Anon. *Croix miraculeuse apparue à Migne, près Poitiers*. Paris, 1827. 35pp.

Anon. [J. F. Barrelle]. *Vie et miracles de Ste. Philomène, vierge et martyre, surnommé Thaumaturge du XIXᵉ siècle*. Amiens, 1835. 144pp.

Aronson, J. E. *Die Kunft das Leben des schönen Geschlechts*. Berlin, 1817. 300pp.

*Generalien Sammlung der Erzdiözese Müchen-Freising. Die oberhirtlichen Verordnungen und Allgemeine Erlasse*. Vol. I, 1821-47; Vol. II, 1847-56.

Kolping, Adolph. *Kalender für das Katholische Volk*. Cologne, 1860-66.

Rienle, Franz Karl. *Lexikon der christlichen Glaubens- und Sittenlehre*. Augsburg, 1796. 2 vols.

Steffens, Karl. *Volkskalender*. Frankfurt a.M., 1841; Leipzig, 1860; Berlin, 1871.

**IV Complainte Literature**

*Bibliothèque National de France*

Ye 973 (17)

1. *Croix de mission plantée à Bordeaux*, 25 avril 1817.
2. *Sainte Philomène* (shown as protectress of the home).

*Le Musee des Beaux-arts* (Orléans).

A. 6705 *Croix de mission d' Orléans*.

A. 6715 *Croix miraculeuse de Migné*.

**V Selected Books and Periodicals**

Abel, Wilhelm. *Massenarmut und Hungerkrisen im vorindustriellen Europa*. Hamburg, 1974. 427pp.

Agulhon, Maurice. 'Mise au point sur les classes sociales en Provence'. *Provence Historique*, 20 (1970), pp.101-8.

*La Sociabilité Méridionale (confréries et associations dans la vie collective en Provence orientale à la fin du XVIIIᵉ siècle*. Aix, la Pensée Universitaire, 1966. 2 vols.

*La Vie Sociale en Provence Intérieure au Lendemain de la Révolution*. Paris, 1970. 531pp.

*Une Ville ouvrière au temps du socialisme utropique: Toulons de 1815 à 1851*. Paris, 1970. 368pp.

Ammermüller, Eva. 'Meckenheim-Merl: konfessionelle Unterschiede der Taufnamen?' *Rheinisches Jahrbuch für Volkskunde*, 21 (1973), pp.9-113

Anon. *La Croix de St. Martin*. Avignon, n.d. (1898). 15pp.

Anon. [Latapie, M. Abbé]. *Ste. Philomène de Montdoumerc*. Cahors, 1958. 55pp.

Aubert, R. *Le Pontificat de Pie IX (1846-1878), Histoire de l' église*, XXI. 592pp.

Barral, Pierre. *Les Agrariens Francais de Méline à Pisani.* Paris, 1968. 385pp.

Bertier de Savigny, Guillaume de. *The Bourbon Restoration.* Translated by Lynn M. Case. Philadelphia, 1966. 499pp.

Böck, Karl. *Johann Christoph Beer, 1690-1760. Ein Seelsorger des gemeinen Volkes. Münchener Historische Studien Abt. Bayerische Geschichte,* bd. II. 1955. 125pp.

Böck, Robert. 'Die Marienwallfahrt Kösslarn und ihre Mirakelbücher.' *Bayerisches Jahrbuch für Volkskunde* (1963), pp.33-57.

Borneman, Ernst. *Sex im Volksmund.* Hamburg, 1971.

Bouchard, Gérard. *Le Village Immobile: Sennely-en-Sologne au XVIIIe siecle.* Paris, 1972, 386pp.

Boulard, F., and Remy, J. *Pratique Religieuse Urbaine et Régions Culturelles.* Paris, 1968. 213pp.

Camp, Wesley D. *Marriage and the Family in France since the Revolution.* New York, 1961, 203pp.

Chaline, N. -J. 'Une image du diocèse de Rouen sous l' épiscopat de Mgr. de Croy (1823-1844).' *RHEF,* 58, 160 (Jan.-June 1972), pp.53-71.

Charpin, Fernand. *Pratique religieuse et formation d' une grande ville: le geste du baptême et la signification en sociologie religieuse, Marseille, 1806-1958.* Paris, 1964. 332pp.

Cholvy, Gérard. 'Le Legs Religieux de l' Ancien Régime au Département de L' Hérault.' *Annales du Midi,* 85, 113 (July-Sept. 1973), pp.303-26.

Daumard, Adeline. *La Bourgeoisie Parisienne de 1815 à 1848.* Paris, 1963. 661pp.

Depauw, J. 'Amour illégitime et société à Nantes au XVIIIe siècle.' *Annales,* E.S.C. 27, 4-5 (July-Oct. 1972), pp.1155-82.

Dewaepenaere, Claude-Hélene. 'L' Enfance illégitime dans le département du Nord au XIXe siècle.' *L' homme, la vie et la mort dans le Nord au 19e siècle,* pp.141-76. Paris, 1972.

Droulers, Paul S. J. *Action pastorale et problèmes sociaux sous la Monarchie de Juillet chez Mgr. d' Astos.* Paris 1954, 445pp.
    'La Presse et les mandements sociaux avant 1848.' *Cahiers d' Histoire* 9, 4 (1964), pp.385-97.

Eich, J. *Histoire religieuse du départment de la Moselle pendant la Révolution.* Metz, 1964. 309pp.

Engelsing, Rolf. *Zur Sozialgeschichte deutscher Mittel – und Unterschichten.* Göttingen, 1973. 314pp.

Faugeras, Marius. *Le Diocèse de Nantes sous la Monarchie Censitaire (1813-1822-1849).* Foutenay-Le-Comte, 1964. 2 vols.

Flandrin, J. C. *L' Eglise et le controle des naissances.* Paris, 1970. 137pp.

Fortin, André. 'Aspects de la vie sociale du Pas-de-Calais durant le second empire.' *Revue du Nord,* 204 (Jan.-Feb. 1970), pp.17-32.

Fried, Pankraz. *Herrschaftsgeschichte der Altbayerischen Landgerichte Dachau und Kranzberg im Hoch-und Spätmittelalter sowie in der frühen Neuzeit.* Munich, 1962. 178pp.

Gaerte, W. *Volksglaube und Brauchtum Ostpreussens.* Würzberg, 1956. 128pp.

Gelu, Victor. *Marseille au XIX^e siècle.* Edited by L. Gaillard and J. Reboul. Paris, 1971. 410pp.

Hartman, Mary S. 'The Sacrilege Law of 1825 in France: A Study of Anti-clericism and Mythmaking.' *JMH,* 44, 1 (March 1972), pp.21-37.

Henning, Friedrich W. *Dienste und Abgaben der Bauern im 18. Jahrhundert.* Stuttgart, 1969. 183pp.

Hilaire, Y. -M. 'Les missions intérieures face à la déchristianisation pendant la second moitié du XIX^e siècle dans la region du Nord.' *Revue du Nord* 46 (1964), pp.51-68.

   'Le recrutement ecclésiastique dans la première moitié du XIX^e siècle: Le diocèse d' Arras represente-t-il un cas original?' *Bulletin de la Société d' Histoire Moderne,* 67^e Année, 14 series, pp.13-19.

   'Remarques sur la pratique religieuse dans le bassin houiller du Pas-de-Calais dans la deuxième moitié du XIX^e siècle.' *Communication de M. Hilaire au colloque Charbon et Sciences humaines,* pp.265-79. N.p., n.d.

Hinrichs, Carl. *Preussentum und Pietismus—Der Pietismus in Brandenburg-Preussen als religiös-soziale Reformbewegung.* Göttingen, 1971. 473pp.

Huot-Pleuroux, P.*Le Recrutement sacerdotal dans le diocèse de Besançonde 1801 a 1860. Besa de 1801 à 1860.* Besançon, 1965. 516 pp.

Isambert, F.A. "L'Attitude religieuse des ouvriers Français au milieu du XIX^e siècle." *Archives de Sociologie des Religions* 5 (1958), 7-35.

   *Christianisme et classe ouvrièr.* Paris, 1961. 243pp.

Katz, Ruth. 'The Egalitarian Waltz.' *Comparative Studies for Society and History,* 15,3 (Nov.-June 1973), pp.368-77.

Kermann, Joachim. *Die Manufakturen im Rheinland, 1750-1833.* Bonn, 1972. 745pp.

Klenk, Willy. *Das Dorfbuch von Mulsum.* Frankfurt a.M., 1959. 293pp.

Kramer, Karl -S. 'Eibelstadt und Wilster.' *Volkskultur und Geschichte,* Berlin, 1970. pp.106-19.

Kuret, Niko. 'Der Slowenische Anteil am Pannonischen Hochzeitsbrauchtum.' *Burgenländische Forschungen,* Heft 61, pp.111-17.

Kyll, Nikolaus. 'Zur Geschichte der Kirmes und ihres Brauchtums in Trierer Lande und in Luxemburg.' *Rheinisches Jahrbuch für Volkskunde,* Jahrgang 20, pp.93-132.

Ladurie, Emmanuel Le Roy. *Le Territoire de l' historien.* Paris, 1973. 542pp.

Langlois, Claude. *Le diocèse de Vannes au XIX<sup>e</sup> siècle, 1800-1830.* Paris, 1974. 629pp.

'Les effectives des congregations féminines au XIX<sup>e</sup> siècle. *RHEF,* 60 (1974), pp.39-64.

Le Bras, Gabriel. 'Déchristianisation: mot fallacieux.' *Social Compass,* 10, 6 (1963), pp.445-52.

*Etudes de Sociologie Religieuse.* Paris, 1955-6. 2 vol.

*Introduction à l' histoire de la pratique religieuse en France.* Paris, 1942-5. 2 vols.

'La Religion dans la société francaise.' *Aspects de la société francaise,* pp.221-40. Edited by André Siegfried. Paris, 1954.

Le Brun, Jacques. 'Politics and Spirituality: the Devotion to the Sacred Heart.' *Concilium,* 9, 7 (Nov. 1971), pp.29-43.

Lefebvre, Georges. *Etudes Orléanaises.* I. *Contribution à l' étude des structures sociales à la fin du XVIII<sup>e</sup> siècle.* Paris, 1962. 262pp.

Leuilliot, Paul. *L' Alsace au début du XIX<sup>e</sup> siècle.* Paris, 1960. 532pp.

Lohmeier, Geogr. (ed.). *Bayerische Barockprediger.* Munich, 1961. 252pp.

Lottin, Alain. 'Naissances illégitimes et filles-mères à Lille au XVIII<sup>e</sup> siècle.' *Revue d' Histoire Moderne et Contemporaine* 17 (April-June 1970), pp.278-322.

McLaren, Angus. 'Some Secular Attitudes towards Sexual Behaviour in France, 1760-1860.' *FHS,* 8, 8 (Fall 1974), pp.604-25.

Magraw, Roger. 'The Conflict in the Villages.' *Conflict in French Society,* pp.169-227. Edited by T. Zeldin. New York, 1970.

Marcilhacy, Ch. *Le diocèse d' Orléans au milieu du XIX<sup>e</sup> siècle.* Paris, 1964. 493pp.

Mayeur, F. 'Les évêque francais et Victor Duruy: les cours secondaires de jeunes filles.' *RHEF,* 57, 159 (July-Dec. 1971), pp.267-304

Mayeur, J. -M. 'Catholicisme intransigeant, catholicisme social, démocratic chrétienne.' *Annales, E.S.C.* 27, 2 (March-April 1972), pp.483-99.

Metkelbach-Pinck, Angelika. *Brauch und Sitte in Ostlothringen.* Frankfurt a.M., 1968. 172pp.

Möller, Helmut. *Die Kleinbürgerliche Familie im 18. Jahrhundert.* Berlin, 1969. 342pp.

Moser-Rath, E. 'Brauchdokumentation in barocker Homiletik.' *Festgabe für J. Dünninger,* pp.347-65. Berlin, 1970.

Neuman, R. P. 'The Sexual Question and Social Democracy in Imperial Germany.' *JSH,* 7, 3 (Spring 1974), pp.271-86.

Newman, Edgar Leon. 'The Blouse and the Frock Coat: The Alliance of the Common People of Paris with the Liberal Leadership and the Middle Class during the Last Years of the Bourbon Restoration.' *JMH,* 46, 1 (March 1974), pp.26-59.

Panzac, Daniel. 'Aix-en-Provence et le choléra en 1835.' *Annales du Midi* 86, 189 (Oct.-Dec. 1974), pp.419-44.

Pfeilstifter-Baumeister, Gg. *Der Salzburger Kongress und seine Auswirkung 1770-1777.* Paderborn, 1929. 818pp.

Phayer, J. M. 'Lower Class Morality: the Case of Bavaria.' *JSH* 7 (Fall 1974), pp.79-95.

Pilbeam, Pamela M. 'The Emergence of Opposition to the Orléanist monarchy, Aug. 1830–Ap. 1831.' *English Historical Review,* 86, 334 (Jan. 1970), pp.12-28.

Pinkney, David H. *The French Revolution of 1830.* Princeton, 1972. 397pp.

Platt, Gerald, and Weinstein, Fred. *Psychoanalytic Sociology.* Baltimore, 1973. 124pp.

   *The Wish To Be Free.* Los Angeles, 1969. 319pp.

Plongeron, B. 'Archetypal Christianity: the Models of 1770 and 1830.' *Concilium,* 7, 7 (Sept. 1971), pp.78-92.

   *Théologie et Politique au Siècle des Lumières (1770-1820).* Geneva, 1973. 405pp.

Pouthas, Charles H. *La population francaise pendant la première moitié du XIXe siècle. Institut national d' études démographie,* 25, 1956. 225pp.

Price, Roger. *The French Second Republic: A Social History.* Ithaca, 1972. 386pp.

Savart, Cl. 'Pour une sociologie de la ferveur religieuse: L' Archiconfrérie de N. -D. -des-Victoires.' *Review d' histoire ecclésiastique* 54, 3-4 (1964), pp.823-44.

Schieder, Wolfgang. 'Kirche und Revolution.' *Archiv für Sozialgeschichte* 14 (1974), pp.419-54.

Schiffhauer, J. 'Das Wallfahrtswesen in Bistum Trier unter Bischof Joseph vom Hommer (1824-36).' *Festschrift f. Alois Thomas,* pp.345-58. Trier, 1967.

Schnabel, Franz. *Deutsche Geschichte im neunzehnten Jahrhundert.* Freiburg, 1954. 4 vols.

Sevrin, E. 'Croyances populaires et médécine supranaturelle en Eure-et-Loir au XIX<sup>e</sup> siècle.' *RHEF,* 32 (1946), pp.265-308.

   *Les missions religieuses en France sous la Restauration.* Vol. I, St. -Mandé (Seine), 1948; Vol. II, Paris, 1959. 336, 531pp.

   'La pratique des sacraments et des observances au diocèse de Chartres sous l' épiscopat de Mgr. Clausel de Montals (1825-1852).' *RHEF,* 25 (1939), pp.316-44.

Sewell, William H., Jr. 'La classe ouvrière de Marseille sous la Seconde République: structure sociale et comportement politique.' *La Mouvement Sociale,* 76 (July-Sept. 1971), pp.27-63.

   'Social Change and the Rise of Working Class Politics in Nineteenth Century Marseille.' *Past and Present,* 65 (Nov. 1974), pp.75-109.

Shorter, Edward. 'Différences de classe et sentiment depuis 1750. L' example de la France.' *Annales, E.S.C.,* 29<sup>e</sup> année, 4 (July-Aug 1974), pp.1034-47.

   *The Making of the Modern Family.* New York, 1975. 369pp.

   'Female Emancipation, Birth Control, and Fertility in European History.' *AHR,* 78, 3 (June 1973), pp.605-40.

   '"La Vie Intim" Beiträge zu seiner Geschichte am Beispiel des kulturellen Wandels im den Bayerischen Unterschichten im 19. Jahrhundert.' *Kölner Zeitschrift für Soziologie und Sozialpsychologie, Sonderheft,* 16 (1972), pp.530-49.

Siegfried, André. *Tableau politique de la France de l' ouest sous la Troisième République.* Paris, 1913. 535pp.

Tilly, Charles. *The Vendée.* Cambridge, Mass., 1964. 373pp.

Tilly, Richard. 'Popular Disorders in Nineteenth Century Germany: A Preliminary Survey.' *JSH* 4, 1 (Fall 1970), pp.1-40.

Trenard, L. 'Aux origines de la déChristianization: le diocèse de Cambrai de 1830 à 1848.' *Revue du Nord,* 47 (1965), pp.399-459.

Trenard, Louis, and Hilaire, Y. -M. 'Idées, Croyances et sensibilité religieuses du XVIII<sup>e</sup> au XIX<sup>e</sup> siècle.' *Bulletin de la section d' histoire moderne et contemporaine,* Fascicule V (1964), pp.7-27.

Turin, Y. 'Enfants trouvés, colonisation et utopie. Etude d' un comportement sociale au XIX<sup>e</sup> siècle.' *Revue Historique,* 244, 496 (Oct.-Dec. 1970), pp.329-56.

Vargote, Antoine, and Aubert, C. 'Parental Images and Representations of God.' *Social Compass,* 19, 3 (1972), pp.431-44.

Veit, L. A. and Lenhart, L. *Kirche und Volksfrömmigkeit im Zeitalter des Barock.* Freiburg, 1956. 332pp.

Vergote, Antoine *et al.* 'Concept of God and Parental Images.' *Journal for the Scientific Study of Religion,* 8, 1 (Spring 1969), pp.79-87.

Vovelle, Michel. *Piété baroque et déchristianisation.* Paris, 1973. 697pp.
'Problèmes Méthodologiques posés par l' utilisation des sources
de l' enregistrement dans une étude de structure sociale.' *Bulletin de
la section d' histoire moderne et contemporaine,* Fascicule III (1961),
pp.49-106.

'Le Prolétariat flottant à Marseille sous la Révolution Francaise.'
*Annales de Démographie Historique,* pp.111-38. Edited by P. Goubert.
Paris, 1968.

Walker, Mack. *German Home Towns.* Ithaca, 1971.

Wright, V. 'Religion et politique dans les Basses-Pyrénées pendant la deuxième republique et le second empire.' *Annales du Midi,* 131, 94 (Oct.
1969), pp.409-42.

Zeldin, Theodore. 'The Conflict of Moralities: Confession, Sin and
Pleasure in the 19th Century.' *Conflicts in French Society: Anti-
clericalism, Education, and Morals in 19th Century France,* pp.13-50.
Edited by T. Zeldin. London, 1970.

Zender, M. 'Gestalt und Wandel von Heiligenverehrung und Wallfahrt an
Main und Rhein.' *Festgabe f. Joseph Dünninger,* pp.425-59. Berlin,
1970.

# INDEX

Abraham a Sancta Clara, 21
Anti-clericalism, 96
Aristocracy, 14, 78, 101, 104, 115, 133
Aronson, J.E., 27
Arras, 114, appendix 2
Artisans, 135-8
Ascension Thursday, 69
Austria (Burgenland), 16, 19, 22
Avignon, 114, 121, 123

Baptismal records, 41-2
Bastardy, *see* Illegitimacy
Bavaria, 19, 32ff, 55-7, 69ff, 86-7, 89
Beauce, 103-4
Birth control, 97
Birth rate, 62
Bourbons, *see* 'Canticles' and 'Legitmacy'
Bourgeoisie, 91; and dancing, 119, 126-7; and religion, 101, 115ff, 123, 126, 133-4, 152; and sex, 25-7
*Brautlauf* (dance), 84
*Bravades,* 127
Burgenland, see Austria

*Calvaire,* 140-3
Canticles, 114, 117
Capitalism, 54-6, 91
Carlists, 121ff
Celibacy, 19
Charles X, 124-5
Chartres (diocese), 95-6
*Chateau d'Amour,* 83
Christocentrism, 78, 94, 100, 113ff, 122, 126, 139, 142, 149
Church attendance, 71, 96
Church membership, 71, 75-6, 94-9, 156
Class, 39-40, 42, 134, 154, appendix 2
Common people, *see Gens du peuple*
Confession, 97, 99
Cosmic view, 21-2, 26, 104
Cotters, *see* Day labourers
Cross cult, 107-8, 140-1

'Dance of Virginity and Marriage', 84-5
Dancing, ch. 5, 59, 98, 149, 154; and

the liturgical cycle, 84-5; erotic, 84-6, 89ff; pre-modern 82-5; modern, 85ff; frequency, 89, 127; opposition to, 113, 117-22, 126-7; and the bourgeoisie, 119, 126-7
Dating, 58-9, 85
Day labourers, 20, 33-5, 37-40, 45-7, 51-2, 60-1, 104-6, 131-2
Dechristianisation, 11, 76, 94, 97-8, 101, 109 n.1, 130-1, 137, 141, 147 n.114, 152
Dietramszell, 34ff

Economy (rural), 53-4
Enclosure system, 24, 54

Faith, 73
Family, 14, 22-3, 37-8
Famine, 16-19, 21, 86
Farm hands, 39-40, 46-7, 51, 72
Farmers, 17, 20, 25, 33-5, 40, 46, 52, 62-3, 77, 86, 103, 132
*Fasching,* 88
Foundlings, 10, 25, 100, 106
Freud, S., 151
Friends of Light, 153

Gars (Bavaria), 16-19
Gelu, Victor, 115
*Gens du peuple,* 121-6

Hardenberg, Prince Karl A., 68
*Heimgarten,* 14-16, 40-1, 52-3
Holy Days, 87-8
Holy Veil (of Trier), 77-8, 150

Ideology, 104, 136
Illegitimacy, 10-11, 17-18, 25, 32, 34, 51, 63, 74, 76, 100, 106, 150; dechristianisation, 108-9; ecclesiastical punishment, 72; fines, 18, 24; ratios, 18, 21, 32-3, 37, 42-3, 55, 102
Industrialisation, 43-5, 52

July Monarchy, 152
July Revolution, 11, 117, 120, 123, 127, 152-3

*Kermesse, see Kirchweih*

174